PLEASE RE~~TURN~~

THE
GAMES
THAT
CHANGED
THE
GAME

The Evolution of the NFL in Seven Sundays

 BALLANTINE BOOKS • NEW YORK

THE
GAMES
THAT
CHANGED
THE
GAME

Ron Jaworski

with GREG COSELL
and DAVID PLAUT

Copyright © 2010 by Ron Jaworksi

Introduction copyright © 2010 by Random House, Inc.

Published in the United States by ESPN Books, an imprint of ESPN, Inc., New York, and Ballantine Books, an imprint of The Random House Publishing Group, a division of Random House, Inc., New York.

BALLANTINE and colophon are registered trademarks of Random House, Inc.

The ESPN Books name and logo are registered trademarks of ESPN, Inc.

Library of Congress Cataloging-in-Publication Data
Jaworksi, Ron.
    The games that changed the game : the evolution of the NFL in seven Sundays / Ron Jaworksi, with Greg Cosell and David Plaut.
        p.   cm.
    Includes index.
    ISBN 978-0-345-51795-1 (hardcover : alk. paper)—ISBN 978-0-345-51797-5 (electronic)
    1. National Football League—History. 2. Football—United States—History. I. Cosell, Greg. II. Plaut, David. III. Title.
    GV955.5.N35J39 2010
    796.332'64—dc22   2010031008

Printed in the United States of America on acid-free paper.

www.ballantinebooks.com

www.espnbooks.com

9 8 7 6 5 4 3

Book design by Mary A. Wirth.

Foreword

STEVE SABOL

president, NFL Films

Football may be a team sport, but it is a coach's game. Although Plato compared the human soul to a chariot pulled by the two horses of reason and emotion, coaching in the NFL is mostly a one-horse show. It is obsessed with reason, with rational calculations, with game plans and play sheets. For nearly a century, professional coaches have been designing different ways to arrange eleven men on a field, either to advance or stop the ball.

Today the coaches in the NFL are the most progressive leaders in sports. They are constantly innovating and embracing every new technology. Football changes more than any sport we have. It was Richard Nixon's favorite sport; it was Hunter S. Thompson's favorite, too. Football coaches will try anything—the good ones will for sure. They're gonzo. Hank Stram once told me, "I'm a coach of fixed and unbending principles, the first of which is to be flexible at all times." Great coaches can do with their players what a magician does with a deck of cards: shuffle the familiar into unexpected patterns.

This book is about seven coaches and seven games in which their innovative game plans not only decided the outcome but also transformed history, because they accelerated in a matter of hours the usually longer evolution of strategy and planning. Football will always be a game of blocking and tackling, as Vince Lombardi once made quite clear. But, as this book points out, it's also a game of imagination and ingenuity.

I will not go into the details of each game because the gentlemen who have researched and analyzed them—my friends Ron Jaworski, Greg Cosell, and David Plaut—have already done so. All of us who watch *Monday Night Football* know that Ron Jaworski understands and explains the game at a level of detail never before reached on television. Perhaps even more important is his ability to make others understand the game as well. For more than two decades, Greg Cosell has clarified the nuances of NFL strategy as creator and executive producer of the *ESPN NFL Matchup* program. *Sports Illustrated*'s Peter King calls it "the one pregame show that should be essential viewing for the real fan." Dave Plaut has worked with me at NFL Films for thirty-five years. He has won numerous Emmy awards for both writing and directing. His knowledge of the league's history is encyclopedic.

There is no inevitability to history; someone has to seize and turn it. In the following pages, you will read about men who met the challenge of the present, and in so doing shaped the future. These seven memorable games are the wildfires of NFL history—the embers of which continue to burn far beyond the original blaze.

Contents

Author's Note

The research and writing of *The Games That Changed the Game* took place over a three-year period. Thirty-six years of my first-hand experiences in the National Football League, as a player and a broadcaster, along with targeted film study, are the primary information sources for this book. I studied coaching tape from the seven featured games, as well as more than two dozen additional games relating to each chapter's subject matter. Where available, the network broadcasts of the selected games have also been viewed, along with all existing footage of those games, as shot by NFL Films cameramen.

In the following pages, I have made a number of educated guesses and observations, based on my coaching tape breakdowns. To substantiate the accuracy of my evaluations, I also contacted those who have knowledge of—or were directly involved with—the chosen games. More than sixty interviews were conducted with current or retired coaches and former players. Information and quotes from well over a hundred additional interviews were derived from transcripts and produced programs housed in the NFL Films archives.

Introduction

I still remember it, still feel it, though I never saw it coming—the hardest hit I ever took in a football game. It was late October 1980, the season that our Philadelphia Eagles team went to the Super Bowl, and we were playing the Chicago Bears at home. We'd called a pass that required a five-step drop, plant, and throw. Unfortunately, Chicago's secondary had covered all my receivers, so I was forced to hold on to the ball a few tenths of a second longer than normal. Defensive end Mike Hartenstine got a good running start and drilled me in the back. My neck snapped, then my knees buckled. I landed face-down on that horrendous Veterans Stadium turf, the league's worst playing surface; nothing more than a slab of dull green-colored concrete.

Back then, team medical staffs weren't as cautious about concussions as they are today. I was helped to my feet and actually returned to the lineup, a little woozy but still capable of running the offense. After another pass play broke down, I scrambled and got whacked again, this time by safety Doug Plank—a guy you'll be hearing more about later. His tackle wasn't nearly as vicious as Hartenstine's, but it finished me for the day. I was rushed to Paoli Hospital.

The Hartenstine hit was so vicious that when I arrived at the emergency room, there was already a doctor waiting for me, one who wasn't connected with the team or even the hospital staff. He turned out to be an off-duty neurologist who had seen the tackle on television while watching the game at home. He had jumped in his car and drove to the hospital immediately, figuring I'd need his help.

When I watched the play on TV the next morning, I realized why that neurologist had raced down to the ER. I had no idea the blow had been so brutal. Getting hit is part of the game, so when you get clobbered, you just get up and keep going. It wasn't until I looked at the replay that I could see the full impact of that collision and realized I was lucky to still be in one piece. And after studying the coaching film a few days later, I completely understood not just how it happened but also why it happened the way it did.

Game film is the great truth teller. Every play puts responsibility on the athletes on the field—eleven on offense, eleven on defense—and all must do their jobs in order for the play to be successful. The only way to accurately see and evaluate each player's performance is to watch what is referred to in the coaching profession as the "All-22" tape. In these tapes, every player is visible, and they are filmed from both sideline and end zone angles. If you study and interpret them correctly, they reveal everything. With few exceptions, television coverage doesn't show this wide angle, so it can't fully reveal the design of the play or the scheme. To truly understand what is happening, the All-22 is the best way to assess NFL plays and players. Ask any sleep-deprived coach, or any player who has missed his assignment and gotten chewed out for it in a film session: The "Eye in the Sky" doesn't lie.

Football is a chess match, with moves and countermoves. You're constantly challenging the opposition, trying at all times to be at least one step ahead of him. You would love for every offensive play you design to score a touchdown, but it doesn't always work that way. In fact, it rarely works that way! An offense will run plays that you know aren't going to pick up much yardage, but you *have* to run them to set up another play for down the road. You run certain plays to see how the defense reacts. You show certain formations to help a quarterback understand how defenders will align against that formation. How do they adjust to a particular motion? Do they increase the number of defenders up front? Do the safeties drop deeper? What are they doing against a specific motion, formation, or player? The offense makes its move; the defense reacts.

When you look at coaching film (and people still do call it that, but with today's team cameras, the accurate term would be "coaching tape"), what you see over time are repetitive plays. It's important to recognize them and the patterns they indicate. Let's take the blitz, for example. As a quarterback, I would study a 10-play package of my opponent's blitzes, always looking for pre-snap indicators, alignments, or movements made before the snap that would tell me what they're trying to do. It's impossible for defenders to mask their intentions long enough; eventually, they'll tip their hand. If the quarterback is patient enough and has studied thoroughly, he should have a good idea of what's in store.

But the guys on defense are pretty smart too. The quarterback has to be sure his opponent isn't playing mind games by disguising intentions with misleading looks. Defenses have certain fronts they'll blitz from, where the ends, tackles, and linebackers set up, and how the positioning of the secondary ties in with these fronts. And if the quarterback has done enough repetitive studying, he will recognize their camouflaging tricks and be able to react instantaneously on game day.

Because of modern technology and the large size of NFL staffs, teams will break down their opponent's previous four games into a variety of categories. Players and coaches will spend hundreds of hours preparing for Sunday's game. While the coaches draw up the game plan, players follow a regimen that is both physical and mental. Players know going in that they're going to get hit, so they combine film study with daily practice, running, weight lifting, and treatment for the bumps and bruises they already have. They have to gear up equally for both the physical and the cerebral aspects of the game.

Preparation for my television work on ESPN requires a totally different mind-set from what was required during my playing days. There isn't a Mike Hartenstine lurking outside our broadcast booth ready to knock me down twenty times, so I don't have to worry about *that* problem anymore. And I don't put in as many hours as the players do. But I do watch tape, and a lot of it—maybe twenty to twenty-five hours per week. The more you watch, the greater an understanding you gain of what teams are trying to accomplish. When I make a comment on *Monday Night Football* or the *NFL Matchup* show, it's based on rigorous study. When I break down a play, I try to gear my comments specifically toward what I saw on tape earlier that week. Before kickoff, I've already formed in my mind a template of what I expect to see, so when it happens on the field that Monday night, I'm already familiar with the teams' formations, motions, and personnel packages. From tape study, I have a better understanding of what kinds of plays will be called and the goals each team seeks to accomplish.

In recent years, fans have become sophisticated and want to learn more about the intricacies of the game. Now, I don't mean this disrespectfully, but even the most dedicated fan could never understand football at the same level as the players and coaches who make their living at it. It's simply impossible. As much as I have learned through my own film study, it doesn't even begin to scratch the surface of what players and coaches consider as they put their game plans together and prepare for specific situations. If Joe Fan watches the first quarter of action and then declares, "This is what they're doing," that's only an educated guess at best. Heck, a lot of times the players *themselves* aren't always sure what their responsibilities are. You can diagram a play, practice it all week, and all of a sudden face a different look during the game, and an adjustment must be made on the fly. In their own postgame critiques, *coaches* aren't always completely sure what happened until they ask the player. "What call did you make in the offensive line? What did the quarterback tell you in the huddle?" Nothing is ever 100 percent certain in football—not even in the minds of the coaches and the players, let alone the fans. And the truth is, it's only getting more complicated.

From what I've observed, today's game is a hell of a lot more complex than it was when I played. The biggest change I've seen since 1973, when I entered the NFL, is the deployment of personnel packages. My first few years as a Los Angeles Rams quarterback were a stroll in the park compared to what today's quarterbacks face. Back then, the same eleven guys played defense, the same eleven on offense, and there were almost no substitutions. Any deviation from that approach came as a complete shock to the opposing team. A perfect example: Our Rams team was playing the Miami Dolphins in the Orange Bowl, and L.A.'s coaches put a wide receiver named Ron Jessie in the backfield as a running back. Miami's defense was so stunned that it was forced to call a time-out, as if to say, "What do we do? There's a receiver in the backfield, and he shouldn't be there!"

All we did was take our regular back Jim Bertelsen out of the game and replace him with Jessie, who went in motion prior to the snap. This seems simple enough to anyone today, but back then this baffled the Dolphins. And bear in mind that this wasn't some run-of-the-mill team we were playing. This was the famous "No-Name Defense" made up of guys like Nick Buoniconti and Dick Anderson, many of the same players who'd won back-to-back Super Bowls in 1972 and 1973.

Today defenses must be ready for exotic personnel changes on every snap. Defenses of old were four down linemen, three linebackers, and four defensive backs. Now you can have three linemen, five linemen—or no linemen. You can have two guys with their hands on the ground or four with their hands on the ground. One play later, you get no one with his hand on the ground! You can have five defensive backs or six or even eight! That's twenty-first-century football.

The National Football League is ever changing. And these changes don't just happen year to year or even month to month; they occur every week! When I start looking at tapes of last Sunday's games, I almost always spot something I haven't seen before: a new scheme, design, or concept. I have incredible respect for the men in the coaching profession, guys who are constantly looking for an edge, a different way to win. And when somebody comes up with something new—a little twist that leads to a big play—word travels fast. In the coaching world, innovators are the ones who win "street cred." I talk to a lot of people during the season who'll say, "Boy, did you see what so-and-so did last Sunday? That was an amazing scheme!" And when coaches receive calls of congratulations from friends and colleagues the Tuesday after a game, that's the highlight of their week. Getting approval from within the coaching fraternity is the highest honor they can receive.

More and more, such innovations are necessities, not luxuries. The pace of today's NFL demands it. The players are better than ever: bigger, faster, more explosive. And, as the game matures, pro football is becoming a more wide-open, pass-first game, because that's what the fans want to see and that's what the league mandates through its rule changes. In my rookie year, it was perfectly legal for a defender to beat the hell out of a receiver 20 yards downfield. Now if a linebacker's *fingernail* touches someone after five yards, he gets a flag.

I've been connected with the NFL for over thirty-five years, and in that time I've seen teams that can play the most primitive football and be very successful doing it. Why? Because their personnel is better. They could line up and win simply by physically overwhelming their opponent. That still happens nowadays when elite teams go against the weaker ones. But overall, today's teams are more competitively balanced, thanks—among other things—to free agency, the salary cap, and improved scouting. And because the talent differential is so razor thin, most successful clubs have to work hard to develop schemes that give them the advantage.

The truly great coaches beat their opponents with design. They don't necessarily need the biggest, fastest, or strongest players—although that always helps! But when they don't have those personnel advantages, the brightest coaches can win because they have confidence in their ability to construct plays or defensive schemes that create crucial mismatches. *This is the underlying strategy in today's NFL.* It's how games are won or lost, and it can be more important than having the best players. Games aren't always won by the more talented team; they are won by the team that recognizes favorable matchups and exploits them.

I travel a great deal for my work, and sometimes I reach a point during flights when I just can't read anymore or stare at my laptop. During those times, I shut my eyes and go over the key concepts I will want to stress in a future *Monday Night Football* broadcast or TV program. On one particularly long and boring flight, I began cataloguing some of the coaching innovations I'd noticed in recent games. That got me to thinking: What have been the major strategic concepts of the last fifty years that helped the NFL evolve into the game we see today? Who created them? When did they take place? Why did they happen at that particular time?

I began making a mental list of the game's most important tacticians. My first version was pretty long, because so many coaches have devised strategic twists over the years. Eventually I was able to put a handful of men into a group of the game's most creative thinkers. They were really astute guys who conceptualized the game as a series of puzzles to be solved; visionaries who had the intelligence and the courage to go against standard conventions.

At the end of this exercise, I arrived at a list of seven coaches. I'm sure fans and football writers could come up with more candidates of their own, but here are the people I believe have done the most to influence the way the modern game is played: Sid Gillman, Bud Carson, Don Coryell, Bill Walsh, Buddy Ryan, Dick LeBeau, and Bill Belichick.

Their ideas seemed radical at the time of their inception but are now commonplace throughout the league. The concepts they devised weren't created by spontaneous combustion; in virtually every case, it took months or even years for these ideas to fully blossom, and these guys likely got input and advice from their own coaching staffs and peers around the league. All of them owe a huge debt to the coaching legends who laid the NFL's foundations: George Halas, Curly Lambeau, and Paul Brown, among others. And many of the approaches crafted by my group of seven are being expanded and tweaked today by a new generation of coaches who've copied the basics, then added touches of their own. After all, like I said: Pro football is a game that changes constantly.

While it took time for these ideas to fully develop, they gained credibility and wider recognition in signature games, the effects of which had lasting influence far beyond the final score. Studying each of these games can help fans better understand the profound impact that these coaches have had on today's pro football. I had three criteria for making my selections:

- They introduced schemes that were surprising and innovative at the time.
- They used the scheme to dominate a highly regarded opponent.
- Their innovation had long-term and leaguewide impact.

These were games that alerted everyone to the fact that something different and exciting was happening on the field. Seen in historical hindsight, these seven coaches—and the significant moments of these seven games—have had a lasting influence in shaping the modern NFL.

I have always been an inquisitive guy. From the time I was a kid, I always asked "Why?" I liked learning about how things worked—a bicycle, a clock, an engine. I couldn't take these things apart and repair them if my life depended on it; I'm certainly not Mr. Fixit! But I have always had a deep interest in breaking things down, and understanding the nuts and bolts. I am going to apply that natural curiosity, along with my football experience, to helping you understand what happened in these seven games and why they've become so important to pro football's development.

I am fortunate that coaching tape still exists for virtually all of my game selections, because the All-22 look is still the most accurate way to evaluate what happens on the field. Through comprehensive film sessions, I will attempt to explain the strategic and historic developments that occurred in each game. I will break down drives and individual plays to illustrate what coaching innovations were taking place and how the opponent reacted to them. I'm also going to pick the brains of former players and current and retired coaches to get their views about these games and the schemes that made them significant. And I'll provide background and context on each coach, his team, and the NFL of that era—crucial elements that created the right conditions for these radical changes.

As the games are analyzed, patterns will begin to emerge. Strategic concepts will start to connect as the work of one coach influences another. The world of pro football is relatively small—everybody knows everybody. The generational ties and bonded loyalties that are forged go a long way toward explaining how creative football people with open minds find one another and encourage innovation. Those relationships provide the support system that is necessary for ideas to flourish.

After the final game chapter, I'll peer into my "crystal football" and make a few predictions about future football trends. I'll let you know who might become part of the next generation of geniuses. I'll also venture a guess about trends you could be seeing in the next few years, as today's coaches continue to react to the game's infinite fluctuations. This culture of never-ending improvement is what makes the NFL exciting, and it's a major reason why pro football has become and will continue to be America's most popular sport.

THE
GAMES
THAT
CHANGED
THE
GAME

Sid Gillman's Vertical Stretch

COURTESY OF THE SAN DIEGO CHARGERS ARCHIVES

**1963 AFL CHAMPIONSHIP
BOSTON PATRIOTS vs. SAN DIEGO CHARGERS**
Balboa Stadium, San Diego, California — January 5, 1964

Dick Vermeil was my coach with the Philadelphia Eagles for six years. He is the most influential person in my football life. Dick believed in me when others did not. He taught me how to be a leader, how to do things right, how to be tough enough to survive in the brutal world of the NFL.

Dick also gave me the greatest gift any quarterback could ever ask for. At a critical point in my career, he brought in Sid Gillman to be my position coach. If there were a Mount Rushmore for pioneering football geniuses, Sid Gillman's likeness would be on it. Sid, quite simply, is the father of the modern passing game. Every passing guru—from Al Davis and Don Coryell to Bill Walsh and Mike Holmgren—owes him a debt of gratitude. Every fan who loves "the bomb" should be grateful to Gillman. I know I was. For two years, I was the lucky re-cipient of Sid's incredible knowledge, and I'd equate my experience with him to be the same as a physics student getting daily one-on-one tutoring from Albert Einstein.

Sound far-fetched? Not really. More than any other coach of his day, Gillman understood the *geometry* of the game. Sid designed his receivers' routes to *look* different, while the distance of the quarter-back's throw remained the same. In Sid's scheme, receivers positioned themselves by using the hash marks. How much space those receivers left between their own tackle or tight end was critical. It insured that a quarterback's throw on specific routes would never vary in distance. Sid achieved this by emphasizing alignment and formation. Specific details were drilled over and over until they became second nature to his players. This is an expected element of pro football now, but it wasn't back when Sid coached the Rams and Chargers during the 1950s and 60s. He reinforced the legitimacy of these concepts by send-ing assistant coach Tom Bass to consult with a mathematics professor at San Diego State University in the early 1960s. Their mission: to fig-ure out *geometrically* where players needed to be on every passing route so that the ball would be in the air the same length of time.

Every passing game concept today stems from Gillman's under-standing of timing, rhythm, and anticipation. It's keyed by a three-, five-, or seven-step drop by the quarterback, drops whose distances are directly linked to the route depths of his receivers. It may be Sid's most lasting and critical contribution to pro football: He took this seem-ingly simple concept and made it a *science*. Joe Collier, who coached against Gillman with the Patriots, Bills, and Denver Broncos in the American Football League, readily admits, "Everybody had to work like hell to keep up with him. We were forced to be more creative on defense because of Sid."

Sid's passing attack was among the first to use the entire field ver-tically *and* horizontally. He divided the field into sections, based on fa-vorable passing angles. He had his split end and flanker (what wide receivers were referred to before 1970, when NFL publicists discarded those terms for the sake of uniformity) line up outside the numbers—the better to stretch the field from sideline to sideline. Sid's credo was

"The field is one hundred yards long and fifty-three yards wide. We're going to use every damn inch of it and force the other guy to defend all of it." He advanced a critical concept that all quarterbacks abide by today: the "best-located-safety" principle. By that, he meant a passer should throw the ball to the receiver who is located the farthest from either safety on the field. The principle worked for his Chargers quarterbacks, it worked for me throughout my pro career, and it's still a cardinal rule for today's NFL passers.

It helped that Sid landed in the perfect environment in which to develop these bold concepts. After he was fired by the Rams in the late 1950s, his coaching days appeared to be over. "I was looking at starting a career in stocks and bonds—a new profession that didn't quite appeal to me," Sid confessed. But then, beginning in 1960, a group of businessmen formed a rival league to compete with the NFL, and Sid was one of the first coaches hired. The new American Football League was a blank slate, with no precedent, no tradition, no history. Its coaches were handed lumps of wet clay and told to create something exciting. That was all a guy like Sid needed to hear. The NFL was a ground-oriented league in 1960, so the AFL decided that it could attract fans by passing—a lot. As Sid told me on more than one occasion, "People wanted to see us throw the ball. They didn't give a damn who caught it, but they wanted that ball in the air." The AFL became a 100-yard laboratory for this pigskin Ph.D. to conduct his football experiments.

In an era when the prevailing wisdom was "Three things can happen when you pass—and two of them are bad," Sid ignored that mind-set and passed more often so he could *set up* his running game. He put backs in motion, threw to backs in the flat—even sent them on "Go" routes up the field and down the middle. Sid asked himself, "Why do we always need our backs and tight end to block, then release? Hell, just let 'em go right away." That gave Sid's teams more receivers downfield than defenses of that era could cover, but it also left fewer pass blockers. Gillman compensated for reduced protection by putting the responsibility on his quarterbacks to throw quickly when pressured (known today as making a "hot read") to the backs and to the tight end. This concept was pivotal to his philosophy—and unique.

Few tight ends regularly ran vertical routes before Sid Gillman came along. Gillman believed that the success of any passing game depended on how well it dominated the hash mark areas with a pass-catching tight end. Time and again Sid preached, "You put a real tough tight end with good hands in the hash area, and there won't be anyone who can cover him. Then you really control the passing game." This forced defenses to respect the interior of the field, which opened up passing lanes for the other receivers. Sid's first tight end with the Chargers was Dave Kocourek, a guy who averaged between 16 to 19 yards per catch every year. He was often shadowed by Mike Stratton, a six-time AFL all-star linebacker who played for the Buffalo Bills. "Kocourek was a tall, rangy guy—very good size for a tight end at that time," said Stratton. "Because the Chargers' other receivers were so talented, opponents abandoned man-to-man and were forced to play more zone coverage, leaving Kocourek open to run plays down the seam in between everybody. He was almost impossible to stop."

The Chargers were also innovative *off* the field, as they were the first pro team to hire a weight trainer. "We really got the jump on the rest of football back then," said Ron Mix, the Chargers' Hall of Fame offensive tackle. "Most coaches discouraged weight lifting because they thought you'd get 'muscle bound' and tied up, interfering with your flexibility. Not many players worked out year-round, but, because of Sid, many of the Chargers did, and it gave us a huge strength advantage in games." More than a few of Gillman's peers viewed this type of training—and many of his passing schemes—as too radical and irresponsible. As Bill Walsh so accurately noted, "Sid was so far ahead of his time, people couldn't totally understand what he was doing."

I certainly didn't have that problem. Sid's brilliance was obvious from the minute I met him. He was almost *too* smart; a mad professor of sorts. He'd scribble so quickly on the blackboard that I'd have to slow him down. It wasn't just *what* he taught—but *how* he taught it. Before Sid came to the pros in the mid-1950s, most coaches would fire up the film projector and focus on an opponent's overall strategy. The *big picture*. Sid ignored that approach. He asked his players to study the *details*. Where is the linebacker? What's his depth from the line of scrimmage? Which leg is the strong safety putting his weight on? How are the cornerback's feet positioned and which way is his head turned? What is he looking at? Other coaches spent their time getting an overview of all eleven defenders. Sid preferred to zero in on one guy at a time to pick up the right clues. If you could crack the code, every player on the field revealed something crucial. Once I was able to apply this knowledge, things really took off for me.

My first eureka moment with Sid came during an off-season practice. I made my first throw, and Sid bellowed, "Let me see your grip!" I'd been throwing the ball the same way for twelve years. But Sid was going to mold me from the ground up, starting with the basics. "Let's see your fingertip control. Shit, Ron, your palm's touching the leather!" We spent the rest of the session working on my throwing mechanics, my drop, and the proper way to stand under the center. It was days before we even started working on play design. Sid wanted his quarterbacks to be fundamentally sound before he'd move on to anything else.

He was also a demon about repetition. Gillman drilled you and drilled you until you ran a play without even thinking about what you were doing. His passing system was based totally on precision. I had to have that ball out to the receiver at a specific point every time. And my receiver had better snap his head around when the pass was released or he was going to get whacked in the face mask. With the Eagles, I was blessed with one of the best receivers I ever threw to in Harold Carmichael, a four-time Pro Bowler, but Sid pushed him just as hard. By the time he got through with the two of us, I could have gone out to the practice field with Harold and completed those passes blindfolded. That was Sid's mantra: Do something so many times the exact way each time, and you'll perform the same in any game situation.

Nobody could make adjustments on the fly like Sid. When the Eagles walked into the halftime locker room, Sid already had everything we needed on the chalkboard: fronts, coverages, hints, indicators. I believed in him so much that I just *knew* the changes we made during halftime were going to work. He was unmatched in his ability to figure out the opponent's game plan and recognize what a team was trying to do to us that day.

The 1980 season was my finest in the NFL. I posted my best stats, was named Player of the Year, and got the Eagles to their first Super Bowl. None of this would have been possible without Sid Gillman. To this day, I still hear his voice in my head when I think about the core principles of the passing game.

And to think that there once was a time I couldn't stand the guy! Of course, that was years ago when I was a kid growing up in Lackawanna, New York—deep in the heart of Buffalo Bills country, where the team that everyone hated (but also grudgingly admired) was Sid's San Diego Chargers—the most glamorous team in the early years of the AFL.

Even back in the 1960s, I was a football nut, and my team was the Bills. I lived and died with their every move. When I was twelve, I worked a paper route for the *Buffalo Courier-Express* to earn enough money to buy a season ticket to home games at War Memorial Stadium. In 1963 a season package for one seat cost $21, and I threw a lot of papers at a lot of front porches to raise the dough. Every Sunday when the Bills were at home, I took a bus by myself into town, transferred to another bus that dropped me off at Jefferson Avenue, then walked the rest of the way to "the Rockpile," as the stadium was affectionately known. I sat in the end zone—section 23, row 13, seat 3. I rarely missed a game from 1963 until the time I went to college in 1969.

In the AFL's early years, every team had a home and away game with all the other clubs, so even though Gillman's Chargers were in the Western Division, they came to Buffalo once a year. You couldn't miss Sid on the sidelines. On warm days, he wore these cool sunglasses, and even on dreary afternoons in Buffalo it seemed like Sid always had a nice tan. But what stood out most was his trademark bow tie. I don't think I ever saw Sid in a necktie, even after he retired. But his sharp wardrobe didn't keep him from arguing with refs or yelling at a player for making a mistake. Frankly, I'm not sure what he was so upset about, because the Chargers won most of the time in Buffalo, at least early on. The first Bills-Chargers game I ever saw was another San

Diego victory, a 1963 game where fullback Keith Lincoln and receiver Lance Alworth scored touchdowns. Those guys were so good—I hated them! And San Diego had other great players too: a terrific offensive line led by Mix, high-stepping halfback Paul Lowe, and two giant defensive linemen in Earl Faison and Ernie Ladd, who always seemed to be sacking our quarterback Jack Kemp for big losses.

Ironically, Kemp had played for Sid during the Chargers' first three seasons, taking them to league championships in 1960, when the franchise was in Los Angeles, and in 1961, its first year in San Diego, both of which they lost. He ended up in Buffalo midway through the '62 season when Sid tried to sneak Jack through waivers after an injury, and the Bills scooped up Kemp because of a loophole in the rules. Lucky for me—and for Buffalo. Jack eventually led the Bills to league championships in '64 and '65, beating Sid's Chargers in both title games. How's that for payback?

After Kemp retired in 1970, he ran for Congress in our Erie County district and represented us for eighteen years. When I was selected in the second round by the Rams in the 1973 draft, one of the first phone calls I made was to Jack's congressional office to seek his advice. He was extremely helpful and gave me great suggestions about adapting to pro football. That was the beginning of a long friendship that lasted until his passing in the spring of 2009.

Jack loved to tell stories, and I heard more than a few from him about Gillman. The ones that really stuck with me related to his dealings with racial prejudice, and they explained a lot about the kind of person Sid was. He graduated from Ohio State in the mid-1930s and always dreamed of becoming a head coach in the Big Ten. But according to Jack, three different Big Ten schools turned down Sid's applications because he was Jewish. Because of that, Jack said, Sid was very sensitive to any type of discrimination. That's probably why Gillman was one of the first pro coaches to actively scout historically black colleges, sign those athletes in significant numbers, and assign them roommates by position, not by race. This was in 1960, when teams like the Washington Redskins didn't have *any* black players. Sid's early Charger teams probably had more African American athletes on their roster than any other pro team—in any sport.

With so many black athletes playing for Sid, it was no surprise that the team often had trouble getting all its players into the same hotel in cities like Dallas and Houston. The same was true with restaurants and theaters. Jack told me about the time Sid bussed the team to see some action movie the night before a game in a southern city. The players all sat down on the main floor, but then an usher told Sid that the black players would have to move to the "Negro section" of the balcony, which was separated from "white only" seats by chicken wire. Sid went nuts. "We do everything as a team!" he screamed at the usher. "If we can't sit together, we aren't staying here!" He then informed all the Chargers—black and white—that they were leaving the theater, and the whole squad got up, marched out into the lobby, and onto the street.

Moments like this obviously earned Sid a great deal of respect from his players. But they also played hard for him because his innovative coaching tactics made them look good on Sundays. The Chargers won five division titles in their first six years. "You never wanted to let Sid down because you knew he was doing everything he could on and off the field to put you in a position to be successful," said Mix. "At training camp, you could go by his room at any hour, and you'd see his projector light on, with Sid studying film. He was tough, very demanding. During film sessions, his comments could be brutal, running the action again and again if you missed an assignment. There was always an air of tension at meetings and at practices because of the intensity he brought. If he saw any diminishment in effort, he was on you. It seemed like he had eyes in the back of his head; he could spot a mistake halfway across the practice field and would start yelling. With Sid, you had to be alert, aware, focused—and you had to produce."

The Chargers had one of their most productive seasons in 1963, setting team records for points scored and rushing yardage. They'd rebounded from a losing record the year before to go 11-3 and win the Western Division. Up to that point, there had been no AFL playoff games, only a championship match. But in '63, my beloved Bills and the Boston Patriots finished the season tied for first, so they had to play each other to determine who would meet the Chargers a week later for the league title. I was there at the Rockpile three days after

Christmas—little Ronnie Jaworski in his customary end zone seat, bundled up tight and ready to root on his heroes. It was typical late-December weather in Buffalo: a hard snowfall and below-freezing temperatures. The conditions were awful, and so were the Bills. The Pats crushed them, 26–8, and even after I thawed out at home, I was depressed over the loss for weeks.

Watching Boston dominate my team so completely, I thought the Pats might have a chance in the championship, even though the game would be played in San Diego. Boston probably had the best-run defense in the AFL, often forcing opponents to throw between thirty and forty times a game. The Patriots also blitzed the most of any team in football, sometimes on more than half of the snaps! Their main weapon was future Hall of Famer Nick Buoniconti, one of the quickest and smartest linebackers who ever played the game. This was, of course, before he was traded to Miami where he anchored their renowned No-Name Defense.

Boston's defensive line coach in '63 was Marion Campbell, who would later be my head coach in Philadelphia after Dick Vermeil retired. Marion recalled, "In our two regular-season games, the Chargers really hadn't caught up to all our blitz packages. Nobody really had. Hell, we blitzed a lot because we could get away with it. We blitzed our way to the championship game." Contributing to the blitz pressure was the Patriots' outstanding defensive front, featuring Houston Antwine, a six-time all-star and a member of the AFL's all-time team, along with Bob Dee, Jim "Earthquake" Hunt, and Larry Eisenhauer.

Eisenhauer had his own nickname—"the Wildman"—for his fanatical playing style, but also for incidents like the time he ran onto a snowy turf for pregame warm-ups dressed only in his helmet and a jockstrap. The Wildman and his Patriots teammates played hard on and off the field. "After we beat the Bills, we got back to Boston and had a fabulous party. I think it went on for two days," Larry recalled. "We had a mediocre record, but here we were one game away from our first league championship. Because our weather in Boston was so bad, and since we had no indoor practice facilities, we flew out to San Diego three or four days before the game. Well, San Diego is a great area with the beaches and all the other places to go. Maybe we got a little distracted."

There was no way that Sid Gillman's team was going to be distracted. They had already lost two title games to the Houston Oilers in 1960 and '61, and Sid wasn't going to let that happen again. But how would he get more production out of his offense? During the regular season, the Patriots had played competitively in two close losses to the Chargers, holding Sid's squad to just 97 rushing yards and a total of 24 points. The answers would come from perhaps the finest game plan Sid Gillman ever devised. Sid even gave it a name, as he did with all his game plans. He called it "Feast or Famine," because he knew that either Boston's blitzers were going to pile up sacks, turnovers, and negative yardage, or his Chargers were going to beat those blitzes for big plays.

Even late in his life when I knew him, Gillman had a flair for the dramatic. He loved Hollywood films because, growing up in Minneapolis, his father owned several movie theaters, and free admission wasn't Sid's only fringe benefit. When he got older, Sid seized the cans containing newsreel films as soon as they arrived each week, cut out the college and pro football game footage, then spliced the reels back together while keeping the football footage for his own library. This practice was highly illegal, but somehow Sid pulled it off. The newsreel companies never discovered that their films had been tampered with.

For the Boston Patriots, Gillman had far more complex trickery up his sleeve. Remember Tom Bass, the Chargers assistant that Sid instructed to pick the brain of a college math instructor about geometric angles on a football field? In 1963 Bass was still at San Diego State, working for a rising star in the coaching ranks named Don Coryell. Tom would be hired for the Chargers backfield coaching job a few months later, but for the AFL championship he was a press box guest at Balboa Stadium. From that vantage point, Bass witnessed what he considers "the finest example I have ever seen of one team totally destroying another team's character. Sid took Boston's greatest strengths and turned them upside down. The 1963 AFL Championship is a game any coach or fan should study to see what perfection is on a football field."

I had only hazy memories from watching the game as a twelve-year old, so when I took my first look at the coaching tape, I was expecting to see a wild aerial game with exotic gadget calls. What I got instead was a fairly basic passing attack that included some of the same bread-and-butter plays Sid had us run with the Eagles nearly twenty years later! The plays themselves weren't exactly groundbreaking, but Sid's timing in calling them and their pre-snap design were revelations. Sid Gillman used his team's passing history—what the Patriots expected to see—to set the opponent up, then destroy it with his running game. A game that was predicted to be close was decided in its first nine minutes.

Watching from my parents' house outside Buffalo, I had no idea that the Chargers-Patriots game was nearly postponed. "The original players' shares were about to be reduced because the league decided to put the game on local TV, even though it wasn't a sellout," Ron Mix recalled. "Our cut was based on tickets sold, so the smaller gate receipts meant guys on both sides would be getting a lot less. I had meetings with Patriots player rep Tom Addison throughout the week, and both of us talked to our teammates about the possibility of going on strike. We hadn't even formed an official players' union yet! Obviously Sid wasn't too happy with me about this, especially during a time when he wanted his team to give its complete focus to game preparation."

Fortunately, a compromise was reached the Friday before the game. The league agreed to pay out shares based on what they would have been if Balboa Stadium was close to a sellout. Nearly fifty years later, Mix laughed about the entire episode. "It's comical to think about how hard we were fighting over what was really nothing but chump change. But none of us made much money in those days."

Being distracted by the player share dispute wasn't Gillman's only worry. The centerpiece of his game plan, Keith Lincoln, was hardly the picture of health. "I drove to the game with my wife and told her I was feeling flu-ish," he recalled. "I felt a little bit off and was concerned whether I'd have enough stamina to play the whole game."

Before the first quarter was even completed, it was the Boston Patriots who felt like throwing up.

1ST HALF

Chargers Series No. 1
1st Quarter: San Diego 0, Boston 0

San Diego began the game's opening drive on its own 28. Paul Lowe and Keith Lincoln were split in the backfield, with quarterback Tobin Rote under center. Tight end Dave Kocourek lined up adjacent to left tackle Ernie Wright, with split end Don Norton in the slot and flanker Lance Alworth to his outside (the slot being the gap in the offensive line between the tackle and the customary receiver on that side). Sid called this his "east" formation, because it put two wide receivers on the right (or east side, as if you were looking at a map), and it made Kocourek the weakside receiver. This forced Patriots safety Ron Hall, whose regular assignment was covering the opponent's strong side, to rotate over to where San Diego's two wideouts were aligned. The problem for Hall was that he normally covered slower tight ends, not speedy receivers like Alworth or Norton. Mismatches like this would hurt the Patriots all day.

The aggressive Boston defense was eager to make an impact right away, so it stationed outside linebacker Jack Rudolph on the line of scrimmage, head-up on Kocourek—and put the other outside backer, Addison, directly over Norton. Rote could clearly see that a blitz was coming, the first of what would be numerous Patriots "red dogs" (the common term for blitzing with a linebacker in the 1960s). Following the snap, nearly the entire Patriots seven-man front went straight for the quarterback. Rote faked a toss to Lincoln and faked an inside trap to Lowe—two fakes on the first play!—then drilled a swing pass to Lincoln on the right side of the field. Both Addison and middle linebacker Buoniconti took the bait on the trap and charged toward Lowe, leaving Lincoln open to pick up a dozen yards.

This first call was Gillman's philosophy in a nutshell. Years later, veteran San Diego sportswriter Wayne Lockwood wrote a terrific magazine piece on the '63 championship game plan, and in that story Sid told him, "You're not just looking to see where you want to throw the ball or run the ball. What you're looking for is reaction and over-reaction from the defense. The reason for that is I want the big play. I don't want the little play, the average play. I want the big play."

Sid didn't have to wait long for the Chargers to bust one. On the second play of the game, with the ball resting on the Chargers' 40, Boston brought an eight-man front that included all three linebackers and Hall from his safety position. Once again, both wide receivers lined up on the same side, but this time on the left. Lowe ran in motion to their side, wreaking havoc in two different ways; Addison ran with Lowe, away from where the play was eventually headed, and Lowe's movement also caused itchy defenders Rudolph and defensive end Bob Dee to go offside. As they jumped, Lincoln ran an inside trap, with left guard Sam DeLuca pulling behind center Don Rogers. Rogers buried defensive tackle Jesse Richardson, and with Addison following Lowe, there were no second-level defenders left in the middle of the field. Even with flu-like symptoms, it wasn't hard for Lincoln to run through open space for a 56-yard gain before being tackled inside the 5.

In their two earlier meetings, San Diego hadn't put either of its backs in motion, deciding it was better at that time to rely on them as pass blockers instead of challenging Boston's rugged run defense. Not today, as far as Sid Gillman was concerned. "Motion, movement, and a lot of traps," he said. "That's what we figured could beat them. We'd fake the toss and run the trap inside." The Chargers would come back

Inside Trap

Gillman exploited Boston's aggressive blitzing tactics with a fake toss to Lowe following a quick count that caused Dee and Rudolph to jump offside. Patriots linebacker Addison followed Lowe, creating a hole for Lincoln to run the trap. Note that Sid positioned both of his wide receivers on the left side, a common alignment today, but very rare in 1963.

to this frequently, and blitz-crazy Boston got torched almost every time. "Having our backs in motion was a new look for them," recalled Lincoln. "I think it really confused their linebackers. It gave us just a split-second where they'd freeze and gave us the opportunity to hit them quick."

Two plays later, Rote dived in on a quarterback sneak, and San Diego had the early lead. After the Chargers defense limited Boston's attack to a net of minus 5 yards on *its* first possession, Gillman's offensive unit took over at its own 41.

Chargers Series No. 2
1st Quarter: San Diego 7, Boston 0

The Patriots defense began the drive with another blitz, but this one got the results its coaching staff was accustomed to seeing. Outside linebacker Rudolph lined up with his hand on the ground, making him a defensive end on the right side. In the middle Buoniconti blitzed the inside (also known as the "A-Gap," the space between the center and the right guard), giving Boston a six-man rush. Buoniconti was successfully contained, but tight end Kocourek failed to block Rudolph, who dropped Rote for an eight-yard loss.

The Patriots had all of thirty seconds to enjoy their defensive success. The spot of the sack placed the ball in the middle of the field between the hash marks, and Boston chose to line up a conventional four-man front. On second and 18, Paul Lowe simulated an inside trap, drawing attention from part of the defensive line. Buoniconti ignored Lowe, blitzing the backfield and colliding with left guard DeLuca. That was too bad for Nick, because the play was a toss outside to the left, with Lincoln running behind Ernie Wright. Wright weighed 270, a pretty good size for an offensive tackle back then, but he sure didn't run like a guy that big. Defensive end Larry Eisenhauer remembered just how quick Ernie was on this play. "The two best tackles I went up against in the AFL were Jim Tyrer [who played for the Kansas City Chiefs] and Winston Hill [of the New York Jets] because they had quick feet. But Ernie was just as fast as they were. He could lead the sweep as well as a guard."

Lincoln was about to electrify the crowd again, but Wright was the true hero of the play. Pulling out on the perimeter, Ernie steamrolled Rudolph with a block that got Lincoln free on the edge. What made the block even more impressive was that Rudolph wasn't really Wright's assignment on the play. But with Rudolph heading his way, Ernie had no choice but to take him out. After Rudolph went down, Wright threw *another* block on Patriots defensive back Dick Felt, leaving no one to stop Lincoln as he broke free for a 67-yard touchdown run. "Our basic play was the outside toss—our key play, the one we dared you to stop," said Gillman. "We had so much speed with Lincoln and Lowe."

The game was barely four minutes old, but already Lincoln had racked up 123 rushing yards on just two carries. The Chargers had scored on their fourth and sixth plays from scrimmage to take a two-touchdown lead. The Patriots answered with their first score of the game, a 7-yard run from Larry Garron, set up by a long pass reception from Gino Cappelletti. Maybe most important, the four-minute drive gave Boston's defense a chance to catch its breath and try to figure out a way to slow down the Chargers.

Outside Toss

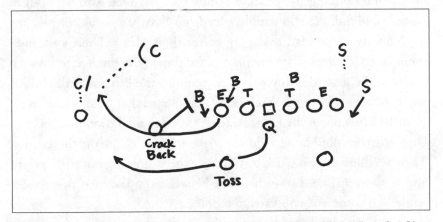

Lowe fakes a trap inside, while Patriots linebacker Buoniconti aggressively blitzes San Diego quarterback Rote. Chargers left tackle Wright pulls out to lead the way for Lincoln, blocking two different Patriots defenders in the process. Lincoln's long scoring run put San Diego ahead 14-0 just minutes into the game. This outside toss was a Gillman favorite. We were still running this in Philadelphia nearly two decades later with me pitching the ball to Wilbert Montgomery.

Chargers Series No. 3
1st Quarter: San Diego 14, Boston 7

From their own 27, the Chargers ran two plays that picked up only 4 yards. Faced with their first third-down situation of the game, the Patriots' defense played the percentages, anticipating a pass. Both their scouting reports and firsthand game experience verified that for most of the '63 season, "pass-first" San Diego usually threw on third-and-long. Well, Sid crossed them up again. He guessed correctly that Boston would be blitzing its front, while the secondary was in "man free" coverage—that is, three defensive backs playing man-to-man on the two wide receivers and tight end, with the free safety available to help where needed. Gillman put Lowe in motion, and Rudolph ran with him step-for-step while leaving his assigned spot. After the snap, Lincoln ran an inside trap, following guard Pat Shea, who sealed off Eisenhauer. Lincoln burst through Rudolph's vacated area for an 11-yard gain and a first down.

Lincoln's gain resulted in the ball being spotted on the left hash mark, which gave the Chargers plenty of room to operate on the right side if they chose to run their next play in that direction. Sure enough, Rote dialed up a play called "Toss 78 Y-Man 0": a pitch to Lowe running behind pulling right tackle Ron Mix. "We liked Ron Mix out in front," said Sid. "If you couldn't lead our toss, you couldn't play for us. Nobody could lead that play better than Mix." There's no finer moment to illustrate why the man nicknamed "the Intellectual Assassin" was the first AFL lineman inducted into the Pro Football Hall of Fame. Mix blasted cornerback Bob Suci so hard that he shoved him almost 10 yards down the field, clearing the edge for Lowe. Slot receiver Don Norton eliminated Addison to get Lowe clean on the corner. Then Mix finished his work by blocking the stumbling but still upright Suci a *second* time. Lowe then ran between the last two Boston defenders to complete a 58-yard touchdown.

The Chargers were blessed with terrific talent on their front line, but they were also well schooled by a guy named Joe Madro, a little genius who was with Sid every place he was a head coach. Tom Bass learned their system after joining the Chargers. "The two of them devised at least three different ways to attack every hole in the line. Ace, deuce, trey, jack, queen, and king were the names Sid and Joe used.

"The beauty of it was that all of those methods were interchangeable, in that you could run the same base plays—which Sid referred to as his Dirty Dozen—but none of them ever looked the same. Three different players of ours could come at a blitzing linebacker, and he never knew which one it would be. Let's say we were going to run off tackle with Mix leading. We could double-team block it and kick out with the fullback. That's one way. Another would be for Ron to block down along with the tight end, then pull for the kick-out with a guard. Or we could block down with the tight end and pull Mix for the kick out. It's all the same play, going to the same area, but with three totally different looks. It was as confusing as hell for the defense."

Confusion certainly must have been the prevailing condition in the Patriots' defensive huddle to this point. The Chargers had scored three touchdowns on their first ten plays, only three of which had been passes, to rack up 204 yards. Boston had geared its blitz package to shut down the pass, and the Chargers had gone with the run. "What had worked for us against them in the regular season sure wasn't working in the championship," admitted Marion Campbell. "When you blitz, the other team can beat you for a touchdown on a single play, where against a more sound defense, you can keep their gains manageable." But did the Pats scale back on their blitzes? Hell no. This was who they were. It had gotten them to this point; they weren't going to change their approach in the middle of a championship game. That strategy played perfectly into Gillman's hands.

Boston's head coach, Mike Holovak, was a defensive-oriented guy. The funny thing was that Mike had the nicest, most gentlemanly personality of any coach of that era, but he liked his defense to play very aggressively. "Sid *wanted* them to blitz," said Tom Bass. "Where most opponents were scared to death of the Patriots, Sid *welcomed* their blitzing. Look, Boston's defensive backs were pretty good, but if your line can block the blitz, there aren't many people who can hold up in the secondary."

Following Lowe's touchdown run, Boston's offense sputtered and was off the field in three plays. The Chargers' next series didn't produce a touchdown—or even a first down. But the Balboa Stadium crowd didn't seem to mind, cheering wildly as the eventful first quarter ended.

Chargers Series No. 5
2nd Quarter: San Diego 21, Boston 7

The Patriots' offensive problems continued on their first series of the quarter; they notched only one first down before being forced to punt again. With a little over ten minutes to go before the half, the Chargers got the ball at their own 26. For the first time against Boston (outside of goal-line offense) San Diego went to a one-back, three-receiver set. The personnel was exactly the same, only this time Lincoln—not Don Norton—was aligned in the slot. Next to Keith was Lance Alworth, who'd been thrown to twice but had yet to catch a pass. As the single back, Lowe motioned toward the slot side. Following the snap, Rote took a five-step drop and hit Alworth on a curl route for 8 yards. The play worked because Lowe flared to the outside, drawing coverage while Lincoln sealed the inside coverage to keep the passing lane open for the completion. I know what you're probably thinking: What's the big deal? Today's NFL offenses run this pattern all the time—and you're right. It's called a flat/curl route combination with a seam seal. But no matter what they called it back then, I can assure you that not many pro teams included this in their playbook. Sid Gillman did.

On the next play, the Chargers returned to their split-back formation. Rote brought his team to the line and then went to a quick count before Boston could settle in. The call was an inside handoff to Lincoln. Don Rogers cleared away Buoniconti, and DeLuca bowled over Houston Antwine. Lincoln was staring at a hole you could drive a dump truck through. He didn't hesitate, bursting into the secondary, where he wasn't stopped until he'd ripped off a 44-yard gain. "We made Lincoln look like Superman," admitted Larry Eisenhauer. "But it wasn't just him. He had a great line blocking for him. Inside, outside—they were running us to death. They weren't passing that much, and we were baffled. *What's going on here?* This wasn't what we had prepared for. I still have visions of all those thunderbolts flying by me: over, around, all over the joint. It was embarrassing."

Lincoln wasn't quite done on the drive. On the next play, he again lined up in the slot in a three-wide set. Lowe went in motion toward the wide side of the field, and Tom Addison followed him. In Addison's vacated area, Rote gunned a slant pass to Keith that put the ball just outside Boston's 10-yard line. This time, though, Boston's red-zone defense held, and the Chargers were forced to settle for a George Blair field goal. Boston matched that score with a Cappelletti field goal on its next possession, so with less than three minutes to play before halftime, the Chargers were given one final opportunity to pad their lead.

Chargers Series No. 6
2nd Quarter: San Diego 24, Boston 10

After picking up a quick first down that got San Diego to its own 45, Lowe ran a sweep that gained just a yard, giving the Chargers a second and 9. Gillman then went back to the same play that had opened the game. Off a quick count, Rote faked the toss to Lincoln, faked the inside trap to Lowe, then fired a swing pass to Lincoln in the flat. I suppose Boston considered this a "moral victory" when Keith got "only" 24 yards on the play, but I spotted several noteworthy features in the call: First and foremost, that the Patriots continued to overreact to San Diego's fakes, taking themselves out of the play while the Chargers burned them on the back side. I was also impressed with the athletic ability of San Diego's offensive line. This time both Rogers and Shea pulled to the outside and gave Lincoln a convoy to follow.

The Chargers were moving the ball well enough on their own, but they got additional help when a pass interference penalty put them on the Patriots' 14-yard line. From there, San Diego scored its first passing touchdown of the afternoon. Don Norton lined up as a tight-end, creating a two-tight-end balanced set in front of a split backfield. Meanwhile, Alworth was flanked wide to the outside. Lowe ran in motion away from Norton, and after the snap, Lincoln and Lowe both released to the wide side, drawing four different Boston defenders to that area. Rote briefly looked in that direction, then narrowly avoided a charging Jack Rudolph as he threw back-side to Norton on a tight-end screen. With all the Patriots busy reacting to Lincoln and Lowe, there were no second-level defenders in Norton's way, and he waltzed into the end zone for the score. It was another example of what Sid hoped for from Boston's defenders: reaction and overreaction.

The half ended with San Diego ahead, 31–10. The margin was unexpected, given how competitive the two Patriots-Chargers regular-season games had been. What was even more surprising was how that big lead had been built. Tobin Rote had thrown only 11 passes the entire half. And yet the Chargers already had four touchdowns and 328 total yards! I could only hearken back to what Sid told me time and again in our quarterback meetings with the Eagles: "You've got to be able to pass to be able to run. When a coach says he's got to establish the run first, he's full of shit!" Sid was an impatient man. He wanted big plays, he wanted them often, and he felt they all derived from putting the ball up—or at least *convincing* the opponent that was his intention. He simply had no patience for the "slow and steady" approach. I remember one time in Philadelphia, he sat fidgeting like a kindergartner while our offensive line coaches talked through the base running plays for that week's game plan. After those coaches finally left the room, Sid rolled his eyes at us quarterbacks and wailed, "I don't know why we waste all that goddamn time trying to gain three yards!"

In today's NFL, the passing game dominates, but you have to realize how radical Sid's thinking was back in the early sixties. NFL teams like the Bears and the Browns were heavily ground oriented, and the Green Bay Packers' success under Vince Lombardi inspired numerous teams to rely on a run-first approach. Sid's trademark was the air game, but when a team like Boston "sold out" with blitzing schemes designed to stop the pass, Sid switched tracks. While the Pats focused on pressuring the passing attack, the Chargers outfoxed them with traps and tosses on running plays.

Clearly Sid had been concerned about Boston's defensive speed and constant blitzing. He didn't want short corners for their linebackers to tee off on his aging quarterback (Rote was in his fourteenth pro season in 1963), which would have been the case if San Diego had spread its formations. So he kept his formations tight, which also provided enough protection for Rote. Sid further rattled Boston by having

Rote call quick counts out of the huddle to eliminate any of the Pats' pre-snap movements that might have raised doubt or hesitation in the minds of Chargers' blockers. Gillman wisely believed that it was better to be proactive and take away any Patriots disguises or deception. It also amped up the tempo of his offense, which kept the Pats back on their heels. It was pro football jujitsu: turning your opponent's strengths against him. By using motion and deception, he never allowed Boston to get defined looks. The Pats' aggression and speed sent them off in one direction while the play went somewhere else.

2ND HALF

The Patriots had the ball twice early in the third quarter, but both drives ended with three-and-outs for Boston. An obvious beneficiary of the Chargers' defensive efficiency was Keith Lincoln. "People made a fuss over my performance that day," he said, "but a lot of that success came from the fact that we got the ball back quickly and often. Boston's defense didn't have time to rest, and our offensive unit was in a rhythm. We pretty much had a hard time doing anything wrong that day." All told, a half dozen Patriots possessions ended with three or fewer plays being run before the ball went back to San Diego's offense.

Chargers Series No. 2
3rd Quarter: San Diego 31, Boston 10

Boston's first-half tactics had produced disastrous results. The Patriots had blitzed on fourteen of San Diego's twenty-six plays from scrimmage, and on those fourteen plays the Chargers had gained more than 200 yards, with an average of 14.6 yards per play. But what other choice did the Patriots have? They were trailing by three touchdowns and needed turnovers quickly. The only way to do that, thought Mike Holovak and Marion Campbell, was to keep the blitzes coming and hope for a fumble or a pick.

On the second play of the drive, Rudolph and Eisenhauer broke through to sack Rote for a 5-yard loss, putting San Diego in a third-

and-7 situation. Sid was never afraid to return to successful plays again and again—and he did right here with the swing pass to Lincoln that had opened the game. Once more Rote effectively faked the toss and trap, then fired to Keith—this time on the short side of the field. The reduced operating space was not a problem, because Ernie Wright had moved quickly to get out in front and lead the way. Don Norton also helped out, running a route with a "rub" element to it: obstructing Buoniconti so that he had to fight through traffic to get to Lincoln. Nick arrived way too late, and Lincoln's 32-yard play put the ball in Boston territory.

Still the Patriots kept blitzing—and for one of the rare times that day, they stifled a Chargers running play. On first down, Lincoln was snowed under by Houston Antwine for a 3-yard loss. But Sid wasn't worried, because his next call was the perfect counterpunch to Boston's relentless red dogs. San Diego called a Go route for Alworth, by far the most athletically gifted player on the field that day for either team. Boston sent six men on the play, but Gillman kept both his backs and tight ends in to block. Eight-man protection almost always wins out when the other team sends only six. And Alworth had only single coverage to beat. The defender was Bob Suci, who'd led the Patriots that season with seven interceptions. Yes, Suci was the guy that Ron Mix had buried twice on Paul Lowe's touchdown run, but on this play, Suci had Lance well covered. Rote's throw was right on target, but, hell, nobody's perfect. Alworth could not come up with the catch, and the Chargers faced a third-and-13.

I've said that Sid liked going back to the same plays over and over if they were working. Well, this time he repeated the *exact* play he had just run! He had that much confidence in Alworth and his blockers. I don't think the Patriots expected to see the same play on back-to-back calls. As was the case on the previous down, the Chargers kept both Lincoln and Lowe and the tight end to block Boston's blitz. Good thing they did, because Buoniconti blew by Wright and was headed for Rote. Fortunately, Tobin was saved by none other than Lincoln, who added to his already outstanding performance by crumpling Buoniconti with a devastating shot. Rote fired downfield, again to Alworth, but the Pats' pressure had forced Tobin to airmail the pass just over

Lance's head, with Suci right on him. But the gifted future Hall of Fame flanker leaped into the sky to pull down the ball just above Suci's helmet, then breezed past him for a 48-yard touchdown.

There were so many great individual efforts on this play that it's easy to lose sight of an essential Gillman principle at the core of its success. A major factor that influenced what formations and personnel Sid used was where the ball was spotted in relation to the hash marks. Back then the hashes were split out much wider on the playing surface than they are under today's rules, so there was a clearly defined short side closer to the sideline (the "boundary") and wide side ("the field"). Sid's formation and personnel choices were heavily influenced by where the ball was spotted on each play.

Because San Diego called this play toward the boundary, Suci was on an "island"—the lone defensive back in a specific area. Even though most of San Diego's skill players stayed in to block, there was no way another defender could make up the necessary distance to come across and give over-the-top help to Suci. Positioned across the field on the wide side, Boston's other DBs simply had too far to run to get to Alworth. *This* was what Sid meant when he said his goal was to force defenses to cover every inch of the football field.

The Chargers had one more series in the third quarter but got only past midfield before punting, content to carry a 38–10 lead into the final quarter. This brief lull is a good opportunity to mention something that really jumped out at me when I watched the game tape. Keep in mind that this championship was played nearly fifty years ago, and even though many of Sid's offensive concepts remain as fresh and vital today as they were back then, in one area the modern game is radically different. As explosive as the Chargers were that afternoon, they still relied on fairly basic personnel—with two backs, one tight end, and two wide receivers—on almost every play. The formations stayed pretty much the same too. By contrast, twenty-first-century NFL offenses are all about personnel packages and formation variation. When you watch a game today, it's not unusual to see fifteen different formations (with all kinds of shifts and motions), and as many as a half dozen personnel packages in the first fifteen plays of the game!

There are a number of reasons why you *didn't* have that kind of variety in 1963, the most basic one being the sheer lack of manpower. "You never saw three-receiver sets then because we didn't have enough guys," Tom Bass recalled. "There were only thirty-five players on each roster. You weren't going to put your substitute wideout on the field and run the risk of them all getting hurt at the same time. So what Sid did was put Keith Lincoln in motion and have him go out to a receiver's spot. That was considered wildly innovative at that time."

The next season, Bass got the privilege of being Lincoln's position coach, and learned firsthand how talented he was. "I can't overemphasize what a valuable asset a player like Lincoln was to Sid's scheme. Besides being an outstanding blocker and runner, he was also a great route runner and receiver. When linebackers covered him, it was an absolute mismatch. Keith had the quickest start of anybody at his position. He could be up to full speed in three steps! A lot of his catches came off play-action. The quarterback would fake to Lowe, Lincoln would pretend to block, then release. Most people from those days who are still around will say that Keith Lincoln was the best route runner among AFL backs of that era."

Chargers Series No. 4
4th Quarter: San Diego 38, Boston 10

After San Diego's defense stopped the Patriots on downs, the Chargers took possession at their own 30 with a little more than ten minutes remaining in the game. At this point, Sid pulled Tobin Rote for his backup: second-year quarterback John Hadl. But that didn't mean Sid was ready to call off the dogs—not by a long shot. He never stopped being aggressive in any game he ever coached, and I think this goes back to his Ohio State days, in the late 1930s when he was a staff assistant for a guy named Francis Schmidt. Coach Schmidt loved gadget plays with end-arounds, tackle- and guard-eligible calls, and multiple laterals. Those Buckeyes teams scored so often and won by such wide margins that he earned the nickname "Close the Gates of Mercy" Schmidt. He was clearly a major influence on Sid's wide-open philosophy and take-no-prisoners attitude. Schmidt was inducted into the College Football Hall of Fame in 1971.

Sid didn't show any mercy to the Patriots, even though the outcome of the '63 title game was no longer in doubt. After a running play picked up 3 yards, the Chargers came to the line of scrimmage and, for the first time the entire day, were in the conventional offensive set of that era: two split backs, a tight end next to the right tackle, and the two receivers split. There was no slot receiver, and nobody went in motion. But even from this standard formation, the Chargers torched Boston. Sid had Don Norton line up a good 5 yards outside of where the yard numbers were imprinted, the better to "spread the field" horizontally and create wider gaps in the Patriots' secondary. Like Rote before him, Hadl ran a quick count to negate Patriot defensive presnap movement, then took a five-step drop, waited patiently for Norton to clear on an inside slant, and gunned it to him for a 30-yard gain. Once more, Boston's defender was simply too far from Norton to close quickly, and the Chargers burned him.

San Diego eventually advanced to the Patriots' 25 where it faced a fourth-and-2. Sid could have kicked a field goal or tried to run for the first down. He did neither. The Chargers came out in a two-tight-end look (granted, Alworth was aligned as one of those tight ends; not the ideal blocking choice if the call were a short-yardage run), and Norton again lined up well outside the numbers. So the defense was fairly certain that Sid would be passing. The Patriots went to a six-man front, with outside linebackers Addison and Rudolph lined up as defensive ends. Hadl ran a play-fake to Lowe, causing Buoniconti to hesitate briefly—a costly decision because Keith Lincoln was his man-to-man responsibility in pass coverage. Lincoln used his amazing burst to blow past Nick on a circle pattern. Hadl ducked away from the blitzing Rudolph and lobbed the ball to a wide-open Lincoln for another touchdown.

To everyone's surprise, Sid then had holder Tobin Rote try to throw for a 2-point conversion from point-after kick formation, but Rote's high pass sailed out of the end zone. Sid was asked in the locker room why he made that decision with a 34-point lead. He claimed it wasn't a designed play; that Rote had merely mishandled the snap and was trying to salvage the attempt by throwing. Maybe that's true, but judging by San Diego's cold-blooded demeanor throughout the game, I have to wonder.

Chargers Series No. 5
4th Quarter: San Diego 44, Boston 10

The Chargers' defense was still playing hard in the final minutes, stopping Boston's next possession near midfield. San Diego began its final drive of the day on its own 20 and called again on Lincoln, who responded with an 8-yard pickup on a sweep. Sid was just about ready to take out Keith for good, but not before allowing his star performer one last encore play. Hadl called the toss play to Lincoln, who swept right. Both Norton and Alworth appeared to position themselves for run blocking. Mix pulled out in front to make it look like a sweep. On a day when he'd virtually done it all, Lincoln added to his accomplishments by lofting an option pass 20 yards downfield to reserve tight end Jacque Mackinnon. After Mackinnon's catch, Sid sent in backup fullback Gerry McDougall so that the man of the hour could receive a well-deserved curtain call. A moment later, the Balboa Stadium public address announcer informed the crowd that Lincoln, to absolutely no one's surprise, had been voted game MVP.

Okay, I'm thinking that with his usual flair for the dramatic, Sid has made this grand gesture to give Lincoln the royal sendoff. Now he'll just run out the clock. Nope. Guns blazing to the end, Hadl threw deep to Alworth near the goal line, but Dick Felt batted it away. After Felt knocked down a shorter pass headed for Lance, the Chargers faced third-and-10 at midfield. Run a halfback dive into the line and kick it away? Not a chance. Sid flexed Mackinnon a few yards away from Mix, which kept the big tight end clear from being jammed by a linebacker once the play began. After the snap, Jacque initially ran a vertical route, then broke left to run a deep crossing pattern. The deep cross was not common for tight ends of the early sixties, who generally lacked the speed to beat defensive backs. Mackinnon didn't have that problem. Hadl fired to his left, and Mackinnon took off for a 33-yard completion. Hadl then threw on *four* consecutive plays, moving the ball just outside the goal line, where he dived in for the touchdown. Following the extra point (a conventional kick this time), the carnage ended, with the Chargers winning, 51–10—the widest margin of victory of any title game in the AFL's ten-year existence.

The final statistics were even more one-sided. Boston gained 263 yards in total offense, while San Diego exploded for an astonishing 610 yards. Of those, 318 yards had come on the ground—a staggering total for a team renowned for throwing the deep pass. But Sid knew that for this game his running attack would best counter Boston's blitzes, and the numbers bear him out. The Chargers ran sixty plays, and the Patriots blitzed on twenty-eight of them, or 47 percent of the time. San Diego gained 352 of its yards when Boston was blitzing, and scored four of its seven touchdowns off red dogs. These inflated numbers had a profound effect on the way Marion Campbell coached defenses the rest of his career. "I realized that this much blitzing can't be your whole system," he reflected. "It totally changed my philosophy. It's easy to just let 'er rip with the blitz, but we got hurt badly with that. If it fails, like it did against the Chargers, you've got nothing to fall back on. From then on, I only coached a controlled system where the other team was going to have to earn every score on its own."

Individually, the best numbers belonged to Lincoln. The same guy who'd told his wife on their drive to the stadium that he didn't think his flu-like symptoms would keep him in action very long amassed one of the finest single-game performances in pro football history: 206 rushing yards and 103 receiving yards, plus the 20 extra yards from his option pass completion. His 329 yards in total offense remained a postseason record until 1971, when Kansas City's Ed Podolak surpassed it with 350 against the Dolphins on Christmas Day in a divisional playoff between the two former AFL teams. But Podolak needed two additional overtime periods to break Keith's record! "San Diego didn't put up those kind of numbers simply because we blitzed so much," claimed Campbell. "A lot of it had to do with their speed and personnel. In the end, good players are going to win for you. But here's where you really have to give Sid credit. Some coaches have good material but don't know what to do with it. Sid really knew how to get the best out of all those great players."

The mood in the Chargers' locker room was nothing less than total elation. It was a sensation Ron Mix hadn't enjoyed before that game and hasn't enjoyed since. "I don't know if I ever felt younger, stronger, or faster than that day. If you do your job right, you should feel tired after the game. I don't remember ever feeling fatigue. The whole experience was invigorating—as if a shot of adrenaline came into your body every time one of our players did something spectacular. It was thrilling to be a part of it. Anybody who plays in any sport, no matter the level, will at some point do something perfect. In our case, it happened to us as a team. Everybody had the game of their lives."

The team's championship ring would eventually bear the engraving "1963 AFL and World Champions." "If anyone wants to dispute that claim, just let them play us," Gillman roared.

"Sid wanted to play the NFL champion Chicago Bears right then and there," recalled Bass. "If that game had taken place, I think the Chargers would have held their own. I don't know if they would have won, but it would have been competitive. The rout over the Patriots gave the AFL a lot of publicity they never would have had otherwise. It really got people's attention."

Coincidentally, the idea of an AFL-NFL showdown was mentioned in a *Sports Illustrated* story just a couple of weeks before the Patriots-Chargers game, in an issue that featured Rote and Lowe on the cover. The day after crushing Boston, Sid attempted to set up a "World Series of pro football" by writing NFL commissioner Pete Rozelle. Rozelle had been Sid's general manager when Gillman coached the Rams in the 1950s. Sid's letter referenced the Vatican's recent Second Ecumenical Council, in which Pope John XXIII sought to reverse years of bitterness between Catholicism and Judaism by stating, "The Jews should not be presented as rejected or accursed by God." Sid noted pointedly, "Pope John was a great man because he recognized the 'other league.'" Rozelle sent Sid a telegram the next day with his reply: "Yes. But it took a thousand years." Clearly, the NFL owners had no interest. To them, the AFL upstarts were poaching on their turf. Why give them any credibility by acknowledging them as equals? And why risk playing them, where the veteran league could be handed an embarrassing defeat?

The two leagues wouldn't meet head-to-head for another three years. But more than any game prior to the New York Jets' upset win in Super Bowl III, in January 1969, the Chargers' rout of Boston forced the established NFL to begin taking this "other league" seriously. And it opened the eyes of even the most conservative critics, who grudgingly admitted there just might be something to Sid Gillman's innovative schemes.

After completing my film study of the Patriots and Chargers, I still marveled at the fact that a Sid Gillman team amassed 610 yards by relying more on the run than the pass. It was the most yardage ever gained by any of Sid's teams in any professional game where he was the head coach. In Wayne Lockwood's magazine feature about the '63 championship, Sid confessed, "No game plan works *that* well. I think it was just one of those days more than anything else." In his wildest dreams, Sid never believed that three of his first ten plays would go for 56, 67, and 58 yards. Every one of those calls was designed with the idea that, executed correctly, the play would pick up anywhere from 10 to 20 yards. Had the Chargers not jumped out to such a commanding lead so early, I'm sure Sid would have put the ball up much more.

But he didn't have to. His tosses and traps were killing Boston's blitz, so San Diego kept running. This brings me back to the brilliance of Gillman's game plan. Against the rest of the AFL in 1963, the Chargers' bombs-away approach piled up points and lopsided wins. But in two narrowly won regular-season games against Marion Campbell's red-dogging defense, San Diego scored only 7 and 17 points. If Sid continued to run this same offense, he was likely to end up with another nail-biter—and no guarantee they'd come out on top a third time. Gillman simply could not take that risk. He desperately wanted to win a championship, so he altered his team's approach. The Chargers changed their look, putting men in motion and calling runs that initially resembled familiar pass plays. Boston came into the game dead certain that it knew exactly what the Chargers would use against it, but Sid turned that defense on its head. For Gillman, it was a melding of ideology and pragmatism, being secure enough to know he would have to set aside the passing plays he loved for the benefit of team success. The result was a coaching triumph any way you want to define it: numerically, artistically, historically.

Nineteen sixty-three was only John Hadl's second year in pro football. Even though he ran for one score and passed for another in the championship game, it was strictly in mop-up duty as Tobin Rote's backup. By the time I met John in 1973, he was a battle-tested old pro. In my rookie season with the Rams, he was a fantastic role model, winning the NFL MVP Award while leading the Rams to their best record in team history. John took me under his wing and taught me plenty about the quarterback position. He also shared more than a few "Sid stories," many of them about what a hard-ass and taskmaster he could be.

"I never had a day off during football season after I became the starter," John remembered. "I'd get to the Charger offices at 8:00 AM and still be there late in the evening. Sid could be pretty tough on me in film sessions—he'd rip my ass and tear it apart. For a while I didn't say much, but it finally got to the point where we'd really go at it. The great thing about Sid was that you could have tremendous arguments with him—screaming and yelling where both of us would get upset. But when those meetings were over, he was already onto the next thing, we'd go to practice, and he was fine. He could really turn it on and off. Deep down, I think Sid enjoyed that give-and-take. I loved Sid, and have tremendous respect for what he did and what he stood for. When I got into coaching myself, I used the Gillman offense for my own teams. It's always been good, and it's always current. After I stopped playing for him, we saw each other all the time and became great friends."

I also enjoyed a warm relationship with Sid at the end of his coaching career. After the 1986 season, I became a free agent and went out to San Diego to meet with the Chargers about playing another season or two. Sid and his lovely wife, Esther, insisted that I stay with them at their home up in La Jolla, and it was truly a memorable experience. Sid showed me his collection of jazz records, the biggest and most comprehensive music library I'd ever seen. It was all meticulously catalogued and alphabetized, from Cannonball Adderley to Lester Young. But that was nothing compared to what I saw after Esther served us dinner. When he was with the Eagles, Sid had told me about his game film archives, amassed over fifty-plus years in coaching, but I had never seen them. He had all these reels of footage, broken down by play selection, personnel, formations—you name it. Once we finished eating, Sid took me into his office, where all his treasures were stored: his personal "wine cellar." More than six hours later, we were still up there, poring over his celluloid history of pro football. It was an evening I will never forget.

As I stood over his shoulder, it struck me that I was actually this close to him years earlier when my Bills team finally won their first championship by beating Sid's Chargers in the 1964 AFL title game. After the final gun sounded, I slipped through the crevasses of War Memorial's rickety snow fence and ran onto the field with thousands of other fans. I remember seeing Jack Kemp being carried off on the shoulders of his teammates. I shook hands with a few of the players, and center Al Bemiller gave me his chin strap. I felt like I was almost part of that Bills team; it was one of the happiest moments of my life. But I was also just a few feet away from a disconsolate Sid Gillman, miserable from the cold and obviously despondent over his team's 20–7 defeat. He brushed past me for a fleeting moment, and then he was gone. I was only thirteen at the time and certainly didn't feel sorry for him—I was exhilarated about my team winning a title. But I will never forget the heartsick expression on Sid's face.

Years later, when he coached me with the Eagles, I never missed an opportunity to gently remind Sid about that '64 game—or the one the following year in which Buffalo beat the Chargers again, this time in a shutout, to win its second straight AFL championship. I'd keep those memories tucked in my hip pocket, and sometimes when Sid would bug me over some boneheaded thing I'd done in practice, I'd get my revenge by teasing him about those back-to-back losses. He'd wince, but I also believe he appreciated how much of a fan I was of the AFL era. I think Sid respected me because I understood where he came from and what he'd accomplished to make his team and that league a success.

I was deeply saddened when I heard that Sid had passed away right after New Year's Day 2003. He was buried at Hillside Memorial Park in Los Angeles, a cemetery that's also the final resting place for numerous Hollywood legends. Comedians Jack Benny and Milton Berle, dancer Cyd Charisse, singers Al Jolson and Dinah Shore—even Moe Howard of the Three Stooges—all have their graves at Hillside. I can't think of a more appropriate place for him to spend eternity. Sid Gillman was a football genius, but he was also a master showman, someone who loved making bold statements with his words, his wardrobe, and his actions on a football field. In a way, Sid, you're kind of back where you started—almost like being in one of your dad's Minneapolis movie houses. Only this time, you're not up in the projection booth swiping football newsreel film clips. No, you're right in your element, alongside some of the greatest entertainers in show business history. And if those spirits could talk, they'd probably agree that you were their football counterpart, as skilled as anyone at giving the crowd every reason to stand up and cheer.

Bud Carson's Cover-Two Defense

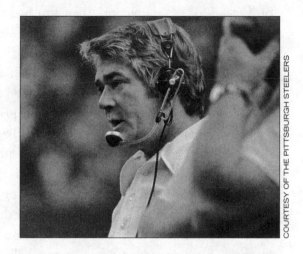

COURTESY OF THE PITTSBURGH STEELERS

1974 AFC CHAMPIONSHIP
PITTSBURGH STEELERS vs. OAKLAND RAIDERS
Oakland Coliseum, Oakland, California — December 29, 1974

On December 20, 1975, nearly seventy thousand fans filed into the Los Angeles Coliseum for a rare Saturday night game that millions more would watch on national television. The opponents were the defending Super Bowl champion Steelers and the hometown Rams. First-string quarterback James Harris was still nursing a bruised shoulder, so L.A. coach Chuck Knox turned to a second-year passer local sportswriters had dubbed "the Polish Rifle" but everyone else called Ronald Vincent Jaworski. Nearly two years since my college days at Youngstown State, I was, at long last, finally getting my first starting assignment in the National Football League.

Both teams had already wrapped up playoff spots, but it was still a game each of us wanted to win. I know I did. This was my best chance to prove that I could play in the NFL, even though I'd be facing one of the greatest defenses in league history. All week, I'd felt that knot in the pit of my stomach as I studied game film of Pittsburgh's Steel Curtain defense. I thought points would be very tough to come by—and boy, was I right.

We squeaked out a 10–3 win that wasn't decided until the fourth quarter. With six minutes to play, I spotted wide receiver Harold Jackson for a 38-yard completion, then finished the drive myself with a quarterback draw for the game's only touchdown. It snapped a Steelers eleven-game winning streak, although they started a new one a week later: three straight postseason wins that earned them their second straight Lombardi Trophy in Super Bowl X.

The Steelers won those championships primarily because of their defense, a unit with talent to burn that utilized a number of revolutionary concepts, including one that many current teams still rely on: Cover-Two. The acknowledged master of this concept was Pittsburgh's defensive coordinator, Bud Carson. His unorthodox approach not only won Super Bowls but also forced the eventual adoption of new rules—rules that morphed the NFL from caveman football to the sky show we watch today. Carson first installed Cover-Two as a college coach during the late 1960s, initially viewing it as a *rushing* defense against the option because it placed both cornerbacks on the line, creating a run-stuffing nine-man front. Bud took it with him to Pittsburgh when Chuck Noll hired him in 1972, and it helped produce one of the finest defenses in league history: the Steel Curtain.

The Steel Curtain was anchored by a front four that could pressure the passer all by themselves and that was a critical component of the Cover-Two concept. Confident that they'd force enemy quarterbacks to throw in a hurry, Carson was able to add other innovative wrinkles. His first change involved redefining the secondary's responsibilities. There were two predominant coverages in the NFL back then, the first being the "three-deep zone." The other was "man-free," which is man-to-man coverage on all eligible receivers, with a roving safety available to help out wherever needed. In both of those traditional coverages, the cornerbacks were responsible for defending any vertical routes, but not in Cover-Two. Carson called for both corners to move up to the line of scrimmage, across from their targeted receivers. Meanwhile, the two safeties dropped deeper than normal to patrol their designated halves of the field. With the corners lined up directly across from their opponents, they could jam, then reroute, a receiver, potentially ruining his designated pattern. The two safeties were, in essence, the "safety net" if the receivers got by those jams.

Before Carson, most secondary run support came from the safeties, but that changed in Cover-Two. The rolled-up corners made this scheme very effective if the offense ran the ball wide, because tight-covering defensive backs could take away plays designed to bounce to the outside. Cover-Two was even more effective on passing plays. The Steelers had corners who were big, physical athletes. Mel Blount and J. T. Thomas could jam receivers at the line and disrupt their patterns. And this was all perfectly legal. Until this tactic was outlawed in 1978, defenders could be much more physical all over the field. They could ride receivers or the tight end and reroute them any-where in the pass pattern. This made quarterbacks sitting ducks for the Steel Curtain's legendary front four of Joe Greene, Ernie Holmes, Dwight White, and L. C. Greenwood.

Another critical component of Cover-Two was Carson's deploy-ment of the inside linebacker. Bud realized that with his corners set tight to their opponents and his safeties split, voids were created in the intermediate and deep middle of the field. That weakness was ad-dressed after Pittsburgh drafted middle linebacker Jack Lambert in 1974. With his off-the-charts height and speed, Lambert was the pro-totypical Cover-Two linebacker, and he made all the difference in Car-son's defense. Teammate Andy Russell claimed that "Lambert was the first linebacker who could blanket tight ends man-to-man, and run with them down the middle." With Lambert smothering the likes of All-Pros Raymond Chester and Russ Francis, the safeties were free to beat up other receivers trying to make catches.

Pittsburgh's safeties were required to be hybrids. They needed range and instincts to defend against the pass, but also the athletic tal-ent to attack downhill, with speed and control to stop the run. This may be why Carson's Steelers defenses are remembered by many as being big and tough. They were physical, all right, and I still have bruise marks from that '75 game as proof! But the reality was that the Steelers of the midseventies were comparatively small for that era, particularly at the linebacker position. Speed and intelligence, more than size, were the strengths of Steelers defenders.

Being smart was essential for anyone who played Cover-Two. In Bud's first years, he stressed another new concept called route progression. Carson taught his guys to understand that defense on all pass routes was based on an understanding of where receivers line up. Are they next to the strong-side tackle? Side by side? Inside where the tight end was? Pre-snap alignment dictated post-snap route combinations. Then Bud established specific drop adjustments for the linebackers and the secondary. Angles and spacing were essential to his system, and Carson's players were drilled constantly to make sure that they were in the right position at the correct distance to cover receivers. The Steelers were especially adept at reading plays before the snap and were rarely fooled by traps or misdirection. Carson also kept them on their toes by changing entire alignments on the fly, sometimes in the middle of games! His players were bright and talented enough to adjust.

"A lot of times, you didn't even know what coverage you were going to play when you came out of the huddle," admitted Tony Dungy, who was a rookie defensive back with the Steelers in 1977, Carson's final season in Pittsburgh. "It depended on the formation the offense was in, and you had to get those checks on the run. If we could be in a better defense, Bud didn't want to be stuck in something that wasn't as good, and he expected us to change it. One of his favorite statements was, 'I know this is a hard concept, but if we're smart, we can handle it.' What were we going to say? That we couldn't handle it? Nobody would say, 'This is really too hard, Bud. We can't do it.' You would take the challenge because he'd always lay it on that way; that if we were as smart as we thought we were, we could get it done." This strategy of using "proactive reaction," virtually nonexistent in the NFL of the early seventies, is widespread in today's game.

Given his background, it almost seemed preordained that Leon "Bud" Carson would one day coach in Pittsburgh. This son of a steelworker was born in Freeport, Pennsylvania, about a half hour drive from Pittsburgh's city limits. He played defensive back for the

University of North Carolina, then served two years in the marines. After his discharge, he coached high school ball until his alma mater brought him back as a Tar Heels assistant in 1957. He made another stop at South Carolina before moving on to Georgia Tech in 1966. The next year, the Yellow Jackets put Carson in charge, succeeding college coaching legend Bobby Dodd. Bud suffered through two losing seasons before taking a 9-3 Tech team to the Sun Bowl in 1970. But after slipping to 6-6 with a bowl loss in '71, Carson was fired.

Steelers head coach Chuck Noll quickly contacted Bud to see if he was interested in returning to his western Pennsylvania roots as defensive backs coach. Carson agreed to join the staff, which also included two brilliant football minds in line coach George Perles and linebackers coach Woody Widenhofer. Noll began 1972 as both head coach and defensive coordinator but soon realized he was spreading himself too thin, so at midseason he put Bud in charge of the defense. The '72 Steelers went on to win their division, making the playoffs for the first time since 1947.

Noll and Carson were a perfect football marriage. Chuck was a firm believer in zone coverage, not the predominant man-to-man schemes of the era. "Right after he was hired, Bud met with Noll, and Chuck told him what kind of defense he wanted to play, given the talent we had," recalled safety Mike Wagner. "Noll's philosophy was not to try and trick the other team but to out-execute them. Bud stuck to this as well, making changes here and there but not straying too far from his principles. Chuck liked the concepts of Cover-Two and thought this scheme could become the foundation for everything he wanted to do on defense. Before then, I didn't even know what Cover-Two was. I had never played it in college, although Jack Ham had played some at Penn State. Even if you don't want to admit that Bud is the father of Cover-Two, he definitely deserves all the credit for refining it and giving it discipline."

Players could tell right away that Carson was brilliant. They also recognized he could be a son of a bitch. "Bud was a tough customer; businesslike and to the point," said Dungy. "He didn't mind getting on anybody and everybody. He was a great guy to learn from, as long as you didn't take it personally. In my rookie year, we were playing the

Browns. We had the lead when I came in to replace Wagner, after he got hurt. It was a scheme we had worked on in practice the whole week. I messed it up, they scored, and I came back to the bench. Bud said, 'Coach Noll ought to fire you, but before I let him do that, I'll cut you myself tomorrow. I'm not going to lose my job because you can't do what you're supposed to do.' If you had feelings that could be hurt easily, you didn't want to play for Bud Carson."

Jack Ham remembers the shouting matches—and there were a lot of them. "To watch us in practice, you'd have thought we were a dysfunctional defense, but out of all that came a solid game plan and a solid defensive football team," he said. "You'd better have a thick skin with Bud. It didn't matter if you were an All-Pro or a backup, he'd scream at you. If you got beat physically, that was one thing, but what drove him crazy was if you made a mental error. He'd go nuts. But he was also receptive to other people's ideas. He wasn't a my-way-or-the-highway kind of guy. He was confident enough in his abilities as a coach that, if you had something that made the team better, then he was all for it."

Because of Carson's open-mindedness, the Steelers' defense was the first unit to figure out how to shut down a particular third-down pass play that had been difficult to stop. On third-and-short, offenses would isolate a running back on a linebacker, who was in man-to-man coverage. If the linebacker played too far outside, the halfback would break his receiving route inside—and vice versa. The play almost always resulted in a first-down completion, because the linebacker backed off in a cushion. Since ballcarriers were usually better athletes with superior open field skills, linebackers *had* to play loose; otherwise, a missed jam could easily result in a touchdown.

But then Andy Russell came up with a solution. "I remembered how I'd covered [Baltimore halfback] Tom Matte. He was a good receiver, but he wasn't any faster than me. So what I did was jump up in his face as the ball was snapped, not allowing him an inside move. Then I'd be able to run with him as I pushed him down the sideline. I thought this might also work against fast backs like O. J. [Simpson], [Ed] Podolak, and Jim Kiick. I explained it to Bud, and he liked the idea. So Ham and I developed a new technique called the 'hug-'em-up.' When the ball was snapped, it would almost be like a blitz, and the backs would set themselves for a blitz pickup. It turned out this technique worked beautifully. We really stopped them on those third-down plays. The year after I retired, I traveled to lots of stadiums as an announcer for NBC. Coaches would come up to me before the game, asking me if I could teach their guys the hug-'em-up.'"

Because he was so receptive to new approaches, Carson could also be flexible with his own. "Bud would never let an offense dictate to our defense," said Wagner. "When he put the game plan in, he was constantly changing what we did, given what he saw on film, or what he anticipated the opponent would do. I remember one time before a game, Noll came up to me to remind me of my responsibility in a particular coverage. I laughed and shook my head, telling Chuck, 'Forget it. Bud just changed it in the tunnel.' Bud was so intense. He was always trying to come up with a better scheme."

Some of that flexibility stemmed from Carson's own paranoia. "He never wanted opposing coaches to know what we were doing," said Russell. "He had a real phobia about them being able to anticipate the defenses we were in. Usually an opposing offense would send guys in motion, in the hopes that the defense would switch to a zone. A lot of defenses responded this way back then. Then the quarterback had a better picture of what he was facing. Bud didn't want us to do that. He wanted us to be able to change every time the offense moved. He wanted us to switch to the defense that would best stop their best play from that specific formation.

"By Friday, Bud would finally decide on what defenses he wanted us to play. He would give us a bunch of 'automatic' checks. So if the other team came out in an I formation, Ham and I would play 'defense number one.' If they moved to where the fullback was behind the center and the halfback was to his right, then Bud had us in 'defense number two.' If they moved to a split backfield, then it was 'defense number three,' and so on. Theoretically, it was possible we could change the defense five times before the ball was snapped. And this had never been done, because in the old days, everybody just checked to the zone. Carson simply would not let them know what we were doing."

One time on a flight to Cincinnati for a game with the Bengals, Russell was cramming like a nervous college student, trying to memorize all of Bud's defensive checks. Road stadiums were too loud for Steelers defenders to rely on hearing the middle linebacker shout out the changes, so the entire front seven had to automatically know how to react to any formation. "We're standing in the tunnel for introductions," Russell recalled, "and Carson informs us that he has completely changed the calls. All of a sudden, we've got five brand new checks. We start the game with these new calls, which I'll refer to as the *Sunday* afternoon checks—as opposed to the *Friday* afternoon checks.

"We play the first quarter, and Bud thinks [Bengals offensive coordinator] Bill Walsh is getting a feel for what we're doing. So he says, 'We're going to mix and match. Every other series, I want you to play the Friday checks, then switch back on the next series and call the Sunday checks. Got it?' Now, I'm not saying we were a bunch of rocket scientists, but if you didn't have some relatively smart guys on defense, we couldn't have done this. We got mixed up a few times, but overall we had a pretty good game that day—and I really don't think anything like that had been tried before. I remember years later being at a party in San Francisco with Walsh. I told Bill that story, and he was absolutely flabbergasted. He couldn't believe it. Bill said, 'Now I understand why I couldn't figure out what you guys were doing!'"

Opponents were constantly frustrated playing against Carson's defenses. "I saw [Redskins quarterback] Billy Kilmer at a golf tournament, and he gave us a great compliment," remembered Wagner. "He said, 'We always know exactly what defense you're in. We call the perfect play against that defense—and we still can't beat you.' A lot of that came from our flexibility. Our playbook was kind of a joke. There was so much Bud taught us on the field that was never written down or diagrammed. You always felt you were better prepared because you had someone like him calling the shots. We loved his philosophy of aggressive play. That was his signature. Bud Carson was a coach who made me better. And he made me realize that the mental aspect was the key to everything."

As I've said, the foundation of Carson's defense was Pittsburgh's front four, and its cornerstone was future Hall of Fame defensive tackle Joe Greene. He was nicknamed "Mean Joe," but he wasn't just some mindless monster in the middle of the line. "I was the guy who was communicating the stunts, formations, and whatever we were going to do at that particular time," recalled Greene. "It wasn't coming from the sideline. We already knew what our responsibilities were, but they constantly changed, based on sets, formations, and down and distance. When the quarterback would make his call, we could make our calls and be on point instead of lagging behind, playing guesswork with what may or may not be thrown at us. We also had the talent, but the kind of communication amongst us was the key to our success."

Because of their skill set, Pittsburgh's front four could apply sufficient pressure all by themselves. "We'd play a four-man front on first down, which was unorthodox at the time," said defensive end Dwight White. "We thought we were better than the other teams were—individually, one-on-one. And if we could find a situation where four guys could ultimately end up one-on-one, we did it, because Joe could take up two blockers all by himself. He's the guy in the middle clogging up everything. Joe took away the whole interior of the offensive line, making the ballcarrier run outside, going toward the sideline, where we wanted him to go anyway."

At the other defensive end was L. C. Greenwood, who, according to White, "was more like a basketball player. Out of the eleven of us on defense, he was probably the most mild mannered and aloof to what was going on, but was an incredible athlete. He was fast and had a long reach. People would try to block him, but you could only block half of him, because there was so much of him that linemen almost needed to say, 'You take this piece, and I'll take the other piece.' *My* disposition was a lot different. I personalized it with the guy in front of me. I'd say to him, 'You're going to have a bad day today. You can take this ass whipping any way you want to take it, but you're gonna take it.' I probably could have used some anger management counseling. My thought was to just keep coming, with constant pressure. I wanted to keep pounding on you, make you feel that I couldn't be stopped."

The fourth member of the Steel Curtain was Ernie "Fats" Holmes, and had his off-field life taken a different turn, he might have been better than any of them. "Ernie was just as good as Joe Greene," insisted White. "He just never got the publicity and was a different personality. He was the closest thing to a John Deere tractor or a Caterpillar that I've ever seen in my life—he had incredible strength. You couldn't move the guy, and he had a real nasty personality."

White acknowledged the greatness of other famous defensive lines such as the Minnesota Vikings' "Purple People Eaters" and the "Fearsome Foursome" of the Los Angeles Rams, but he felt the Steel Curtain was unique by comparison: "We were four black players, four guys from small schools with common backgrounds. We took great pride in that because of what was happening in the late sixties in the country. Here are four black cats featured on the cover of *Time*. I think that was the first time a unit from a sports team was given that type of profile by *Time* magazine. And it was important to us to be as good as they said we were, because people were watching us."

The front four's dominance meant that Pittsburgh's linebackers rarely needed to blitz. "Our offensive linemen wouldn't dare fire out on play-action, because they were afraid they'd miss a block on Greene and those guys," said Chiefs quarterback Len Dawson. "Then this allowed their linebackers to drop off, to read a pass play quicker. It all centered on the strength of the front four." And Carson made sure the communication between linemen and linebackers was constant. "All three of us linebackers talked to the defensive line," claimed Russell. "We'd say stuff like, 'Play it with your left shoulder, because they're going to be running a 17-U'—and that's exactly what the offense would do. Our line responded, and we shut things down. If you have a sense of what the other team is going to do and react to it quickly, they're going to have to go somewhere else and do things they don't want to do."

Steelers linebackers were coached to "get depth," which made it hard for a quarterback to make out what was going on downfield. They were taught to keep running underneath with the inside receiver, whoever it was. The longer the quarterback held the ball, the deeper the linebackers could drop. The idea was to keep the quarterback from completing passes to the inside; make it hard for him to read the progression. "In those days, it was legal to reroute wide receivers," said Russell. "You couldn't hold them, but you could put your hands on them until the ball was in the air. We spent probably ninety percent of our time rerouting receivers, not letting them go where they wanted to go. You don't see so much of that happening today. Linebackers now pretty much blitz or they drop back to a zone, but don't do the funneling we did back in those days."

Outside linebackers Ham and Russell were each blessed with unique talents that were deeply appreciated by their position coach Woody Widenhofer. "Jack could have been a professional racquetball player," he contended. "He was that fast. Ham was the best player I ever coached. Russell was the smartest." Ham concurs. "I probably learned more football from Andy when I first came in the league," he said, "than all the coaches I had throughout my career."

During the first two years of Carson's tenure, the middle linebacker was a plugger named Henry Davis. "Henry was an underrated linebacker," recalled Russell. "He had a great season in 1973 and made the Pro Bowl. When this rookie linebacker Jack Lambert came to camp in '74, nobody thought he'd take Henry's job." But in an early exhibition game against the Eagles, Davis suffered a serious concussion and never played again. Lambert ended up starting the entire season. Carson had been incorporating Cover-Two principles when Davis was playing in the middle. "But Lambert just played it much better," observed Ham. "Henry was a solid linebacker, but the passing game was not his forte. Henry would knock your helmet off and was big on physical play, but this scheme required a lot more of the middle backer."

At first glance, Lambert wasn't the usual NFL man in the middle. "He looked more like a defensive end that needed to put on weight. He looked out of place," stated Greene. "But then you started to watch him play. He had the ability to be in the right spot all the time. He had to call the signals, and he had to make the checks; and this was a rookie doing this. And I don't know if he brought that tough attitude with him or if it just started to come out. But that attitude was definitely a big part of his success, because at six-four, two hundred eighteen pounds, as an inside backer, he doesn't pass the eye test. But he could play."

With Lambert's arrival, a good Steelers defense became one of the finest in league history. "*Everything* changed for Bud with the arrival of Jack Lambert," declared Wagner. "He was the salvation, the *messiah*. Jack could stay with almost anyone. If that tight end was running down the field, Jack was with him—huffing and puffing, but he was there. Jack's height and ability to get downfield deep allowed the safeties to come pounding in there, to beat up the guy trying to catch the ball."

Almost from the first day of training camp, Lambert's singular talents were evident to Carson. "Bud had me do things that middle linebackers had never done before, mainly in pass coverage," he recalled. "He had me covering tight ends man-to-man, covering halfbacks in a spread formation. He had us doubling wide receivers. Things like that were unheard of back when [Ray] Nitschke, [Dick] Butkus, and Willie Lanier played." All three of these players are in the Hall of Fame, but none of them had anything approaching Lambert's foot speed. A few years later, Carson told a reporter, "Joe Greene was the cornerstone, but Jack Lambert was the catalyst. I'm not sure we ever would've turned the corner had Lambert not come to this football team."

Fans too young to have watched Lambert in action know him primarily from iconic NFL Films footage, growling at teammates with a mouth of missing teeth, while knocking runners and tight ends into next week. He was a tough customer, and I was certainly wary of him whenever my teams played Pittsburgh. But there was more to him than physical toughness. "People think his success was based on all that macho stuff, but that had very little to do with it," said Russell. "He had superb techniques. He knew an offense's tendencies, played them well, and was always in the right place at the right time. The guy had the brains to back up his bravado."

Beginning in '74, Carson placed the responsibility of changing defensive checks on Lambert's shoulders. "It was up to me to make the calls and signals to my teammates," he explained. "That's kind of like being a quarterback on offense. Between Ham, Russell, and myself, we made very few mistakes out there. We were well prepared. We knew our assignments. If we did make a mistake—and we did from time to time—we never made it again." Each of the three linebackers also excelled in the classroom. "Games are won on Tuesdays, Wednesdays, and Thursdays," said Ham. "Those meetings were not the place where you'd take a nap. Maybe we weren't members of Mensa, but we were pretty smart guys who knew what was happening. Sometimes coaches would help you from the sidelines, but we were perfectly capable of making adjustments on the field ourselves. You combine the talent we had with the ability for our guys to disguise our coverages, and you'll make a lot of plays."

Ham and Lambert knew the indicators that could help them avoid being fooled by play-action fakes, and they were happy to share other trade secrets with their teammates. These included reading tackle traps and detecting how the depth of a pulling guard would reveal whether the play was going off tackle or around end. "When a tight end moved a yard outside of formation, Ham explained to me why that would help me predict what kind of pass was coming, and where he was going," noted Wagner. "These guys watched film over and over, looking for stuff like this, and that's what they found: things the average player didn't see."

By jamming receivers at the line, Pittsburgh's corners also made life easier for the safeties. This allowed Wagner and Glen Edwards to drop from their normal areas, which disrupted a quarterback's timing. "We had our corners carry the receivers to the fade area, normally a void area where people tried to attack, where the safety couldn't get to the sideline," explained Widenhofer. "Carrying the receivers to the fade area gave our safeties time to recover to defend any Go route," which set up Edwards and Wagner perfectly. "My interception totals jumped after Bud got there," Wagner boasted. "I played one of those years with a broken thumb and dropped quite a few because of that. Otherwise I might have had twenty interceptions!"

After Carson's arrival, the Steelers annually finished among the league's best in team interceptions, even though the franchise's eventual all-time leading interceptor was still learning how to play within

Bud's system. "Mel Blount was one of the greatest physical specimens I've ever seen," claimed Lambert in a 2001 interview with NFL Films. "I wouldn't be surprised if you'd give him a couple of weeks to get in shape, he could go out and probably play right now. The guy could run like a deer. He was almost as big as I was, playing the cornerback position, but he was about ten times faster than I was."

Unfortunately, Blount's natural talent had him believing that he could get by simply on size and speed. During his first few seasons, he often strayed from the demands of Carson's system. "There were a couple of occasions where Bud was highly critical of Mel's mistakes," Russell remembered. "Bud basically said, 'If you're not going to do what I'm telling you, you're going to have to sit.' "

Early in his career, in a game against the Dolphins, Mel was schooled by Hall of Fame receiver Paul Warfield. "Paul beat him for three touchdowns in the first half, and Mel was in tears," said Russell. "He was shocked. This was impossible! Here was a big guy who ran a 4.4, was a superb athlete, and Paul was turning him inside out. Well, Mel had to learn. It takes a while to understand what you can get away with in the NFL. Bud was constantly telling Mel what he should and should not do, and sometimes Mel just got stubborn with him."

Blount's independent streak was a real obstacle for Carson, because Cover-Two could not succeed with freelancing cornerbacks. "The problem was that J. T. Thomas and Mel wanted to play man-to-man on every play," admitted Wagner. It took a while for the two of them to realize that they would do much better if they bought into Bud's scheme. "With Cover-Two, you had guys who could make tackles at the line of scrimmage," explained Dungy. "Pittsburgh forced the wide receivers to have to block these big corners, as opposed to just being wide receivers out there running pass routes. So it changed the way people could attack. Mel was six foot three and two hundred fifteen; J.T. was six foot two and two hundred fifteen. You tried to draft guys like that who could hit and liked to hit, because they were going to make seventy-five to a hundred tackles a year. They weren't just going to be cover guys."

The corners' massive size was a major problem when other teams tried to run the ball. Bud was always looking for ways to take the best opposing players out of the game, and that's exactly what Cover-Two achieved on rushing attempts. Part of Carson's genius was forcing receivers to block big defensive backs. They couldn't simply run them off. Wideouts now had to run laterally, and most of them weren't such wonderful blockers to begin with. Either way—run or pass—Blount and Thomas spent most Sunday afternoons during the seventies flattening receivers into hamburger patties.

Peter Giunta served on Bud's staff with the Eagles in the early nineties and went on to apply many of Carson's concepts as an assistant coach with the Jets, Rams, Chiefs, and Giants. "Bud always said, 'Never pass up an opportunity to hit a receiver.' He liked Cover-Two because you could hit receivers right from the line of scrimmage. Then the linebackers could hit the tight end to reroute him to where Lambert was. People were not used to seeing teams playing what Pittsburgh did, which was a huge advantage. When you're doing something different from what's going on in the rest of the league, that makes it tough. And he'd mix up the coverage so offenses couldn't detect a pattern; give them different looks." Carson had his defenders sit back seven or eight yards so that quarterbacks couldn't tell if they were in Cover-Two or Cover-Three. "There weren't as many offensive formations, and teams didn't go to three and four wideouts on plays," explained Giunta. "So there weren't as many disguises back then. The offensive looks didn't change that much, which made it easier for the defense to make its calls."

Once the corners effectively jammed the receivers, Cover-Two's second-level defense asserted itself, taking the tight end or a releasing back out of circulation. "Lambert wouldn't stay with the tight end from start to finish if he ran a vertical seam route," explained Ham. "He'd pull off, and if I did my job and flattened the tight end to slow him down, it then took him a moment to take another step upfield. That was enough time for Lambert to be sitting deep enough in the middle. Now the tight end is no longer a factor, and the safeties can move over to the receivers, because there's nothing really threatening them in the middle of the field."

During the late sixties and early seventies, the zone defenses typically had three guys playing deep. When Carson came in, he focused on the rerouting system, supplemented by Cover-Two, which was a zone-man combination. "The idea was that the quarterback wouldn't have much time to throw anyway," said Russell, "so every potential re-ceiver could be covered in those zones. Carson's theory was, 'If you can make them punt, you've done your job. You don't have to be a hero with an interception.' Rerouting was done in man-to-man, even if we did have deep guys playing zone. It was a matchup zone. If a man came into your zone, you didn't back off—you covered him right away."

Carson viewed defensive play in much the same way that Sid Gill-man visualized offenses: through geometric principles. "For Bud, the whole idea was that it's a game of angles," said Wagner. "If you got deep enough, the quarterback would be more reluctant to throw that far, because the angles were different. NFL passers are all about who can fire that sideline route, the comeback, the fifteen-yarder into the seam. You get your hands on the receiver, give him a little shove, and that makes it a much tougher throw for the quarterback."

Cut down the angles, Carson believed, and you eliminated the bread-and-butter routes most comfortable for quarterbacks. "What we did was take away the window to the curl route," said Widenhofer. "We would squeeze that to where the action was. We had landmarks for the safeties on the field. The corners funneled one receiver inside, while the linebackers funneled others outside. This way, the safety could help out on either receiver, because he didn't have as much ground to cover. We were lucky, because the players we had not only executed our schemes but also understood them and why we called them."

Small wonder then, that Pittsburgh's Cover-Two produced on-field results and off-field awards. "In 1976 we had four Steelers from our secondary voted to the Pro Bowl," recalled Wagner. "I'm not sure that had ever happened before."

Pittsburgh's fiercest rival of the 1970s was not a divisional oppo-nent but a team that played its home games more than two thou-sand miles away. From 1972 through 1976, the Steelers and the Oakland Raiders faced each other in five straight win-or-go-home playoff battles. "It was almost like the Steelers and Raiders *were* in the same division, because we met them so often in the playoffs," observed Tom Flores, Oakland's receivers coach during that period. "It was an incredible rivalry because it was the same guys basically playing year in and year out. You'll never see that again, with the way free agency is and the salary cap. They had Noll, and we had [head coach] John Madden and pretty much the same assistant coaches all through the seventies. And there were only seven coaches back then, too. So the philosophies of the teams did not change."

Neither did either team's attitude toward its opponent: Both maintained a healthy mix of disdain and respect. "Just about everybody hated the Raiders," admitted Joe Greene. "The Raiders were at the front gate of the AFC for so many years. Anybody who won the conference championship had to go through [owner] Al Davis's team. In my heart of hearts, it was teams like the Raiders that made *us* a good football team, because they'd beat your ass."

Oakland had fans all over the country, and the emerging Steelers hungered for the success that would bring them a national following

Steelers Base Cover-Two Alignment

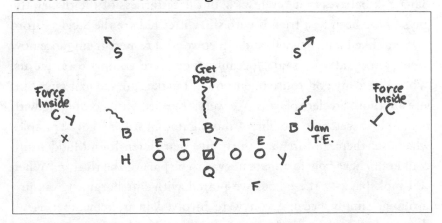

Pittsburgh's defensive line sets up in standard four-man front to apply pass-rushing pressure, allowing outside linebackers (Russell and Ham) to drop into underneath zones where they can disrupt intermediate pass routes. Middle linebacker Lambert drops deep into pass coverage, backed by safety help. This frees cornerbacks Blount and Thomas to roll up tight on opposing receivers, where they can be jammed repeatedly and forced inside, disrupting their pass routes.

too. "During the seventies, they were always the marquee team in Monday night games," stated Dwight White. "Nobody ever went to bed early the nights the Raiders played. They always mounted comebacks, found a way to win. They were our equals, the closest thing to us. And psychologically, most football teams want to beat the people that are the closest thing to you, in order to prove to yourself that we're on top."

Jack Lambert wouldn't have minded squaring off against Oakland every week. "Undoubtedly, the most fun I've ever had in my life was playing against the Raiders," he said. "To me, that was what football was all about. They didn't whine. They didn't cry. They came out and knew it was going to be a bloodbath. It wasn't tricky football, like playing the Cowboys. They came out and said, 'We're going to run right here. Try and stop us.' We had guys on our team that were just as nasty, if not nastier, than some of those guys on their team, and they did some pretty nasty things out there. But I still respected them. I thought the world of [Raiders quarterback] Kenny Stabler and a couple of the other guys that played on their team. I got a chance to meet them at the Pro Bowls and find out that, hey, these are pretty good guys."

Among the Raiders, the feeling was mutual. Running back Pete Banaszak believes that "even with all the bitterness of the rivalry, the guys I have been best friends with since I retired are the Steelers from that era, like Ham, Russell, and Greenwood. I respect them more now than I ever did," he said, "because they were competitors like us. When I have my golf tournament today, I make sure the first guys I invite are those Steelers players. We were obsessed with competing with them. I love watching old film of those games. I still get goose pimples when I see them." More than thirty-five years later, John Madden still couldn't believe how fortunate he was to be part of the rivalry: "When you look back at the games we played with Pittsburgh, it was just thrilling, simply because you were involved in it, remembering all those guys that are in the Hall of Fame who played in those games and made them so great."

You know a rivalry is intense when events away from the action become part of the story. "We were playing them in Oakland one time, and the Steelers had the ball," remembered Banaszak. "[Center] Mike Webster came out of the huddle, bent over to make the snap, but then told the ref he needed to switch to another ball. When the ref asked why, Mike showed it to him. Apparently the Raiders' equipment staff had written on the laces, 'Fuck you Steelers.'" Before one playoff game at Three Rivers Stadium, Al Davis accused the Pittsburgh grounds crew of purposely icing up a previously dry field to slow down Oakland's faster receivers. "Something weird always happened to us when we went to Pittsburgh," Banaszak continued. "One year, our tight end Bob Moore got beat up somewhere and came back to his room with a black eye. Another time, the night before our game, the fire alarm in our hotel suddenly went off at one-thirty in the morning."

But no planned pranks could surpass the damage in the '72 playoff game, when Pittsburgh running back Franco Harris made his famous (or dubious, if you ask Oakland) "Immaculate Reception." With the Steelers trailing, 7–6, in the closing seconds of the game, Raiders' defensive back Jack Tatum got in front of Terry Bradshaw's desperation pass. The ball caromed right into the arms of a happily surprised Harris, who was behind the action. The rookie caught it, then ran 42 yards for a come-from-behind touchdown, giving the franchise the first playoff victory in its largely sorry thirty-nine-year history. Many historians still regard Franco's freak catch as the most famous play in the annals of the NFL. It certainly ranks that high in Pittsburgh!

After losing to Pittsburgh again during the '73 regular season, an angered Oakland squad vowed that it would avenge these back-to-back defeats by cramming the ball down the Steelers' throats. The next time they met, the Raiders were going to run and then run some more behind their storied offensive front known as "the Iron Line." The left side of the unit included tackle Art Shell, guard Gene Upshaw, and center Jim Otto—all eventual Hall of Famers. When the two teams met in Pittsburgh in the '73 divisional playoffs, the Raiders ran the ball an astounding 55 times for 232 yards, crushing the Steelers, 33–14. It was nearly as lopsided the next year, when the Raiders traveled to Pittsburgh in the third week of the regular season. Oakland attempted only a dozen passes all day, while rushing for nearly 200 yards in a 17–0 whitewash. It was the first time the Steelers had been blanked at home since 1964, a span of 146 games.

"They shut us out," lamented Greene. "You pitch a shutout on your opponent's home turf, and you start thinking you're a Super Bowl team. That loss could have shattered our hopes and confidence. This was the same team that beat us so bad the prior season in the playoffs—they booted us right out. Oakland had become our nemesis." Russell was worried that the problem went beyond simply being overmatched. "Losing the game to the Raiders in Three Rivers was rough," he conceded. "They were obviously a very good team, and they appeared to have figured out our offense. That was a crushing loss. We came out of that thinking, *We've got to revamp this whole thing.*"

Andy was referring specifically to Pittsburgh's lackluster offense, which did eventually make a significant change by installing Terry Bradshaw as the starting quarterback. But change was also coming on the defensive side of the ball, and it happened almost by accident. During a Thursday practice session, Greene experimented by dropping into his stance at a 45-degree angle, instead of head-up. "This offset alignment was something Joe developed himself, out of frustration," said Russell. "He hated to get blocked and wanted to make plays. So it occurred to him that, because he was so quick, he should just line up inside, between the center and the guard, tip his shoulder sideways, and when the ball was snapped, he'd just dart through that hole. He was supposed to line head-up on the guard. He jumped in the gap between the guard and center, tilted his body, and just blew through that gap, and it was devastating. It was a beautiful thing to see."

"I discussed it with George Perles," recalled Greene, "and he said, 'Hey, let's just line up in the doggone thing.' We found out that with my lining up in it, I could demand a double-team. The only way you can command a double is to not let the center overblock you, get in across your face. When we did that, I was able to maintain my position and make the guard block me. If he didn't block me and went to the backer, then I could get in the backfield. And if the guard and center double-teamed me, then Lambert was free to make the tackle." This new alignment, called the "Stunt 4-3," was a godsend for the undersized middle linebacker. "Jack looked like a basketball player," noted Ham. "I'm not sure there weren't times he got down to around two hundred. That's pretty light. In the Stunt 4-3, guys couldn't get a real good shot at him. And Jack had great leverage. He knew how to take on a two-hundred-sixty- to two-hundred-eighty-pound center or guard coming out at him. At that kind of weight, it's difficult to make it through the season. But with Greene's help, he was able to do it."

Chuck Noll loved Greene's tilted-nose alignment after just one day of practice. "It started out as a pass technique," he recalled, "but we found out it really screwed up the offensive blocking. It's an aggressive defensive play, because our front four isn't sitting and reading the offense. Instead they're the ones making things happen." And few defensive coordinators of the day were as open minded in their thinking as Carson. Most of them would likely have rejected Joe's idea as too radical. But Bud was willing to adapt, and Greene should *also* be applauded for his unselfishness.

"The key to all of it was Joe, because he could have said he wanted to be an up-the-field rusher," said Ham. "But he bought into the scheme, and that's what made it work. Joe made sure there wasn't much distance between himself and the offensive line—he was really crowding in the neutral zone and didn't allow linemen to pull out. It eliminated a lot of their running plays. Joe would take a real physical beating when he did this. It created a domino effect that made our defense better."

Exactly when the Steelers began running the Stunt 4-3 is open to debate. I discovered NFL Films footage of Mean Joe as a tilted nose in late-November games against both the Saints and Oilers. The history link on the official team website claims that the formation was unveiled in the second-to-last game of the regular season, when the Steelers beat the Patriots to clinch the AFC Central. Greene says he first lined up in it during the '74 divisional playoffs against the Bills. Woody Widenhofer cites its launching point in the AFC championship. "We really didn't put that scheme in until right before the title game with Oakland," he claimed. "It was the first time the Raiders ever saw it, so they weren't well prepared for that at all." No matter who's right, Widenhofer was correct about one thing: Oakland would have surprising difficulty dealing with Pittsburgh's defense in the AFC championship. And at least part of the reason why may have stemmed from the Raiders' subconscious belief that they were already on their way to the Super Bowl.

On the day before the Steelers trounced Buffalo, 32–14, in the divisional round, the Raiders rallied during the final seconds to beat the defending world champion Dolphins in the legendary "Sea of Hands" playoff game. Because it had been billed as "Super Bowl VIII ½," most observers all but awarded the Lombardi Trophy to the Raiders. Russell recalled how completely the Raiders had been swept up in the euphoria. "Madden was quoted as saying, 'When the two best teams in football, Miami and Oakland, get together, great things will happen.'"

Years later, Madden was still disturbed about the way he and his team handled their win over Miami. "It was not a championship

Steelers Stunt 4-3

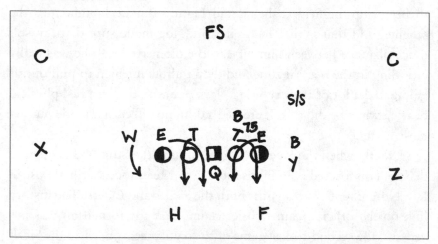

Also referred to as the tilted-nose alignment, where Greene positions himself on an angle between the right guard and center. Greene could "shoot the gap" to stuff the run or sack the quarterback. But in this particular scheme, Mean Joe runs a stunt with defensive end White. White and Greene twist past each other, causing blocking confusion for the offensive line. Weak side backer Russell adds to the pressure by blitzing from his area. On the other end of the line, end Greenwood also executes a twist with a tackle to Holmes. This was too much chaos and talent for most offensive lines of that era to handle!

game; it was just a playoff game. We were so excited and so happy about stopping their streak and beating the Dolphins. I got carried away, and I think the players got carried away," he reflected, "because beating Miami was big. They were the only team that had ever gone undefeated. To beat a Shula team in a playoff, coming off a second straight Super Bowl win—we thought we had won a championship. I still look back at that, and I think I made a mistake in letting our celebration go on too long. Because the next week, we had to play the Steelers in the *real* championship game. I think that lesson was, 'We haven't done anything yet.' Because when it's a playoff game, and you've got a championship game the next week, it *can't* be anything else other than just a game."

The response from Franco Harris was typical of the entire Steelers team: "The Dolphins-Raiders game, I have to admit, was a great game with two great teams. But when Oakland already accepted the crown and said that they're the best, that didn't sit well with us. Even though they beat us earlier in the season, it was like, 'So what? We weren't at our best at that time. We're now a new team, with new spirit.'" A few days after beating the Bills, the Steelers gathered to begin preparations for their title game in Oakland. Chuck Noll got up to address the entire squad, which was usually a matter-of-fact lead-in to the week's preparation. "A lot of guys didn't pay a whole lot of attention, because usually Chuck's style was very businesslike," remembered Ham. "He could've been the chairman of the board of a company, holding a management meeting. For Chuck to go out and say what he did grabbed the attention of that entire room, because it was so unlike him to do this."

Joe Greene was sitting in the front row as Noll began his speech. "He didn't raise his voice. But his voice did change when he said, 'The best team in the NFL didn't play yesterday, and the Super Bowl wasn't played yesterday. The Super Bowl is going to be played in two weeks, and the best football team in the league is sitting here in this room.' It was out of character for him to say things like that, but it was right on the money. It was what we needed."

"You could feel the level of confidence rise in that room—from all the players," recalled Mel Blount. "Chuck *never* said anything like that. But I guess it was something that he saw out there in the Raiders' celebration after beating the Dolphins. That was one of many turning points for the Steelers. He just came right out and said it with such conviction. After that, we had great practices all week."

As the team boarded its charter flight to California, Franco Harris made a promise. "I knew we were going to come back a winner," he said. "And it felt good. I told my teammates, 'After the game, when we get back, it'll be early in the morning. We'll have steak and eggs at my place.' That's what I told them. 'Steak, eggs—and champagne.'"

1ST HALF

1st Quarter: 3 Raiders Offensive Possessions

When the Raiders won the toss, they elected to receive, which made perfect sense. They'd led the AFC in total offense, relying on a near-perfect statistical balance of running and throwing. "You can't play a team like Pittsburgh and just do one thing," observed Madden. "You have to mix the run with the pass, and you have to have confidence when you do run." In its most recent games against the Steelers, the Silver and Black had piled up huge rushing numbers. Why would today be any different? "Madden wanted to dominate the sticks," said Russell. "He wanted to move the ball on the ground. And I always felt Stabler never cared how many yards he threw for. He was quite content to hand that ball off the whole game if it worked."

The fun began on the first play from scrimmage. "The ball is sitting right there, and Ernie Holmes steps over it," said Greene. "Ernie says, 'Eugene! Upshaw!' Upshaw finally turns around because he was in the huddle. Ernie looks at him and says, 'I'm gonna kick your ass!' The rest of us cracked up when we heard this, but when they snapped the ball, it was *on*. Ernie played a lot of great games, but this one really got his juices flowing."

Stabler handed the ball to Clarence Davis, who glided left, behind Upshaw. The next thing you see in the film frame is Holmes leaping over the fray into Davis, joined a split second later by two other Steelers defenders. Oakland picked up 4 yards on the carry, unaware that this would be the *longest* run it would make all day. At the bottom of the pile, Ernie was still busy. "I saw Upshaw at a football camp a few months later," recalled Widenhofer. "He said to me, 'Who is this Holmes? That guy's crazy! First play of the game, he spit right in my face!' Ernie was wired up. He was ready to play that game."

On the next play, Greene lined up in the Stunt 4-3 formation for the first time. This time Davis ran to his right, but with Greene tying up two linemen, J. T. Thomas and Lambert had a clear path and made the stop after only a 1-yard pickup. Facing third-and-5, Stabler called his first pass. Aligned again in the tilted-nose position, Greene teamed with Holmes on a looping stunt. It forced right guard George Buehler to come off Greene and react to Holmes. This gave Joe plenty of outside leverage on Jim Otto. He slammed the veteran Raiders center to the turf with one hand, then crashed through the middle to sack Stabler for an 11-yard loss, forcing an Oakland punt.

"We always claimed Greene was offside when he lined up in the gap that way," said Flores. "He was tilted inward and was such a great player that he usually penetrated. Once that happens, it blows up your double-teams or single blocks, because you have to worry he'll be in the backfield." Bud Carson could not have been more pleased with his defense's first series, but unfortunately for Pittsburgh, the unit was back on the field in short order. Rookie Lynn Swann fumbled the punt return, and the Raiders recovered at the Steelers' 41, so the defense would have to start from scratch.

Given a reprieve, Oakland began with another run. This time it was fullback Marv Hubbard, but he was squashed by Greenwood and Lambert for no gain. On second down, Stabler dropped to throw, looking for nine-year veteran and perennial All-Pro Fred Biletnikoff, just in front of the Oakland bench. As the ball arrived, Thomas pushed in and nearly intercepted the pass. Both Fred and Madden screamed for a pass interference call, but the officials ignored them. The afternoon was young, but this marked the second time that Biletnikoff had been disturbed by a Pittsburgh defender. "I'd been in a Pro Bowl with Fred and saw him putting this tar on his chest and arms," remembered Russell. "He just sprayed it all over himself. It was incredible. He could pick up a ball, and it would stick to his elbow. So during warm-ups before the championship game I said, 'Hey, Fred! Don't come near our bench. We have some buckets of feathers. If you come over there, we're going to tar and feather you with all your Stickum.' I gave him this look of mock seriousness, as if I was really concerned for him. But I was just joking. I made the whole thing up. We didn't really have a bucket of feathers. Now, whether that had any impact on the game, I don't know. But he never ran his signature comeback route toward our bench, I know that."

With third-and-ten coming up, the Steelers went to "nickel" coverage, removing Lambert from the lineup and replacing him with rookie safety Donnie Shell. It was a strategy that Carson would return to several times throughout the day. Even with the extra defensive back, Stabler was able to complete his throw over the middle to wide receiver Cliff Branch for a first down at Pittsburgh's 28. It would be the only first down the Raiders would pick up until late in the half.

Oakland again called a running play to the left, with Banaszak on the carry, but Dwight White smothered him for only a short gain. The next play was also a run to the same side, this time by Davis. Holmes overpowered Upshaw, reached out with one hand and grabbed Davis, slowing him long enough for Lambert to tackle him after only 2 yards. "On those great Steelers teams, I think Ernie Holmes was probably their most underrated player," claimed Madden. "You think of the guys who played on that Steel Curtain line, but Ernie gave us more problems than any of them." On this particular day, Holmes was sporting his trademark haircut: What little hair remained on his shaved scalp was contoured in the shape of an arrow. Ernie claimed the design helped him stay on a straight path to ballcarriers—and it seemed to be working quite effectively so far against the Raiders.

Facing third-and-5, Stabler looked for Branch on a square-in, but Glen Edwards knocked it down just as the ball arrived. The Raiders settled for a 40-yard field goal by George Blanda to take a 3–0 lead. They wouldn't score again until deep into the third quarter. But the Steelers offense didn't exactly set the place on fire during *its* first possession either, punting after three plays. Three-and-out would be a recurring first-quarter trend. On each of Oakland's next two possessions, the Raiders were off the field after little more than a minute, thanks to Pittsburgh's suffocating run defense.

"We did a lot of stunts and con games in the '74 championship," revealed Widenhofer. "We created a new line of scrimmage on almost every run. The Stunt 4-3 created a situation for Lambert where he could go in untouched and make plays. Greene was a cock-nose so that neither the center nor guard could block him by themselves. So what you have is two guys blocking Greene, and Lambert running free." To add to Oakland's bewilderment, Carson occasionally mixed in nickel coverage from a 3-4 alignment, swapping Holmes for extra linebacker Loren Toews. "We did this primarily to give the Raiders a different look, just to mix things up," said Widenhofer. After one quarter of play, Oakland's offense was both confused and abused. In fifteen minutes, it had generated all of 15 net yards.

2nd Quarter: 2 Raiders Offensive Possessions

Throughout the first half, the Steelers ran the ball much more efficiently than their Raiders counterparts, but they didn't have much to show for it. Kicker Roy Gerela, named to the Pro Bowl that year, missed a 20-yard field goal after one sustained drive. However, he later connected on a second try from about the same distance, tying the game at 3–3. Despite the score, the Steelers were winning the battles of both field position and time of possession.

Even with repeated failures in their running game, the Raiders kept plugging. "We had to try to run," said Madden. "You can't just throw on every down. If you give their defensive line a credit card to rush the quarterback, then you make it a lot tougher on yourself." Four of their drives in the first half began with runs, and the trend continued even on second down. I charted four second-and-long situations in the first half where Oakland handed off the ball to a back. The results weren't pretty: Those carries gained 1, 2, 1, and 1 yards. Something else I saw was that, no matter what, the Raiders were committed to running left. "What they did was untraditional," observed Dwight White. "Most teams run to the right. Most people are right-handed, so it's easier to run to the right than to the left. Not the Raiders."

In previous games against Pittsburgh, this strategy had worked. "They knew it was coming, but we still had success because we did it better than they defended it," said Madden. "I know a lot of people used to say we ran to the left because Kenny Stabler was left-handed. That had nothing to do with it. It was because we had Art Shell and Gene Upshaw over there. That's why we ran to the left." Oakland's left was Pittsburgh's right side, which meant that White, Holmes, and Russell were getting the brunt of the action. "One time during that game, Ham came in the huddle, and he was so bored," noted Russell. "He said, 'Let me take a few shots over on your side.' The challenge was there for the three of us to see if we could defeat their best players."

Through virtually the entire first half, the Steelers were winning that challenge—handily. And they weren't just dominating Shell and Upshaw; Pittsburgh's front was clobbering the entire Oakland offensive line. "They changed things up from earlier in the year," conceded Otto. "There were some plays I was assigned to block Lambert, but if he was keeping me from making my route cutoff point, I couldn't get to him in time. We'd try to switch off so the guy closer could block Jack, and I'd take Joe Greene. There were decisions that Buehler or Upshaw and I had to make pretty quickly. We might get one, but not both of them." Buehler was growing particularly discouraged. "I know I got conservative in what I was doing," he lamented. "I was thinking too much instead of reacting. I never did lose my pregame jitters."

On the outside, the Raiders' offensive tackles were having their own problems. Halfway through the second quarter, Oakland was in a favorable third-and-short situation, needing probably no more than a foot to move the chains. Davis took the handoff and wasn't even two steps into the play before Greenwood barreled into his midsection and dropped him for no gain. L.C. was so quick off the ball that right tackle John Vella never even had the chance to lay a glove on him, and Oakland was forced to punt again.

"There were a lot of trash talkers on Pittsburgh," said Otto. "They'd try to get me riled up, but I'd just smile back at them. They'd curse me out, and I'd just try to knock the hell out of them on the next play. At the end of one run, Joe Greene cussed me out, then kicked me square in the testicles—and I've never forgotten that. I didn't think that was very nice." Par for the course in Steelers-Raiders games, according to Banaszak. "Hey, that was football. You couldn't play that style now—because the rules weren't the same. It was just a different game. There'd be twenty guys tossed out today if they did the stuff we did back then."

The Steel Curtain totally shut down Oakland's running attack, but the Raiders' passing game was also having first-half problems. "We were playing mostly man, along with some Cover-Two, which was the only zone we played then," said Wagner. "Probably thirty to forty percent of our defense in the Raiders game was Cover-Two. In Cover-Two, the safeties never backpedaled until we got to our target area. You got there by turning your shoulders and running, not backpedaling. This way you could keep an eye on the receiver, watch the quarterback drop, and figure out where inside receivers may be going. If the safeties are deep enough, they can cover half the field just by going left and right. This is what Bud taught us, to turn and run, a technique you don't see today. It's all about running as fast as you can. How many plays work because the defender is a half step late?"

With a little over seven minutes remaining in the half, the Steelers put together their best drive, highlighted by a pair of Bradshaw completions. A third throw should have given Pittsburgh the go-ahead touchdown, but it didn't count. "John Stallworth caught a pass with just his left hand," recalled Greene. "I think [defensive back] Nemiah Wilson grabbed his right hand, and Stallworth tiptoed down the sideline. He caught it in the end zone, but the referee claimed he didn't have both feet in, and it was ruled out of bounds." Disputed plays weren't reviewed by officials back then as they are now. Otherwise it would have been overturned, because repeat angles on the NBC telecast clearly show that the official blew the call. Mean Joe didn't bat an eye. "The feeling that I had was, it didn't matter. We will still beat you. No fussing. No complaining. That's how I felt. The Raiders weren't gonna win. Not today."

As it turned out, the Steelers didn't get any points following the Stallworth play. A Raiders interception brought the ball to midfield with just under two minutes remaining. The Steelers' defense opened in Cover-Two but yielded the longest play of the half when Stabler hit

Biletnikoff down the left sideline for a 27-yard gain. Two things went wrong for Pittsburgh on the play. First, Blount did not disrupt Biletnikoff's release, which allowed Fred to blow right past him. This prevented Edwards from getting to the sideline in time with safety help. In addition, Oakland's line finally blocked well enough to neutralize all of Pittsburgh's rushers, giving Snake Stabler enough protection to find the streaking Biletnikoff. With the ball on the Steelers' 23 and still over a minute to go, the Raiders were in business. Their next call would also be a pass—and it turned out to be the most pivotal play of the half.

The Raiders broke the huddle, led by the man who'd come to symbolize their franchise during its first fifteen years of existence. Many still regard Jim Otto, with the distinctive number 00 on his back, as the greatest center in pro football history. He never missed a game during his career and was still out there battling the Pittsburgh rush even though his thirty-six-year-old body was breaking down. "My knee ligaments were really a problem, but my plan was to win this game, win the Super Bowl, then have surgery right afterward so I could play in '75," Otto explained. "That would have been my sixteenth year in pro ball. I went into the hospital shortly after we played the Steelers and had bone graft reconstruction in the joint. My rehab was going fine until I got to training camp, and that's where my bone graft came apart. I realized if I tried to play with it, I would not be as effective as I'd always been. I decided that wouldn't be fair to the team, so I retired."

It was at this moment in the title game where Otto's creaky knees betrayed him, costing the Raiders an almost certain touchdown. Stabler connected down the left sideline with Branch, who'd beaten Blount badly to get open. Cliff was forced out at the 1-yard line, but the play was nullified by a tripping penalty on Otto. "I set up for pass protection, and when I planted that foot, the pain in my knee was so severe that I had to lift my leg up," he recalled. "I'm standing on one foot and went over backward with the other in the air because I couldn't stand any pressure on it—and Joe Greene fell over me. It wasn't an intentional trip or leg whip or anything like that. But if you look at the film, you do see Joe trip over me."

Oakland was flagged for 10 yards and never recovered. Pittsburgh held on three straight downs, and then Blanda's 38-yard field goal try was blocked by Lambert. The half ended with the score still 3–3, but by every other tangible measure, the Steelers clearly had the upper hand. Oakland had amassed only two first downs, 65 yards of total offense, and 18 yards on the ground. "They only got twenty-nine rushing yards the whole *game*," Greene bragged. "Something like twenty-one attempts and only twenty-nine yards. I've probably repeated those numbers quite a bit because they were special. The Raiders were just bewildered. They could not believe what was happening to them in terms of our ability to stop the run." This was apparent from a brief exchange between Mean Joe and Buehler. Following one play late in the quarter, Greene shouted to the Raiders guard, "Hey, nice block, George!" Buehler replied, "I know, it's the only one I've got on you today."

It wasn't until after his career ended that Greene could fully appreciate what he and his Steelers teammates were doing to the Raiders that afternoon. "You've heard people talk about being 'in the zone,'" Joe stated in an interview with NFL Films for the *America's Game* series. "They don't know what the hell the zone is about, because you don't *live* in the zone. You *visit* the zone probably once in your life. I don't want to trivialize it. I played thirteen years. I was in the zone *one* time, and that was in the playoff game against the Raiders. And I think our team was in the zone. It didn't matter who we played or where we played them. They were going to lose. That was the most special feeling I ever had playing."

2ND HALF

3rd Quarter: 2 Raiders Offensive Possessions

Oakland got the ball early in the quarter after its defense recovered a fumble on the Steelers' 40, but it failed to take advantage. Once more, the Raiders ran on first down, but Lambert took Hubbard down after only a few yards. "They were on us like fleas on a cat," Marv said afterward. Russell batted away a pass attempt to Clarence Davis in the left flat, bringing up third-and-7. Carson returned to nickel coverage, swapping Shell for Lambert, but Branch beat Donnie on the right side for 13 yards and a first down. I have to tip my hat to the Snake on this one. Greenwood beat Vella easily and whacked Kenny hard on his release, but he still got the pass away in time. "The Steelers made you speed things up and do things you didn't normally want to do," Stabler said. "You always understood that you were going to get pressure and that you had to get rid of the ball."

Stabler's next throw produced far different results. After Holmes stopped a Banaszak run, Oakland was staring at second-and-8. "We did not anticipate they would shut down our running game so well," admitted Flores, "so we ended up passing more than we wanted to, and in the end you're playing into their hands. You could not be careless against Pittsburgh—and you sure weren't going to trick them. Their linebackers were too smart for that."

Smart—and in Ham's case, blessed with unique football talent. "Ham is the greatest outside linebacker that ever played the game," claimed Lambert. "I'm sure there are people like Lawrence Taylor who could rush the passer better. But I watched Jack, not only every game but every day in practice. He did everything right. He played the run and pass the way you were supposed to play them." If you wanted to choose a signature play to define Ham's career, the one he made on the next snap is as good as any.

Stabler dropped to pass, looking to his left for an open receiver. Pete Banaszak was Ham's responsibility, but Jack was well over to the right as the play began. "Ham suckered Stabler into going to Banaszak, and Jack kind of hung back," said Russell. "I couldn't do that, because I didn't have that burst, but Jack could." Stabler fired toward Banaszak, but suddenly Ham appeared out of nowhere to make the interception. He was the last guy Stabler expected to see in that area. "Ham was probably the fastest guy on our team within a five-to-ten-yard distance," Russell continued. "Jack could lag behind a receiver to make it look like the guy was open, then just close to the ball quickly. He made plays look easy, while the rest of us had to dive to make shoestring tackles."

The Steelers, however, failed to cash in following the Ham interception; luckily for them, Jack would make an even bigger play later on. In the meantime, Oakland finally mounted its most successful drive of the game. It didn't start well, as the Steelers blew up run plays on first and second downs. On one of those calls, the Raiders lined up in an I formation, something that Oakland teams almost never did, but even against that set, the Steelers were unstoppable. Holmes absolutely annihilated Upshaw at the point of attack—and was in the backfield so quickly that he literally startled the fullback Hubbard, who was supposed to be blocking someone else. It allowed Russell a clean shot to make the tackle. When Biletnikoff kept the drive going with a clutch third-down reception off a comeback route, it drove home the point that the Raiders' best chance for success was in the air.

"Oakland had to throw," observed Widenhofer. "I don't care who they were playing. With the offensive line the Raiders had, they were going to get protection. And Branch was just about impossible to cover one-on-one. Stabler was a great competitor, and even though I felt we could continue to get good pressure on him, he was still able to complete passes." Even so, the Steelers' secondary was convinced it could handle whatever the Snake threw its way. "Back then we used hand signals for different coverage schemes, and they weren't that complicated," said Wagner. "The Raiders could probably figure out what we were calling. We didn't care, because we had that much confidence in our ability to stop them. We'd yell our coverages out loud so Oakland could hear us, but it didn't matter. We'd dare them to beat us—it was our men against their men."

Unfortunately for Pittsburgh, Cliff Branch was one opponent they couldn't really handle. That season he led all wide receivers in catches and had a league-high 13 touchdowns. "That was the year Cliff really came into his own and became a legitimate NFL star," stated Flores. "The Steelers would roll up a lot to his side so Blount could come up and try to muscle Branch. Cliff was not a big guy, and Mel always tried to engulf him. But if he couldn't get his hands on Cliff, then he was in a lot of trouble."

Branch had caught only one pass the entire first half and wasn't happy about it. "Cliff was the kind of guy who started yelling for the ball before he got his jock on," laughed Stabler. "He'd say, 'Kenny I got this guy, I own this guy. Throw me the ball.'" Starting from their own 30, the Raiders called Branch's number repeatedly, which meant that they'd be targeting Blount on nearly every play. Mel gave Branch too much of a cushion as he ran down the left sideline, and Cliff easily caught the pass for a 20-yard pickup. With the ball at midfield, the Steelers lined up in the Stunt 4-3, with Russell blitzing from the outside. Otto made a tremendous block to negate Russell's charge, and Stabler threw deep again for Branch. Blount was badly beaten on this play too, but he lucked out when Branch couldn't hold on to the ball. With the Steelers in their nickel on third-and-8, Russell blitzed again but was quickly picked up by Banaszak. Stabler went after Blount once more, this time hitting Biletnikoff on a curl for another 10 yards.

"We normally didn't do a lot of blitzing, but because the Raiders had that tremendous offensive line, we had to try," noted Wagner. "When we blitzed, everybody was locked on. There were no safeties in the middle of the field, with pure man coverage across the board. We blitzed more than usual because we couldn't let Stabler stand in that pocket." But that's pretty much what happened on the next play. Stabler took a seven-step drop, getting nearly four seconds before lofting the ball down the left side for Branch. He easily eluded Blount and pulled it in for a 38-yard touchdown.

"Blount could run a 4.4 or 4.5. But Branch was a quick little guy, and it just wasn't a favorable matchup for us," observed Widenhofer. "If he got off clean, he was going to get free. The touchdown came on a first-and-ten, so we were probably playing the run and they went deep. Blount took away the inside dig route that Cliff ran well. But then Branch straightened up and ran past him. We probably should have had safety help over the top, but the safety might have been looked off too."

From the coaching tape, it was apparent that Blount made mistakes both in fundamentals and in judgment. Mel was looking inside at Stabler and wasn't focused on Branch, which allowed Cliff to run past him. With his back turned to Branch, Blount likely anticipated that Cliff was going to run to the post, because he drifted inside as he turned and ran. All in all, the play was a total disaster for the Steelers corner—and his mistakes put Oakland ahead, 10–3, heading into the final quarter.

4th Quarter: 5 Raiders Offensive Possessions

The Steelers responded with a touchdown of their own, rushing eight times in a nine-play drive to tie the game with a Harris run early in the quarter. Now Pittsburgh's defense needed to make a stop, and it did. From their own 30, the Raiders tried to pick on Blount again with another Go route to Branch. This time the Steelers were in Cover-Two, and Mel had support over the top from safety Glen Edwards. As it turned out, Mel didn't need help; he blanketed Branch perfectly. Pocket pressure by Greenwood kept Stabler from driving into the throw, and the pass was incomplete.

The Steelers had Oakland in second-and-10, and didn't expect the Raiders to run. For Carson, it seemed like the perfect time to go with something Stabler hadn't yet seen. Bud dialed up a blitz out of Cover-Zero, which meant that the corners would be in pure man-to-man with no safety help. The idea was to pressure the Snake into hurrying his throw, and Carson achieved this by blitzing Lambert, Russell, and Edwards up the middle. "Stabler thought the safe play was out to [halfback] Charlie Smith," said Ham. "I don't think Kenny ever saw me. He threw it, I intercepted it, and returned it. That's where our scheme really paid off—a little surprise—the unexpected against a smart, veteran team like Oakland. Sometimes just that one play can make all the difference. We weren't going to play it safe by this point in the game, staying back in a zone. This kind of wrinkle was so typical of Bud."

Stabler knew he'd made a terrible mistake from the moment he let it go: "I wish I would've eaten that ball and then punted it, because we had Ray Guy, the best punter that's ever kicked. Just punt the ball and play for real estate, play for field position. Of all the passes I ever threw, the one I wish I could take back most was that one against Pittsburgh. They were just a terrific team—the best team I ever played against."

Ham returned the interception down to the Raiders' 9-yard line, and the Steelers cashed in three plays later when Bradshaw hit Swann over the middle for a touchdown. Pittsburgh's 17–10 lead was its first of the day, but nearly twelve minutes remained—more than enough time for a patented Raiders comeback.

Oakland's next possession began on its own 15. The offense ran on the first play and, as usual, got nowhere. But on second down, Stabler tried something new. He called a designed rollout to both avoid the rush and alter the launch point of his pass. The rollout worked as Branch caught the ball for 16 yards near the left sideline. After a running play, the Raiders were in a manageable second-and-6. The Steelers went to Cover-Two, with Greene aligned in the Stunt 4-3 formation. Mean Joe ran a twist, but Upshaw picked him up to buy Stabler extra time. It allowed Branch to make it look as if he were running another Go pattern, which he then changed to an intermediate in-breaking route. Blount was fooled at first but appeared to recover. Mel cut in front of Branch and nearly picked off the pass, but the Snake made a perfect throw to Cliff, and he broke away for a 42-yard gain. Branch probably would have scored except for the fact that Lambert had dropped deep enough in Cover-Two, allowing him to catch and finally drag down Cliff at the Steelers' 24-yard line.

By now Carson had run out of patience. He yanked Blount from the game and replaced him with rookie Jimmy Allen. Blount would see no further action that day. "Mel was the kind of guy who just wanted to play man, never really paying attention to the scheme," said Wagner. "Eventually he'd blow some coverages. His technique was bad. This didn't work for Bud Carson, who was a no-nonsense guy. If you didn't do things his way, you were out of the game. Let's face it, Branch was one of the fastest guys we ever played against. Blount said he was the toughest guy he ever had to cover. Mel got benched in that game simply because he couldn't stay with Branch in single coverage. In blitz packages, that would be an extremely difficult coverage for Mel. Blount just had a bad game."

Branch caught another pass on the next play to move the ball inside the 20, but Oakland couldn't get any closer. Lambert made a terrific open-field tackle following one short pass, then whacked Stabler on the next play, thanks to a blitz from Greenwood and Greene. "We did get some big gains with Branch, but when you're inside the red zone, the field shrinks," conceded Flores. "And when that happens, I thought that was when the Steelers were at their best. Their two-deep zone, rolling up their corners, and linebackers who could run—put all those things together—when you squeeze the field down to twenty yards or so, there aren't a lot of options to go to." Blanda salvaged the drive with a short field goal to narrow Pittsburgh's lead to 17–13, and there were still more than seven and a half minutes remaining.

The Steelers' offense drained four of those minutes off the clock before punting away, but Oakland did nothing on its next series. "Because we held a late lead, we may have been playing a deeper set," said Russell, "with four linebackers covering short zones and three guys still deep. We probably had three down linemen some of the time. Bud would try different techniques to throw them off stride." The critical stop came on third-and-7, with Greene aligned as a tilted nose and Carson calling a Cover-Zero blitz. This created an alley that allowed Lambert to get in clean, forcing Stabler to chuck it into the seats. "Against a throwing team like Oakland, you'd better be able to defend the passing game with your middle linebacker," observed Ham. "Without that, your Cover-Two's not worth a damn. In that game, Lambert forced Stabler to throw the ball over a six-foot-four guy, adding a little bit of an arc that could force hurries and interceptions. Lambert's height was really important."

Still trailing only by 4, Oakland had one last chance after getting the ball with 1:48 remaining. Branch opened the drive with an 18-yard catch, but on the next snap, Greenwood caved in Oakland's protection to sack Stabler for a 9-yard loss. It was wiped out because of a defensive holding call by Thomas, but J.T. more than made up for it on the next play. When Hubbard stayed in to block instead of running out into the pattern, it gave Russell the green light to abandon pass coverage responsibilities on Marv and blitz the pocket. Andy stormed in on Stabler, who threw it up for grabs. No Raider was nearby as Thomas picked it off, returning it to the Oakland 24. Two plays later, Harris ran up the middle virtually untouched for the game-clinching touchdown.

For a twelve-year vet like Russell, who'd played on many dreadful Steelers teams, the 24–13 win was "the most euphoric moment I think I'd ever felt on a football field. We almost had tears in our eyes. We were so happy and deliriously excited about going to the Super Bowl." It was also meaningful for Greene, who'd also suffered through some lean years. "To think that when you haven't won anything in your history, and then that precise moment when you know that the next ball game will be the Super Bowl, it just doesn't get any better than that. I was floating."

Franco Harris called it "the biggest game of the whole seventies teams, because it really showed what we were about—our character and what we overcame and what we achieved. To go there and to win that game made us realize that we're a really good football team; probably the best. And that really set the tone for what was to come for the rest of the decade. We got home late that night, around two or three in the morning. We weren't tired at all. We were just feeling great. Some of the guys came over to my place, and we had our steak and eggs and champagne, partying till the next morning."

Two weeks later, the Steelers won the first world championship in franchise history by defeating the Minnesota Vikings, 16–6. In that game, Bud Carson's defense set a Super Bowl record by allowing only 119 yards in total offense. If anyone still had doubts about Pittsburgh's defenders—or the system they played in—this performance put them to rest. One of the converts may have been Mel Blount himself. Years later, he confessed, "I had one of my worst games ever when I went against Cliff Branch, and I made some statements about being pulled from that game—that a smart coach would not have done something like that. Going into the Super Bowl, there was a lot of controversy about whether or not I would even play."

Carson ultimately decided to restore Blount to the lineup, and Mel responded with a shut-down performance. He made a key goal-line interception just before the half and worked with the rest of the secondary to allow just one catch to a wide receiver the entire game. It marked a turning point for Blount's career and his success in Carson's defensive scheme. "Before then, Bud and Mel butted heads a lot," recalled Wagner. "I've talked to Mel about this, and he's admitted that he was wrong; that he needed to learn how to work within Bud's system."

After the Steelers chose Michigan cornerback Dave Brown as their first pick in the next draft, Blount realized he'd have to convince Carson that he was fully committed to his program. "I knew that I had to come into training camp in '75 and prove that I was a great player and could play in this league," said Blount. "The results were that I got eleven interceptions and was the NFL defensive player of the year." That interception total remains the franchise record more than thirty years later. Mel went on to make the Pro Bowl five times, won three more Super Bowl rings with the Steelers, and was inducted into the Pro Football Hall of Fame in 1989.

A case can be made that once Blount mastered his Cover-Two responsibilities, the Steelers' defense reached a level of accomplishment few other units have equaled. In a way, they became almost *too* good. In 1976 the Steelers ran off a string of nine straight regular-season wins. During that streak, they allowed the opposition only 28 points! Things weren't a whole lot better around the rest of the NFL, either. With other teams incorporating the aggressive features of Carson's Cover-Two, the majority of games were turning into low-scoring affairs—and fans were getting bored. When fans are unhappy, the owners are unhappy, so they decided to do something about it.

Beginning in 1978, the year that the season was expanded to sixteen games, the league implemented a pair of drastic rule changes to boost offenses. One new ruling assisted offensive linemen, who were now allowed to block with their hands open and arms extended. What was once whistled for a holding penalty now became legal pass protection, giving quarterbacks more time to read defenses before finding their receivers. The other new rule was instituted at curbing abuse by defensive backs, and those changes were aimed specifically with the Steelers in mind. The Illegal Chuck Rule (or "Mel Blount rule," as some called it) prohibited defenders from making any contact with receivers once they ran 5 yards beyond the line of scrimmage. From now on, aggressive defenders like Blount would have to keep their hands to themselves, and once-bullied pass targets were free to run their routes without being mugged.

Blount was more flattered than annoyed by the decision. "I think anytime a player can have such an effect on the game that they name a rule after you, what more can you ask for? It's something my kids can read about; a part of your legacy. And I'm honored that they thought enough of the way I played the game that they would change the rule and call it the Mel Blount rule. When something like that happens, you just have to do things differently. We might have had to disguise ourselves a little bit better to camouflage our defenses, or do whatever was necessary to force a mistake by the opponent. We were still talented enough that we could go on and win championships."

Because the Steelers' defense dominated the 1970s, other teams tried to replicate their success, but with mixed results. "Those clubs never had anything close to the quality of the Steelers players," stated Bill Belichick, who was then a staff assistant with the Broncos. "That was a very sophisticated and difficult defense. There was no way you could run it unless you really knew what you were doing. Guys just weren't leaving Pittsburgh until George Perles took it with him to Michigan State. When I hired Nick Saban at Cleveland in 1990, Nick had run Bud's defense at MSU. When he got to the Browns, we ran that Pittsburgh defense from 1990 to '95, with some modifications. But by then things had changed from when Bud ran it with the Steelers. We had to handle a lot of different problems against one-back, three-wide formations—things that didn't show up that much back in the seventies."

Because of those formations and the Blount rule, Carson's original version of Cover-Two isn't used today, but its core principles are still valid, and the man most successful in adapting those principles was Tony Dungy. Although Dungy spent only one season as a player under Carson, he was profoundly influenced by his philosophy. Many of the building blocks for Tony's highly successful "Tampa-Two" defense can be found in Carson's 1977 Steelers playbook, a tattered but treasured binder that Tony still keeps on his shelf. "This was how I grew up in pro football. That's what I believed in. So when I went to the Vikings in 1992 as defensive coordinator for Denny Green, that's why I said, 'This is how I want to play.' He gave me the go-ahead to put it together.

"Monte Kiffin was on the staff, as the linebackers coach," Dungy continued. "They'd already been successful with a little different style of defense—not much Cover-Two, but a great pass rush. So I said,

'Monte, if we can incorporate your stuff and throw Cover-Two in, I think we can have something special.' It turned out great, because in 1993 we led the league in defense. We also led the league a couple of times in takeaways. But it didn't spread in popularity until after we got to Tampa in '96. And that was where we committed to playing it as a base defense, something people hadn't seen since the seventies."

There were some noticeable differences. Bud essentially told his linebackers, "Read where the receiver goes and follow him." Dungy and Kiffin asked their guys to hit landmarks, move to assigned spots, then come up to make the play. I remember when I was broadcasting Bucs preseason games, I'd watch their guys at training camp. It took them a while to learn this system, but once the light went on, it really fit that team well. Staff assistants Lovie Smith and Herm Edwards carried it with them after they became head coaches. When Lovie's Chicago Bears met Dungy's Colts in Super Bowl XLI, you had both conference champions running basically the same defense. In today's NFL, virtually every team incorporates some element of Cover-Two–Tampa-Two in its defensive schemes.

Whenever Dungy taught it to newcomers, there was initial confusion. "At practices, guys we acquired from other teams would ask, 'If the tight end does this, who's got him?' And we'd say, 'Well, no one's got him. The defense is going to take care of it. The offense is going to complete some passes. If they're patient, and they just dump the ball off, we've got to come up and tackle well. But at some point, one of our defensive linemen will get a great rush, or we'll stop a run and make it third-and-nine. Now they aren't going to be able to throw that six-yard pass anymore. That's what you've got to believe in.' That was foreign territory to a lot of professional teams. They believed they needed an answer to every single route run against them, but we didn't, and that's probably the difference with the true Tampa-Two."

At the end of the 1977 season, Carson left Pittsburgh to become defensive coordinator for the Los Angeles Rams. Ironically, two years later, those same Rams entered Super Bowl XIV as heavy underdogs against the Steelers, but by the end of the third quarter, L.A. was actually ahead. Because Carson knew his former team's defenses so thoroughly, Pittsburgh rotated linebackers after every play so that Bud couldn't steal its calls from the sidelines. The Rams eventually lost, but Bud continued to be successful as a coordinator for another decade until finally achieving his lifetime goal.

He ran defenses for the Colts, Chiefs, and Jets before being named Cleveland's head coach in 1989. In his first season, he led the Browns all the way to the conference championship game but was impulsively fired by owner Art Modell after a slow start the following year—a move that Modell later admitted was a mistake. Carson landed on his feet in Philadelphia, coaching a defense in 1991 that scared the rest of the league to death. Reggie White, Seth Joyner, Eric Allen, and Wes Hopkins were among its biggest stars. Because pro football was becoming more pass oriented, Bud adapted his base schemes to the times, blitzing a lot more in Philly than he ever did in Pittsburgh. Those changes were clearly successful, because that Eagles unit became one of the few to ever lead the league in rushing, passing, and total defense in a single season. Most historians will agree that Carson was responsible for two of the greatest defenses of all time with the '76 Steelers and the '91 Eagles.

Peter Giunta, Bud's secondary coach, remembered a bus ride the Eagles took to Washington for a game with the Redskins. "We were passing the Pentagon, when one of our linebackers, Bill Romanowski, said, 'I think that may be the only building in America that has more defenses than Bud Carson.' So, of course, at halftime of that game, Bud adds yet another defense he thinks up to try to take Washington's better players out of the game. And Romanowski then said, 'You know, I was wrong. Carson has *more* defenses than the Pentagon!' When things weren't going well, Bud would stay very calm, rein things in, and go back to the basic defenses we played best. He was so good at making adjustments; taking away opponents' elements that were hurting you. He did a great job of adapting to the skills of the players he had. He'd add new wrinkles, new blitzes, always trying to be ahead of the offense."

Carson returned to the Rams to finish his coaching career before finally retiring at the end of the '97 season. He passed away in 2005, but his core concepts remain deeply woven into the fabric of today's NFL. "Bud Carson was a guy who had the courage to try things that had never been tried before," said Andy Russell. "Changing the defense anytime the offense moved before the snap of the ball was totally innovative. The Stunt 4-3, route progression awareness, the hug-'em-up, and, of course, everything with Cover-Two. He had an ability to balance an athlete's physical talent with his mental strengths. He always reminded us to use our heads—not to be impatient."

There may have been more dominant performances by the Steel Curtain defense, but I believe that the '74 AFC championship will always be Bud Carson's signature game. And although Tony Dungy wasn't there that day when the Steelers beat Oakland, he learned enough in one year with Carson to become his most enthusiastic disciple. During his thirteen seasons as head coach of Tampa Bay and then Indianapolis—where he won the Super Bowl in 2006—Tony spread the gospel of Cover-Two more than anyone else. But Dungy also recognized Bud's flaws, even while admiring his genius. "As a head coach, he didn't have the right personality for the job. He wasn't going to give you confidence if you didn't already have it. But as far as getting you in position to understand what you had to do and getting you ready to play, he was great. And he knew football. Bud had strong beliefs, knew what he was doing, and wasn't afraid to go against the grain. Bud Carson never felt he had to follow the crowd."

Don Coryell's Roving-Y

COURTESY OF THE SAN DIEGO CHARGERS ARCHIVES

OAKLAND RAIDERS vs. SAN DIEGO CHARGERS
San Diego Stadium, San Diego, California — September 14, 1980

By the end of my fourth NFL season, I was ready for a change. I'd spent each of those years with the Los Angeles Rams and had played well when given the chance. But the quarterback position had been something of a revolving door since I'd arrived: First John Hadl, then James Harris, and, finally, Pat Haden had all seen more action than I had. I had reached the point in my career where I simply wanted to play every day. It was so important to me that I'd taken a 10 percent pay cut in '76 to be eligible for that era's version of "free agency"; that season I made the grand sum of $27,000.

My agent was a fellow named Steve Deutsch, whose family was in the film business in L.A. He was friendly with Michael Klein, the son of San Diego Chargers owner Gene Klein. Steve asked if the Chargers might be interested in acquiring my services, and the answer was yes.

They already had a solid young passer in Dan Fouts, but Dan was about to take on both the players union and San Diego management in separate but equally complicated disputes, so the Chargers thought it might be wise to look for additional quarterback help.

The other team interested in signing me was the Philadelphia Eagles. I knew their coach, Dick Vermeil, from when he had served as the Rams' running-back coach a few years earlier. Throughout the '76 season, Dick was unofficially "recruiting" me through a friend of his in California: a car dealer named Ben Wells, who stayed in constant touch. After the Rams were eliminated from the playoffs, Dick was permitted to talk directly to me, and he pitched me hard.

Ultimately, Coach Vermeil won me over because of the kind of person he is. And to be honest, I also fell in love with Philadelphia. It was an ethnic city like my hometown of Buffalo, with different neighborhoods and cultures. I liked that. I had been offered basically the same money and contract length by both the Chargers and the Eagles. After talking it over with my wife, Liz, we decided we'd head back east to make our new home. To make things official, the Eagles traded the rights for tight end Charle Young to L.A., and the Rams sent my rights to Philly—so it looked like a trade. Since nobody around the league complained about it, it went through. In every meaningful way, the move turned out to be the best thing for me, and I have no regrets.

Well, maybe I do have *one* tiny regret. Had I signed with San Diego, I would have become the triggerman for what is still regarded by many experts as the greatest passing offense in NFL history. Fouts eventually ironed out his contract differences with Gene Klein and was there when Don Coryell was hired to coach San Diego in 1978. Beginning at that moment, Coryell transformed the Chargers into an offensive juggernaut. Any quarterback would have loved to play on those teams. I still lie in bed sometimes and think about what might have been had I gone with San Diego. I look at the numbers Fouts put up, the records he shattered, and think, *That could have been me.*

During our Super Bowl season of 1980, the Eagles flew to San Diego to play the Chargers. It was the first time I got the chance to see the "Air Coryell" offense in person. They beat us that day to snap our eight-game winning streak, but that's not what I remember most about the game. It was one of the few times in my career when I didn't just sit on the bench and collect my thoughts while our defense was on the field. I made it a point to study Fouts and the rest of Air Coryell. They were so much fun to watch—even if they were having fun at our expense. For sheer beauty of timing and rhythm in the passing game, that Chargers team is still the best I've ever seen.

I believe Coryell owes a great deal of his success in San Diego to Bud Carson's famed Steel Curtain defense. Its dominance mandated the introduction of the illegal chuck, or Mel Blount, rule, and liberalized offensive line blocking regulations. These major changes became part of the game in 1978, right at the time Coryell was hired by the Chargers. Don may not have been the first to take advantage of these new rules, but he was the best at taking advantage of them.

Several of Don's philosophies can be traced directly to Sid Gillman: forcing opponents to defend the entire field, emphasizing quarterback pocket protection, and relying on timing and rhythm in the passing game. But then Coryell went a step further. Those liberalized 1978 rules created the perfect climate in which to implement previously unseen formation shifts and men in motion. If defenders were allowed contact only near the line of scrimmage, why not have receivers moving prior to the snap, where they'd be almost impossible to jam? And why limit this to wideouts? Why not running backs or the tight end as well? Motion produced another benefit: If a defensive back or linebacker rotated with the moving player during pre-snap, this was a good indication that the defense was in man-to-man coverage. For a sharp quarterback like Fouts, knowing this even before the play began was a tremendous advantage.

Coryell and his longtime assistant Ernie Zampese looked to force opponents into default, or base, coverages—vanilla defenses they knew how to beat based on film study. So while opposing defenses made themselves predictable, Coryell's offense was anything but. He ingeniously created a system of routes that relied on formation and alignment, not on the receivers themselves. On a given pass play, all five receivers could set up shop anywhere in the formation. If that wasn't enough of a defensive headache, he made it worse by having Fouts pass the ball before the receiver even made his break. How can a defensive back cover his man when the throw is to a spot the pass target isn't even looking at? All these elements made Air Coryell varied, unpredictable, and just about impossible to defend. At least those problems existed only against the Chargers, because nobody else was doing this at the time. Ask former Raiders and Bills linebacker Phil Villapiano about defending against the Chargers, and he simply shakes his head. "They'd run you into the ground," he said. "Coryell would have five receivers that were potential targets on every down, and you can't cover five receivers. It's amazing how Fouts was coached to find the open guy all the time—and believe me, someone was always open."

Nobody else had a tight end like Kellen Winslow, either. Hall of Famers like John Mackey and Mike Ditka were rampaging bulls who could bowl people over after the catch. So could Winslow, but his skills went far beyond brute strength. Kellen was a superb route runner with great hands—practically an oversized wide receiver. There were other tight ends of this period that might also have done well in Coryell's system: Dave Casper, in his days with the Raiders, and Cleveland's Ozzie Newsome being two who come to mind. But they played for other teams that didn't use the tight end (or the "Y," as the position is called in playbook parlance) the way the Chargers did.

Coryell and Zampese set Winslow up anywhere on the field. They put him in motion where he couldn't be jammed. They'd line him up in the slot or out wide against some unfortunate five-foot-eleven, 180-pound corner. How on earth can that guy defend a six-foot-five, 250-pound receiver who runs just as fast as he does? That is the classic mismatch NFL coaches dream about—and in San Diego, mismatches like this existed on *every* play.

Winslow wasn't his quarterback's only choice. There was Hall of Famer Charlie Joiner, who ran the most precise routes of any receiver in that era. And there was John Jefferson, who was as athletically gifted as any target on the Chargers. J.J. could stretch out and grab anything—even overthrows. The Chargers could also run the rock with 245-pound monster Chuck Muncie. You can see why opposing defensive coordinators probably lost a lot of sleep preparing for San Diego.

As I've said many times, if you control the middle of the field, you control the game. It was Gillman's mantra, and it became Coryell's too. The quickest way to the goal line is a straight line, so when you send a target like Winslow down the middle, the safeties must stay home and play honest. And if you then add threats on both outside flanks the way the Chargers could, you put enormous pressure on every defender. This creates advantageous one-on-one matchups, and against a team of talented athletes like the Chargers, that was usually enough to get beat.

Beyond being a brilliant tactician, Coryell was adored by his players, and his teams were a joy to watch. "The most important thing to me about Don Coryell is him as a person," said Fouts. "He actually cared about us as players. A lot of coaches don't even know who you are. They call you by your number. But Don was always a guy who made you feel important, who made you feel that your contributions to the meetings, or the team, or to the locker room was part of the deal, and we were all in this together."

Don Coryell had already enjoyed a lifetime of experiences by the time he arrived on the campus of San Diego State College in 1961. He'd served in both ski and paratroop divisions during World War II, later worked as a lumberjack, then played defensive back and competed as a boxer at the University of Washington. He coached junior college football before taking on the head coach's position at Whittier College from 1957 through 1959. After a year as John McKay's running-back coach at the University of Southern California, Coryell was brought in to revive the Aztecs' struggling football program.

His first hire was Riverside City College assistant Tom Bass, who would run the defense. "I asked him why he wanted to go to San Diego State, because they hadn't won a game in three years! He told me he thought that he could do a lot better than that," said Bass. "Joe Gibbs was a player for us then—he was our tight end and also played linebacker. He also filled in one game at center when our regular guy was injured. We only recruited junior college players, and Joe was one of them. We never even talked to high school kids. We only had thirty-three scholarships back then. It just seemed easier for us this way. Don and I did all the recruiting. It took some of the guesswork out of player evaluation. Everyone we brought in was ready to play."

San Diego State was an independent in those days, which meant that it wasn't tied to specific conference regulations dealing with player transfers or eligibility. "A lot of kids who were recruited by the big West Coast powers got to these colleges and realized they couldn't cut it there, for a number of reasons," remembered Al Saunders, who coached for Coryell with both the Aztecs and Chargers. "Don got lots of players this way, especially receivers. Because of the loose rules, he could get a kid to enroll at San Diego on Wednesday and then play them that Saturday. So Don had to devise an offense where he could get guys in and have them ready to go in just a few days. He devised a three-digit numbering system in his passing tree and could teach a kid the basics of that system in five minutes. Naturally, the player wouldn't know all the route combinations and adjustments, but everybody can count from one to nine."

Gibbs, whom Coryell recruited as a junior college player, said of his mentor, "The way he arrived at the three-digit system and his way of calling the passing game was one of the more enlightening things that has ever been done in football. The system basically was: The higher the number, the deeper the route. Inside cuts were even numbers, outside cuts were odd. That was easy to remember. On the first day Don coached a receiver, that guy could learn basic plays. The idea behind it all was to give the quarterback a visual picture."

San Diego State didn't become a passing powerhouse right away. "At first we were an I-formation team because Don had coached that with McKay at Southern Cal," said Bass. "But by year three, we were throwing the ball a lot more. We really started passing more when Rod Dowhower was our quarterback, and then Don Horn, who was eventually drafted number one by the Packers. Coryell wasn't wed to anything. He saw that passing would help us win. He understood that we could get national recognition—not just by winning but by scoring a lot of points, and the only way to really do that was to throw the ball."

Being in San Diego at the same time as Sid Gillman had little impact on Coryell. "Don didn't spend as much time at the Chargers'
camp as I did," Bass added. "He really was his own innovator. He just
watched a lot of football and picked up ideas that way. He also attended a ton of clinics. In those days, you practically lived at them.
Don had total and complete tunnel vision during football season. I remember the two of us taking a recruiting trip up to Bakersfield. I did
the driving, Don was sitting next to me, and it was two hours before
he said a word. The whole time, he was drawing plays on index cards,
then throwing them in the back seat. He must have gone through
about two hundred of those things. But that was just Don—he was so
totally focused. He really had no hobbies or outside interests, other
than his family."

In 1964 Bass was hired by Sid Gillman to be the Chargers' backfield coach, but Tom wasn't going to leave Coryell empty-handed. He
recommended a young junior college coach named John Madden,
who would serve as Coryell's defensive coordinator for three years.
"John knew Ernie Zampese from Santa Maria Junior College," Bass
recalled, "and after Madden came to San Diego State, he got Ernie to
join the staff as well. Ernie knew Coryell from USC, where he'd played
as a defensive back. Ernie was a lot like Don in that he had no ego. He
never wanted to be a head coach, wasn't big about working on his
own—he most enjoyed working with Coryell. Having played defense
in college really helped Ernie when he coached the offense at San
Diego State and then the pros."

By the late sixties, the Aztecs' passing attack had grown quite sophisticated. Receivers Gary Garrison, Haven Moses, and Isaac Curtis
all excelled in Coryell's system before going on to the NFL. The suc-
cession of passers after Don Horn included Dennis Shaw, Brian Sipe,
and Jesse Freitas—all eventual NFL quarterbacks. According to Bass,
"When Sipe first got to Cleveland, he realized the stuff he was doing
with Coryell at San Diego State was way ahead of what the Browns
were doing."

Coryell had other NFL admirers just up the coast in Los Angeles
as well. "Don was always ahead of his time," claimed Dick Vermeil.
"When he coached at San Diego State, I used to go down there as a

Rams assistant, watch them practice, steal stuff from them, and then put it in our Ram offense."

The Aztecs hardly ever lost with Coryell in charge. During his dozen years at the school, Don posted an astounding record of 104-19-2. At the end of the '72 season, he was hired by the NFL's St. Louis Cardinals to do the same thing he had done in San Diego: revive a moribund football team. Within a year, Coryell took the Cardinals to a division title and their first playoff appearance since 1948. He succeeded for two more seasons by utilizing the same formula that had worked for him in college: putting the ball in the air early and often. "Don would always be yelling, 'Throw it, throw it!'" recalled Cardinals quarterback Jim Hart. "It could be third-and-inches, and he'd come to our huddle during a time-out and tell us to throw it. He loved throwing on every down."

Hart recalled other ways that Coryell displayed his competitive and often combative nature. "We were playing the Eagles, staying at a hotel in Cherry Hill, New Jersey, and the bus driver wouldn't pull into the entrance because he said it was too tight a space for him to get in. Don got mad and said, 'My players aren't going to walk a hundred yards through snow because of you.' He was ready to duke it out! The driver asked him if he wanted to step outside, and Don said, 'You bet I do!' And this was the day before a game!"

When it came to interacting with his players, however, Coryell shunned the tough-guy approach. "I have no interest in intimidating people," he said. "I'd rather help people. I treat a player the way I'd want to be treated, try to help him become a better player by giving him an opportunity to do the things he can do best. I don't think a coach has to be a son of a bitch to be successful. I think you can treat men like men."

For Coryell, it was all about looking after his athletes, even if it sometimes put him at personal risk. Hall of Fame tackle and current broadcaster Dan Dierdorf has his own favorite story about Don's dedication: "We'd just gotten a defensive tackle from Pittsburgh named Charlie Davis, and in his first day of practice, he got in a fight with Conrad Dobler. I don't know what Coryell could have possibly been thinking, because Don's a little guy. He jumped in between these two huge linemen to try and break it up. And Charlie goes with this big roundhouse right, Conrad ducks, and Coryell gets struck right on the bridge of his nose. Blood is spurting everywhere, and the trainer runs out to try to help Don, but he waves him off. He stayed out there and just continued to run practice like nothing had happened."

That same focus and intensity carried over into Don's daily life. "Don lived in a rural area about an hour outside of downtown St. Louis," Hart remembered. "I heard a story where he'd put his garbage in his car so he could stop and deposit it somewhere right outside his house. I think he dropped his daughter off at school and then just continued on downtown, so consumed with football that he completely forgot he had all that trash in the back of his car."

What occupied Don's mind the bulk of the time were his thoughts on how to improve the Cardinals' explosive offense. He was always looking for new ways to exploit such stars as running back Terry Metcalf, receiver Mel Gray, and tight end Jackie Smith. But the creative innovations he'd eventually dream up with the Chargers were still a few years away. "There was nothing of what we know of as Air Coryell in St. Louis," claimed Gibbs, who served as an assistant on both the Cardinals' and the Chargers' coaching staffs. "His scheme in St. Louis was totally different. It was different personnel, different sets, more of the standard split backs. We had a very gifted quarterback in Hart, and Don certainly wanted to throw the football. But we were not in the one-back set. We ran standard formations. The tight ends ran conventional routes. We wanted to be balanced, and it helped having a great offensive line with Tom Banks, Bob Young, Dierdorf, and Dobler."

In the final month of the '77 season, the Cardinals fell apart, dropping their last four games, including a loss to a Tampa Bay Buccaneers team considered to be the worst in the league. St. Louis finished at 7-7 and management abruptly decided to make a coaching change. But Don wasn't unemployed for long. After the Chargers dropped three of their first four games to open the '78 schedule, they accepted head coach Tommy Prothro's resignation and brought Coryell in as his replacement.

It was too far into the season to install his entire offense, so Coryell made a gradual shift by adding selected plays to the Chargers' repertoire. Even so, San Diego won eight of its last nine games, and the team entered the '79 season brimming with confidence. The players were especially excited about the revamped offense put together by Coryell, Gibbs, and Zampese, an attack with roots in another San Diego coach from the past. "Dating back to Sid Gillman, most teams used the passing tree," recalled Chargers running back and special-teams captain Hank Bauer. "It's a numerical system tied into the number of steps of the quarterback's drop. Shorter routes are small numbers. Even numbers are inside routes. Odd numbers are outside routes. The deeper the quarterback's drop, the longer the receiver's route."

Sometimes those routes were deep enough to score long touchdowns. "The first thing in our offense was always the bomb," stated Fouts. "It was built into almost every pass play, where the quarterback initially looks for that chance to hit the big one. And I think if you start with this premise and then work your way back toward the line of scrimmage, that's the Air Coryell offense."

When Coryell began varying offensive formations, Fouts could get pre-snap reads because of the way the defense reacted. "Dan would know probably ninety-nine percent of the time what coverage he faced before taking his drop," said Bauer. "It's much harder to read coverage after the snap when the pass rush is coming and you can't see. As soon as Dan confirmed that coverage, that ball was out of his hand. That's what made it so lethal. If the ball's in the air before the receiver comes out of his break, there's absolutely no way a defensive back—unless he guesses—can make the play. And at that time, nobody in the league had seen that."

The timing of the offense didn't fall just on the quarterback. The line and everyone else had to work together. The launch point, the breaking points, the landmarks on the field—all had to be consistent. If you were supposed to break at 10 yards with your inside foot, you'd better do it just that way. Not 12 with your outside foot, because that wouldn't work. And you had to have the right mind-set to accept that style of coaching: factors such as the depth of the quarterback drops and where the ball was going. The system demanded precision, and coaching it required a lot of repetition.

Let me walk you through a typical play progression to better illustrate the concept. Say that Charlie Joiner is split outside, and there's a corner playing on him. If the corner's playing inside technique, he's in man-to-man coverage. But on which side is Charlie coming out of his break? He'll break it to the outside, because what's the point of coming back to the inside when the defender is sitting there waiting for him and can play the ball? If Joiner pushes him, then breaks outside, it's almost impossible for the defender to make the play.

Of course, none of this happens without a smart, tough quarterback—and in Fouts, the Chargers had someone who fit the bill perfectly. "Dan Fouts had cool, steel-like nerve and courage," stated Bill Walsh, who coached Dan in San Diego during the '76 season. "The great ones can function in that storm of people coming after him. He took a lot of beatings, a lot of pounding, but continued to play, hurt or otherwise. He played more physical football than anybody on his team, including the linebackers, because of all the contact he absorbed. He was the complete forward passer; every element of the passing game was at his command. Dan was not the most gifted athlete to play the position, but hard work and efficiency in his movement more than made up for it."

You know Dan today as a TV analyst, which seems natural, given his lineage. Fouts has been around pro football most of his life. During the fifties, his father, Bob, was the radio voice of the San Francisco 49ers—a job that enabled Dan to be a Niners ballboy at an early age. He chose the jersey number 14 because that's what Y. A. Tittle wore when he played for San Francisco. Later on, Tittle's successor, John Brodie, took Dan under his wing, teaching by example the mental toughness that was required to be an NFL quarterback.

Fouts learned those lessons well, but he was also a born leader. "Dan used to wear this hat during the week," recalled Bauer. "It said 'M.F.I.C.'—Mother Fucker in Charge—and he was definitely that. He was the smartest, toughest quarterback I've ever known. He was always prepared, knew the game plan, and when you got in that huddle, you'd sure better know what you were doing. If the coaches made a mistake, they weren't immune, either. Fouts would come at you. You were held responsible for being prepared."

Opponents also feared Fouts—for entirely different reasons. "You could not take a play off against him, he was so good," praised Dolphins defensive back Glenn Blackwood. "Fouts never eyeballed a receiver; he never tipped you off. His greatest ability was his command of the field. He knew where the holes were, and he put the ball on the money."

Statistically, the ball most often ended up with Joiner, the most technically sound of the Chargers' receivers. Charlie had actually started in the pros as a defensive back with Houston, but he got flattened by Broncos running back Floyd Little during his rookie year. After being carted off the field, Charlie made an immediate career change—to wide receiver. He prospered with the Oilers and Cincinnati Bengals before coming to the Chargers in '76. "When I went to San Diego, I was entering my eighth or ninth year and thought I was almost at the end of my career," said Joiner. "But Coryell's offense fit me so well that it really turned out to be the beginning my career. I played nine more years after that. For me, it was the best offense in the world.

"My job was to make sure that I could keep a safety out of the action to give those other receivers a chance to catch it and turn it upfield. We always knew there was no particular chosen guy on the pass pattern. There were as many as five who had a chance of getting the ball. But you had to run your route to precision, run it believably, force the defense to defend the entire field. If you were open, Dan would get the ball to you. No matter what curves the defense had, one of our five receivers was going to be open."

"The reason Charlie Joiner is in the Hall of Fame," noted Saunders, "is that he could change his direction with the same body lean going full speed. He could get out of a break as fast as he came off the line of scrimmage. Chargers receivers had to outleverage the defender and get quicker separation. That's why the ball had to be thrown *before* separation, so the target could get to the ball before the defender did."

In 1978 the Chargers drafted John Jefferson out of Arizona State University, adding a deep threat to San Diego's passing attack. "I had some real speed coming out of college," said Jefferson. "I was the type of guy who might be covered at first going deep downfield, but once the ball got there, I was able to go up and take it away from whoever was on me—very similar to Lynn Swann with Pittsburgh in his heyday." As a rookie, Jefferson led the league with 13 touchdown catches, and the Coryell system had much to do with that. "In his passing tree, you can give your receivers two or three different routes," explained Jefferson. "In San Diego, the coaches allowed us the freedom to change those routes, depending on the coverage. Dan pretty much knew when we were going to break those routes and when to release the ball. Sure enough, we'd be there. This made it difficult for defenses to shut us down. They might have the proper coverage to stop that *first* route, but when we changed it, we had them beat."

Nineteen seventy-eight was the Chargers' first winning season since 1969, when Gillman had been their coach. Al Saunders pinpointed an even more significant similarity: "Both Sid's and Don's offenses were built on big-play potential, which is the reverse of the 'control the football, move the chains' approach. But look at the stats, and you'll see a pretty good balance with the running game—ground attacks that were very efficient. Unpredictability was vital to their success. Defenses don't want to give up big plays, which made them tend to play more conservatively.

"Both men's mind-set was 'score,' not 'control the game,'" he continued. "So they were ahead of their time by being more aggressive in their calls. I can never remember Don Coryell saying before a game, 'We're going to pound these guys into the ground, we're going to wear them down.' Winning in physical style wasn't his way. You never sensed that Don was going to hold back—he was always aggressive in his play calls. Keep the pressure on the defense. And neither Sid nor Don were in-the-box thinkers. They were willing to utilize players' talents to help them succeed. And that often meant coming up with creative solutions."

Both Gillman and Coryell knew that none of this could take place unless their quarterbacks were well protected, so both placed a premium on quality offensive line play. The 1980s unit of center Don Macek, tackles Billy Shields and Russ Washington, and guards Ed White and Doug Wilkerson was one of the finest in league history. It was so big in size for that era that one local writer nicknamed them "the Five Tackles." Fouts loved them like brothers. "My guys were great players and great people. They really formed a tight pocket for me. We were strong in the middle and had athletic tackles on the sides to run defensive ends away from me. Obviously I knew their importance to our success and to my own well-being, so I'd always take them out to dinner the night before a game. How well they'd performed the week before determined the size of the tab I was going to run up. I'd use this as a motivating tool in the huddle late during the fourth quarter when the game was on the line. I'd say, 'We've got to go down and score, men. What's it going to be: prime rib or pasta?' The big boys always wanted their meat, so to me, those T-bone steaks were the best form of life insurance."

But there were also some noticeable differences between Gillman's Chargers and Coryell's late-seventies model. "I think Sid's was a more deliberate system to get the ball downfield. There were fewer progressions with those Chargers teams—a primary receiver to a checkdown," Saunders noted. "Don's system created more options for the quarterback when he didn't have to throw downfield. When I was with Don, we had screens off of downfield throws. Let's say you had a curl route for Joiner, with the back on a swing pass. The guard would pull out wide. What Don and Ernie did was expand what you could do with underneath receivers. It allowed for more creativity, because as the game evolved, people were utilized in different ways."

It was the next draft that would drastically reshape the look of Air Coryell—and permanently change the NFL passing game. San Diego's two veteran tight ends, Bob Klein and Pat Curran, were showing their age, and the team needed new blood at the position. After orchestrating a deal with the Browns, the Chargers were able to move up in the first round and select the University of Missouri's Kellen Winslow.

"I didn't play high school football until my senior year," Winslow recalled. "Up till then, I was kind of a nerd. I was in chess club and had an after-school job with UPS. Once I finally got out on the practice field, I didn't know what I was doing—I was pretty green. But my chess knowledge actually helped me figure things out. It wasn't till the end of my sophomore year in college at spring practice that I realized I was the 'knight' of a chess board. At that point, the light went on, and football began to make sense to me. There's only so much time and space to get certain things done. You can't be everywhere. The knight is the only chess piece that can move eight spaces in multiple directions. It helped me understand what the wide receivers and backs were supposed to be doing."

During his rookie year in '79, the Chargers used tight ends primarily to shuttle in plays. Their duties were traditional to the position: run blocking and short-to-intermediate routes originating next to either offensive tackle. Winslow caught only twenty-five passes before a leg injury prematurely ended his season. That winter, Coryell and his staff thought long and hard about better ways to take advantage of Kellen's skills. "The Chargers' offensive line coach back then was a guy named Dave Levy," remembered Saunders. "Dave said, 'If you gave me Kellen for a year, I could make him into an All-Pro tackle.' That's how athletic he was. He was a wide receiver in an offensive lineman's body.

"You have to understand how tight ends were being used in the early 1980s," Saunders added. "Their primary function was as a blocker, then to move out to the back side as part of the route and run a drag route. Or they'd run hooks inside, or get open in the flat. That was it. They were all big guys, 'tackles' who could catch the football. Plus, outside linebackers could still grab a guy and smack him around trying to defend the run."

It pained Joe Gibbs to see Winslow's talent being held back by the traditional limits of the position. "When we lined him up at the standard tight end spot and he went to release, he got pounded by the outside linebacker in a 4-3 or the inside linebacker in a 3-4," he recalled. "He had a tough time getting off clean, and we felt we had to do something. So Ernie, Don, our O-line coach, Jim Hanifan, and I said to ourselves, 'Maybe the thing to do is take him off that line of scrimmage and start moving him all over the place.'"

The idea itself wasn't entirely new to Coryell. "I remember at San Diego State when Don, out of nowhere, moved a wide receiver to the tight end position when he thought the guy could get deep in the middle," recalled Tom Bass. "We ended up getting a touchdown on that play. Even then he was thinking this was an alignment that was ripe for exploitation. That got everyone's attention back then."

The experimentation with Winslow began when he was running dummy drills before a 1980 summer camp scrimmage with Dallas. "The Cowboys had a lot of motion, lots of sets," Winslow recalled. "I was working with backup quarterback James Harris on the scout team, and it was hard to mimic what they did before the snap, because a lot of it was impromptu. So they'd hold up a card and say, 'Line up where you want, but end up in this formation.' So we just started playing around with it. Our coaches saw something, and so I ended up in practice running the same routes as the wide receivers. I loved running those routes, the 'skinny post,' the 'deep post'—and there weren't many guys then at six five, 245 who could run these traditional wide-out routes. When you looked at the film, I ran the routes about as well as the wide receivers, although I was usually a step or two behind where they were."

What Coryell and Zampese did with Winslow was to take a player with extraordinary pass-catching ability and create positions in which he could be the primary receiver. "Now you had a guy in the middle of the field who took advantage of personnel matchups or man-on-man matchups," said Saunders. "Back then, either a strong safety or linebacker was going to have to cover him. They didn't play zone defenses then like they do today, giving Winslow much more space to operate. The more Kellen showed what he could do, the more Coryell added to the system. And because of that offense's versatility, everybody could play a part in what was going on. Winslow was a big target, but he was also courageous, catching in a crowd. He was always better than the defender he was going up against."

Turning Winslow into what I call The Roving-Y created a king-sized headache for opposing defensive coordinators, including Denver's Joe Collier, who faced the Chargers twice a year. "During the early years of Air Coryell," he said, "the strong safety wasn't much more than a glorified linebacker; basically a run defender who could cover an average tight end. You put a guy like Winslow out in the slot and he's going up against coverage that's a lot slower than he is. It's not the matchup on defense we liked. So we'd try to give that strong safety some help, like bringing a linebacker out to him or bringing the other safety over to help. Of course, this weakened us in other areas. It forced us to do things we didn't want to do."

San Diego opened the 1980 season on the road with a relatively easy 34–13 win at Seattle. Winslow was barely a factor, catching only two passes for 41 yards. The Chargers were saving him, along with some creative new play calls, for their home opener the following week against the arch-rival Oakland Raiders. "Ernie Zampese was a master at handling top talent," Winslow recalled. "He was quick to compliment and encourage. After I caught only two passes against Seattle, he made a point to say he'd try to get me a lot more in the next game. We were so tied to the team concept that we all knew if you caught two passes one day, you'd get a big increase in another game. Teams would try to take a guy out who did well the week before, so things would open up for someone else."

Rod Rust was the Chiefs' defensive coordinator during the heyday of Air Coryell. As a division foe, he became all too familiar with San Diego's share-the-wealth receiving strategy. "By design, the Chargers went through a rotating 'receiver of the week' scheme," he explained. "What you would see on game film from the previous three weeks was not what you were going to see in your game. If you went back more than four weeks, then you might be able to see what they were more likely to run. They used so many formation variations, moving people around, and there are only so many hours in the week for film study."

During the '80 draft, the Raiders selected a big and physical Penn State linebacker named Matt Millen in the second round. The week-two matchup with the Chargers was only Millen's second professional game, and what he saw that afternoon was the first glimpse of an offensive approach that would profoundly affect pro football strategy. "That day, they ran a bunch of stuff we hadn't seen, hadn't practiced against," Millen confessed. "Today all this stuff is commonplace, but not then. The Chargers' coaching staff was fortunate to have Winslow, and he was fortunate to have those coaches. Had it not been in San Diego, it would eventually have been done someplace else, because it was time. This was the right place at the right time for both."

1ST HALF

1st Quarter

Winslow was not in the starting lineup when the Chargers began their first series. Instead San Diego went with Greg McCrary at tight end, a skilled blocker of considerable size who'd actually caught a touchdown pass the week before in the win against the Seattle Seahawks. From a traditional two-back set, the Chargers ran the ball on their first three plays before missing on a throw to Jefferson. A Raiders holding penalty on a punt gave Fouts a fresh set of downs near midfield, and that's when Coryell called the first of many passes to Winslow.

Kellen replaced McCrary, but he did not line up as a traditional tight end. He was split right outside the numbers as the X, or weakside, wide receiver. Joiner was in the slot to the left, with Jefferson aligned outside of Joiner. Clarence Williams and John Cappelletti were split in the backfield. Raiders strong safety Mike Davis was aligned over Winslow but gave him a generous 10-yard cushion. Davis was a terrific run defender but had limited abilities in open space. "Like the rough beard he always wore, Mike was tough," remembered Tom Flores, who was in his second year as Oakland's head coach in 1980. "But it was a lot to ask of him to go man-to-man all day long on Winslow. He was just a bitch to cover or slow down. Whenever Winslow split out, our rule was for the strong safety to cover him. When possible, we also had a linebacker move out and try to bump him at the line of scrimmage."

Nobody hit Kellen on this first pass, a quick 5-yard hitch that gave him plenty of room to run. Winslow picked up 16 yards and brought the ball into Raiders territory before he was finally brought down by Millen.

"It was the genius of Coryell and his coaches to use Kellen this way, because nobody had ever done this before," claimed Bauer.

"We're playing the Raiders, who played man-free coverage ninety per-cent of the time. That's fine if you're facing a normal pro set, but we come out against them and suddenly shift Kellen outside to flanker. Who goes out to cover him? Are you going to take one of your corners off a receiver and put a strong safety on Winslow? Early on, that's what they did, so the first thing that told us was they're playing man under, free coverage. And we also got a mismatch, because no strong safety could cover Kellen in the open field. They weren't as big, as fast, or as athletic. If they bumped out a corner, then we'd know they were playing zone, and they'd put a linebacker on Kellen, which was even better for us."

"The problem Winslow presented was that he ran like a wide re-ceiver," said Millen. "If you tried to get up on him, he'd just blow past you. He and Davis had some good battles out there that day. But Mike had to play off him, because he didn't want to miss a tackle." There were no more throws to Kellen the rest of the drive, which ended with a 52-yard field goal by kicker Rolf Benirschke. At the time, it was the longest kick in Chargers history. Oakland tied the game on its next drive, then San Diego was quickly dispatched with a three-and-out in its only other first-quarter possession.

2nd Quarter

The Chargers had three less than prosperous possessions in this quarter before finally cashing in just before halftime. Their first series had Winslow line up as a traditional tight end, with McCrary off the line in what we would now refer to as the H-back position. With two runners in the backfield, that meant only one wide receiver, Jefferson, was on the field. Whenever you have two backs and two tight ends to-gether in the lineup, you have what is called "Twenty-Two personnel." San Diego would run a number of plays from this formation through-out the game. After the snap, Winslow ran a drag route in front of un-derneath coverage and picked up 7. The next pass was also intended for Kellen but fell incomplete, due mainly to Millen's aggressive de-fense on the young Chargers tight end. "Winslow was physically im-posing but wasn't a physical guy," observed Millen. "He could run like a little guy. If you put a little guy on him to cover, he'd slap that guy around."

Winslow laughs about Millen's tactics now, but it wasn't funny to him at the time. "I drew mostly Davis in that Raider game, and Odis McKinney as the nickel defender," he recalled. "But whenever it was Millen, he'd grab my jersey every time! Once you came inside, he'd put his hands on you." Millen pleads guilty as charged: "The rules were a little different then. I could beat the piss out of receivers down the field. You'd take your shots. You could get away with a lot more things because it was a much more physical game."

San Diego punted after failing on third down, then did even less on its next series, when Clarence Williams fumbled on the first play. The Chargers quickly forced a fumble of their own to get the ball back. Williams continued to struggle, however, losing 3 yards on a sweep. Facing second-and-13, San Diego came out in a two-back set, with McCrary as the single tight end. Winslow was split left outside the numbers as the X receiver, while Jefferson was out wide on the opposite side. The Raiders responded by going to nickel coverage for the first time, inserting McKinney as their fifth defensive back. For the remainder of the game, he would defend against Winslow whenever Oakland was in the nickel.

"If we saw McKinney on Kellen, Oakland had a huge matchup problem," claimed Bauer. "That's what our game planning was all week: coming up with the formations and movements that dictated coverage, gave Dan a pre-snap read, and provided the potential of creating confusion in their secondary." In this instance, Jefferson worked away from a smart but slower safety in Burgess Owens to make a 7-yard catch. Facing third-and-6, Fouts beat a Raiders blitz, hitting Joiner on a hot read to get the ball to midfield.

Oakland tried to change things up, going to a 3-4 front: rushing four men while dropping its secondary into zone coverage. The Chargers came out in Twenty-Two personnel, with McCrary at tight end and Winslow split left outside the numbers as the X receiver. This time, cornerback Monte Jackson drew Winslow as his assignment. Ironically, Jackson had been recruited by Coryell out of local St. Augustine High School and played for him at San Diego State. On this particular play, Jackson may have shown the Chargers and his former coach too much respect, giving Kellen an even wider cushion than Davis was offering. Winslow ran a 10-yard stop route well in front of the backpedaling Jackson to pick up a first down on Oakland's 40-yard line.

But then its defense stiffened, first sacking Fouts for a 9-yard loss. The Raiders returned to nickel coverage with McKinney on Winslow for the next two long-yardage plays. Both were passes to Joiner, neither successful. San Diego was forced to punt, but the Chargers' defense also stood its ground, getting the ball back for one last drive just before halftime.

San Diego began the series at its own 45, with Winslow aligned in the conventional tight end position and Joiner and Jefferson split wide. "We didn't flip-flop our defensive coverage in those days," explained Flores. "If Jefferson lined up on Lester Hayes's side, then Hayes had him. And if he didn't, then Lester covered Joiner. We didn't chase them all over the field." With both wideouts taking their corners outside, Winslow was able to run a slant pattern unmolested in the middle to pick up 9 yards. On the next play, Kellen lined up tight on the left side and blocked somewhat awkwardly for a run by Cappelletti that picked up a first down. "Kellen wasn't much of a blocker then, but he was a big man," noted Millen. "It wasn't lack of effort—he just didn't know how to block very well. It was only his second year, and, let's face it, most tight ends aren't very good blockers anyway."

Coryell would make far better use of Winslow's talents during the next few plays of the drive. After an incomplete pass in the flat to Williams, the Chargers faced second-and-10. They split Kellen wide right as the X, isolating him one-on-one with Davis. After the snap, Winslow took off on a Go route. Davis covered him perfectly, and the pass fell incomplete, but Oakland had to be startled nonetheless. In the NFL of 1980, tight ends *never* ran Go routes. That was solely the province of wide receivers.

Knowing that this had given Oakland's secondary pause, the Chargers lined Winslow up wide right again on the next play. Sure enough, he took off down the sideline as Jefferson broke free across the field to haul in a 19-yard pass for the first down. Now just outside the red zone, Coryell called Winslow's number once more. Split as the X receiver, Kellen ran a stutter-Go route, another pattern you'd never see from a tight end in the early eighties. This time Davis got beat badly. He was forced to grab Winslow and was promptly flagged for an illegal chuck—the quintessential enforcement of the Mel Blount rule. Three years earlier, Davis's defense would have been perfectly legal.

"The '78 rules changes just killed a team like Oakland," claimed Joiner. "It totally changed how the Raiders game planned for pass defense. They'd always had physical corners that would bump you all over the field. It took away a lot of their aggressiveness; a lot of what they did well. But I think the design of Air Coryell was good enough that we'd still have succeeded even without those rules changes."

Two running plays and a face mask penalty on Oakland put the ball inside the 5-yard line. On second-and-goal, Winslow lined up as the slot receiver on the left side. He broke toward the sideline, taking Davis with him. Fouts quickly threw to the right corner, where Jefferson faced single coverage from Hayes. J.J. then made one of the signature receptions of his career: a leaping, one-handed catch near the corner of the end zone for the game's first touchdown. "I just loved throwing the ball to J.J. because I felt no matter where I threw it he was somehow going to catch it," said Fouts. "He had an incredible ability to focus on the ball regardless of the situation. He made so many catches like this, and that just gave me confidence that I could cut loose and not worry about it, because he was going to take care of me. That carried over to the others too, because all our receivers were competing for the ball, competing for my attention."

For Jefferson, it wasn't that big a deal. "It was just your typical fade route against Hayes, who would bump and run anybody, anytime. He was the best in the league at that. This time he bumped me pretty good; was right on top of me. The pass was over my head. Somehow I went up and got it with one hand, and it stuck."

The rest of Jefferson's teammates, including Hank Bauer, were in awe of the gravity-defying grab. "I always judged players by who you were playing against," he said. "Here's J.J. being defended by 'Mr. Stickum,' Lester Hayes, one of the all-time greats. Fouts was throwing it away, and it was high and gone like a throwaway should be. All of a sudden, out of nowhere, J.J. reaches up with one hand. He keeps his tippy toes down at the end line, in bounds, and catches the point of the football. On the bench, our jaws dropped, and we said, 'What? Are you kidding me?'"

Oakland's Cliff Branch caught a touchdown pass of his own a little over a minute later to tie the game at 10 going into intermission. During my film study of the first half, there were several recurring elements that caught my attention. When you also included penalties, the Chargers had run more than thirty plays from scrimmage. I rarely saw the same formations twice. In the NBC telecast, color analyst Merlin Olsen claimed that the Chargers had utilized forty-five different offensive formations the previous year, an incredibly high number for that era. Olsen made the point that the reason San Diego had so many formations was to isolate matchups on specific Raiders defenders.

Despite those variations, I counted a disproportionate number of Twenty-Two personnel packages used by the Chargers. In that package, both Winslow and McCrary stayed on the same side of the formation, with Jefferson as a single receiver to the weak side. And whenever Winslow was the X receiver to the weak side, Jefferson and Joiner were grouped together on the other side of that formation. Raiders defensive coverage also stayed remarkably consistent. In base personnel, Mike Davis was always matched up on Winslow. In the nickel, Odis McKinney was Kellen's defender.

In their week-one win at Seattle, the Chargers' ground game had gashed the Seahawks for nearly 200 yards. In the first half against Oakland, it was a different story: only a dozen rushing yards against the Raiders' defense. "You have to do what you believe in, what you can do best," said Coryell. "We go into every game thinking that if we think we can run the ball, then we'll run it. But if we don't think we can consistently move the ball on the ground, then we'll throw. And if we *have* to throw the ball on every down because we *know* we can't run it, then we'll throw the ball on every down." That's pretty much what the Chargers did to start the second half—and they were fortunate this decision didn't cost them the game.

3rd Quarter

I studied quite a few games for this book and saw a lot of things that surprised me, both tactically and athletically. But nothing I watched was more shocking than what happened to the Chargers in the third quarter of their '80 game against Oakland. In those fifteen minutes of football, they turned the ball over *five* times: four interceptions plus a lost fumble that the Raiders recovered for a touchdown. In spite of this meltdown, San Diego, incredibly, trailed by only a touchdown heading into the final quarter. Part of it was a strong response by the Chargers' defense. It also didn't hurt San Diego that Oakland's kicker, Chris Bahr, missed a pair of field goals.

Not all of Fouts's four interceptions were his fault. In a couple of cases, his passes could have been caught but bounced off a receiver's hands. Other times it was Oakland's pass rush. "The only way you could really stop us was to put the heat on Dan," explained Charlie Joiner. "You had to find a way to pressure him where he couldn't set up and get rid of the ball quickly. You had to break his rhythm some kind of way." Even after that happened, Fouts possessed the most important talent a quarterback can possess: resilience. "Fouts was a tough, tough sucker," admitted Millen. "You could beat up on him, and he'd just get pissed off. The more you hit him, the better he got."

Even though during this stretch Coryell's offense was as bad as I've ever seen it, there were a number of plays involving Winslow that I found revealing. On a majority of snaps—including the one that allowed the Raiders to force and recover a fumble, then run it in for a score—the Silver and Black was in nickel coverage. Defending the San Diego passing game was clearly the priority, because the Chargers had decided to junk their very unproductive running game. But let's be clear: Oakland's use of the nickel defense was dictated primarily by circumstance—down and distance—not Chargers personnel. When you see nickel or dime coverages today, it's almost always in response to additional receivers in the formation. In September 1980 the concept of having even *three* wideouts, let alone four, wasn't yet a part of the game, although Coryell would seize upon this tactic within just a few weeks of this game, after the team made a significant trade.

During the disastrous third quarter, Kellen still made two fine receptions and would have had a third except for a low throw from Fouts forced by Oakland pressure. The first catch was a 10-yard completion, with Winslow aligned as the X receiver against base personnel. Once again, Mike Davis was giving Kellen a 10-yard cushion—out of necessity, according to Millen. "When you were drafting a safety back then, you didn't say, 'Is this guy a good player in space?' That's because those conditions simply didn't exist. He wasn't asked to do what receivers like Winslow forced on them." Winslow ran a quick 5-yard hitch and had additional room to run, adding another 5 yards before Davis tackled him.

Winslow's other reception was a real stunner for me. Again aligned as the X receiver, with Joiner in the slot on the left adjacent to Jefferson, Kellen ran a traditional wideout's route: the skinny post (similar to a traditional post pattern, but cut off at a shallower angle). Tight ends back then just didn't *do* this kind of thing. It was as beautifully timed a play as the Chargers ran all game. "Dan had a pre-snap read," recalled Winslow. "He knew where I was going to go. It was based on the coverage he saw. It was a fifteen-to-eighteen-yard route. You plant at twelve yards, make the catch at fifteen, and hope to break a tackle." He broke one, all right. The route may have been a traditional wide receiver's pattern, but what happened next was standard tight end fare of the era. After catching the ball in stride, Winslow ran over free safety Burgess Owens and rumbled for 22 yards.

Although neither catch led to anything other than eventual Chargers turnovers, both foreshadowed what Winslow was going to accomplish the rest of the game—contributing to one of the most fantastic finishes of any contest in the Coryell era.

4th Quarter

Coryell had abandoned the running game in the third quarter but decided to give it one more try as the fourth quarter began. Halfback Clarence Williams ran or caught the ball on each of San Diego's first four plays, accounting for 35 yards and a pair of first downs. On the next call, Fouts overthrew Winslow on a deep post pattern, but a Raiders penalty moved the ball up 5 yards. Two plays later, Kellen lined up as the X receiver, with Joiner and Jefferson on the other side and split backs behind Fouts. The Raiders went to nickel personnel, which once again put McKinney over Winslow. Oakland played a man coverage scheme and accounted for Winslow with two defenders. Davis and McKinney played what we call a bracket concept: in-and-out, deep-to-short coverage. Winslow ran an X delay underneath pattern at about 10 yards, where McKinney forced Kellen toward Davis on the inside. The third-year safety, a second-round draft pick out of Colorado, tried to stay with him but slipped and fell. Winslow caught the pass at the 15 and ran untouched into the end zone to tie the game at 17. "On that touchdown, I was going back side to weak side," Winslow remembered. "Oakland wanted to put pressure on the quarterback, so we knew what defensive coverages they were in almost every play."

After an end zone interception by the Chargers' Glen Edwards to stop an Oakland drive, Winslow made a huge impact on San Diego's

Roving-Y Skinny Post Pattern

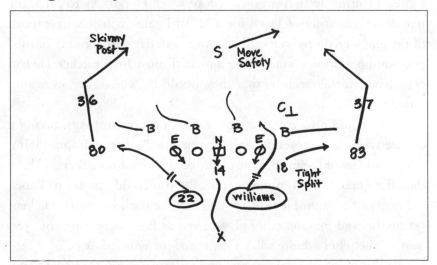

Post patterns of any kind weren't routes typically run by tight ends until Winslow's arrival. Winslow begins the play lined up away from the right tackle, not the conventional spot where most tight ends were located in the 1970s. As Winslow runs this shortened post he gets help from Jefferson, whose route effectively drives free safety Owens away from Winslow's area. The Raiders have four linebackers available, but none have the speed to stay with the faster Winslow on the post route.

next series. On second-and-10, Coryell had Kellen line up as the X receiver, this time on the left side of the formation. The Raiders went to nickel coverage, with McKinney shadowing the San Diego tight end, and Kellen burned him with an inside curl route for 11 yards. Oakland continued to stay with the nickel—in essence removing a run defender, and the Chargers took advantage as Williams picked up substantial rushing yardage during the drive. To the Raiders' dismay, the extra man in the secondary wasn't doing much to stop Fouts, who found Jefferson for 11 more yards and then hooked up with Winslow again.

Winslow's ninth and final reception of the game was one of his best, given Oakland's defensive formation. The Raiders rushed only three men, dropping eight defenders into coverage. It was an interesting and unusual concept deployed by their defensive coordinator, Charlie Sumner. Davis was the over-the-top safety, with future Hall of Famer Ted "the Mad Stork" Hendricks buzzing out from his normal linebacker's position to get underneath Winslow. This was a zone concept, but had a double-team element to it. It was creative stuff, although none of this mattered to Kellen. He ran an intermediate dig route, sprinting away from the six-foot-seven Hendricks to catch the ball directly in front of Davis for a 22-yard gain. Winslow gave much of the play's credit to Fouts: "Dan moved safeties with a pretty darned good pump motion—kind of like a pickoff move for a pitcher. He had confidence in the receivers that they would be where they were supposed to be."

"You could also try to double Kellen on certain plays, taking a chance with single coverage on everyone else," observed Tom Flores. "You could favor the inside part of the field with a linebacker and have the safety take him from the outside. Or you could just try to knock the crap out of him. He was a tough guy; he took his shots. He kept getting up and making more plays. Even as he was beating you, you couldn't help but admire what a great athlete Winslow was."

At this point, the Raiders reverted to base personnel to try to stop San Diego's suddenly vibrant running attack. It didn't work. The Chargers had found their rhythm on the ground, and five straight running plays eventually got San Diego into the end zone to take a 24–17 lead. On four of those plays, Winslow lined up as a conventional tight end and blocked efficiently. On the final call, he aligned wide right, taking defenders with him on a short route as Clarence Williams swept around the vacated area to score the go-ahead touchdown.

Winslow's influence was evident throughout that final drive. His presence had a profound impact on both San Diego's running and passing games. The Raiders switched back and forth between nickel and base coverages to try to stop whatever the Chargers and Winslow were doing—but never quite succeeded. From across the field, Tom Flores could do little more than tip his cap to a talented opponent. "The NFL is a copycat league," he noted, "and people would say, 'Did you see that? Maybe there's a way our guy can do that too.' Then I'd say, 'We don't *have* that guy!' We did have Raymond Chester, who was more of a power-type tight end who'd block your head off, then catch the ball downfield, and outrace you to the end zone. Nowadays you see more tight ends like Winslow and fewer like Chester."

At that moment, though, the Raiders were mighty glad they had

Intermediate Dig Route

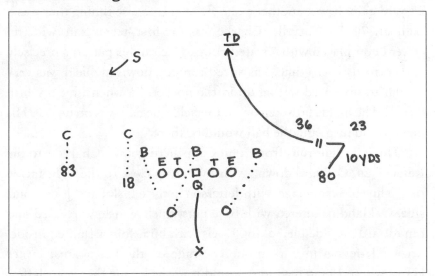

Winslow's 25-yard touchdown catch against Oakland came on this play. Coryell has Kellen lined up as the X wide receiver, a much different position than any other tight end of that era would align. Note that Joiner is lined up close to the line on the left side, which was also a highly unusual origination point for a wide receiver of that period.

Raymond Chester in their lineup, because it was his touchdown reception with thirty-nine seconds remaining that tied the game at 24, sending the contest into overtime.

Overtime

The Chargers won the toss but gave the ball back on their very first play when Fouts's pass was tipped by the Raiders, then caromed off Jefferson's hands to Millen for an interception. Oakland ran on five straight plays before being stopped on a third-down pass attempt. Chris Bahr entered, hoping to redeem himself after missing four other field goals, but he failed for a fifth time when his kick was partially blocked, allowing San Diego to take over on its own 33.

Fouts opened the drive with a pass to Williams for 11 yards, but then Clarence was dropped for a 6-yard loss on the next play. Facing second-and-16, the Chargers split Winslow out left as the X receiver, matched up against McKinney. Kellen cleared out the middle by running to his left, essentially carrying two defenders with him. This left Joiner with single coverage, and the crafty veteran beat his man for a 28-yard gain. It was another example of the precise timing that was a hallmark of Air Coryell. "Charlie was the first 'technician' wide receiver I ever played with," stated Fouts. "He ran his patterns precisely and correctly *every* time. His speed running down the field was very similar to my speed setting up in the pocket. So when I hit my fifth step, and he hit his fifth step down the field, the ball was on its way. His head would turn, and the ball would be there."

Three straight runs from John Cappelletti got the Chargers to the Raiders' 24. On third down, Winslow set up close to the right tackle on the line of scrimmage, with Jefferson in the left slot and Joiner outside. Oakland countered with base personnel. Winslow released and ran toward the sideline, taking Davis with him. Joiner slanted inside, leaving Jefferson in one-on-one coverage on the left against Lester Hayes whose 13 interceptions would lead the league that year. Jefferson broke to the corner and made a spectacular leaping catch directly over Hayes. "I caught it even though I was looking right into the sun," recalled Jefferson. "I was on the ground, and for whatever reason,

Hayes just stopped. So I simply rolled into the end zone, and the referee put his arms in the air."

The partisan crowd erupted as Jefferson bounced up off the turf to celebrate the winning score. "J.J. wasn't the fastest, he wasn't a burner, but he had body control and great hands," said Bauer. "Jefferson was one of the few guys in the NFL who could 'take the judge to court.' He used to beat Lester Hayes down, and it would just drive Lester the Molester crazy. We loved it. We fed off it. And this time, it got us a W in overtime."

Going back through my notes, I counted Winslow lining up wide as the X receiver on 27 of the Chargers' 78 snaps from scrimmage. That means Kellen was performing as a wide receiver on 35 percent of his team's plays. Forget that this was an astounding total for 1980. You wouldn't even see so many alignments of this kind in the NFL today by a Dallas Clark or Antonio Gates. San Diego's 30–24 overtime victory was, in historical context, Kellen Winslow's coming-out party. The way he was deployed that afternoon by Coryell was unlike anything ever witnessed in an NFL game.

Two weeks after defeating the Raiders, San Diego traded for New Orleans running back Chuck Muncie. "He may have been the most gifted running back ever to play the game," according to Bauer. "As a Chargers announcer, I've watched every one of Ladainian Tomlinson's carries. I've seen Barry Sanders, Marcus Allen, Emmitt Smith, O. J. Simpson. You name them. And I still say Chuck is the baddest runner I have ever seen. He'd have been the best of all time if he'd stayed out of trouble off the field. Just imagine what we could do now with Kellen, three wides, and a back like Muncie. The defense tries to shut down our passing game with six defensive backs, their safeties dropping—and just one linebacker. They're all going out wide, covering Kellen and the other receivers. We'd just run the stretch play all day, and Muncie would kill them."

Muncie's arrival handed Coryell, Gibbs, and Zampese another lethal weapon and sparked even more creative ideas. "That led to us putting another tight end in the game and making him the 'ace' back, then putting in different formations all over the place," explained Gibbs. "That was the evolution of the one-back offense. Of all the people I ever coached with, Coryell was never afraid to try anything. He was very progressive and let his coaches try any idea." Among those suggestions were all kinds of personnel shifts; pre-snap moves that totally baffled San Diego's opponents.

When the Chargers put Winslow in motion prior to the snap, it gave San Diego several distinct advantages. It's considerably harder for a defender to cover someone when he's forced to move with him before the snap. It's much easier standing still, when he can square up and set himself before the play begins. And the player in motion knows exactly where he's going to go, while the defender can only guess. It's also harder for the defender to change direction. Then there was the basic physical mismatch between Winslow and the defenders of that era. "Kellen was taller and faster than anyone opponents put on him," said Saunders. "He was at his best in a contested environment. He used what we called 'basketball skills' better than any tight end of his time. He could wall off a defender to make the catch. Kellen would run a route right into a defender and knock him back, then break off. Now he'd be open, get the ball, and in the open field he could really run. He was too big for a lot of those defenders to take on.

"A defense had to account for all that shifting—Winslow shifting from backfield to tight end, backs in motion. Don wanted to get an advantage before the snap. Some teams did that with cadence or audibles. Don's movement created mismatches and confusion with the defense. When I first got to San Diego, I asked Ernie Zampese why they did so much shifting and movement. His reply was, 'Sometimes we just do it to do it.' When you shift or go in motion, that causes at least two checks by the defense. So what happens if someone doesn't hear the check or hears it incorrectly? Now he's out of position, or you have the wrong defender in place."

From week to week, the Chargers added more components to their offense, which drove opponents out of their minds. And it wasn't just an endless parade of men in motion. Coryell was now clustering his receivers in unorthodox ways, utilizing what are known as combination routes. These were patterns linked to the location and grouping of his pass targets, determined by where they lined up in the formation, and with whom they were bunched: other wideouts, tight ends, or even running backs. Winslow appreciated the cerebral nature of these innovations: "That's all it really is: a time-space continuum. An offense has to exploit that time and space. And the more you have to think about it as a defensive player, the less effective you are at covering all options. As an offense, when we ran plays of simplicity in a complicated way, we improved our odds."

Broncos defensive coordinator Joe Collier tried to crack the Chargers' code twice a season, with only mixed results. "Coryell's teams never showed you the same thing twice," he stated. "They always seemed to come out with new formations, new motions, new shifts. What we had to do was to play a pretty vanilla defense until we figured out what the hell we should be doing against them. The plays they ended up with would be the same plays they used all year. But it was their *way* of getting into the plays that caused doubt in our defenses."

Rod Rust faced the same problems positioning his Chiefs' defenses. "Against the Chargers, the first thing you had to worry about was getting lined up properly," he explained. "My last year in Kansas City, we finally figured out what we needed to do, and that was basically by thinking *We don't care where anyone is*—whether Kellen was lined up as an X or Z. We were going to line up with our corners outside, safeties inside, linebackers in the box. We were going to defend the one they gave us rather than saying, 'You'll cover this guy, you cover that guy'—because if you do that, you're already behind the curve. I'd made that mistake too many times before. This enabled our players to compete with their *players* rather than compete with their *coaches,* trying to figure out where to line up. The genius of what San Diego did was that their players knew what to do better than the defenders, because they moved people around in atypical locations. If you could eliminate the indecision, your defense had a much better chance against them."

Every NFL offense ever devised can be stopped, however, even Coryell's Chargers. "One way is by having our offense beat itself with turnovers," revealed Bauer. "Otherwise, it was because some teams were good at stopping our run. Then those teams could press our pass pocket, because we didn't roll the pocket that much. They'd have to guess, take a chance of their own by giving us a false look on defense. The teams that put pressure on Dan were the ones who gave us fits. Whether it was overloading personnel, an individual mismatch, blitzes, stunts, you've got to press the pocket inside, get in the face of the quarterback, and make him move his feet. The other thing is, if you've got physical corners that can get a good jam on our guys releasing, our timing routes could get disrupted."

Obviously, teams did find ways to defeat the Chargers, because San Diego never reached the Super Bowl during Coryell's tenure. Some believe it was because the defensive units never performed at the same high levels as the offense. "During practices, Don was focused on throwing and running the ball—never on defense," admitted Tom Bass, who served four years as Chargers defensive coordinator. "This was true at San Diego State and in the pros. He was very friendly with the players in the locker room, kidding around with them, but as far as worrying about defensive schemes or trying to coach these guys—no chance. He never wanted to be briefed about defensive game plans; it was totally up to me. He was so in love with the other side of the ball, especially in the eighties when he had the kinds of players he had with the Chargers. In planning and designing defense, he simply had no interest."

Although Coryell never won a Lombardi Trophy with his schemes, several of his disciples did. Joe Gibbs went to Washington the very next year, carrying Coryell's system in his briefcase. He added his own wrinkles to the offense and won three Super Bowls with it for the Redskins. When Zampese coached with the Rams in the late eighties, he taught the system to a young staff assistant named Norv Turner. A few years later, Norv ran Coryell's exact system as offensive coordinator with the Dallas Cowboys and claimed back-to-back Super Bowl titles in 1992 and '93.

When people discuss the great quarterbacks of all time, Troy Aikman rarely gets a mention. But I think he was the ultimate timing and rhythm passer. He wasn't a good deep thrower but was very accurate in short and intermediate passes. He was a bigger Dan Fouts—with a stronger arm—who could throw the skinny post, the square-in. The eighties Chargers offense didn't do much with sideline throws. They were an inside route–running team. But Troy's accuracy on those deep comebacks made them a major part of the nineties Cowboys offense, especially with Michael Irvin, who ran very good routes. That was just a fun offense to watch. Norv has since utilized the Air Coryell system everywhere he's been, and he's still running it today with quarterback Philip Rivers and the explosive twenty-first-century version of the Chargers' offense.

In 1999 Dick Vermeil's St. Louis Rams won a championship by basing their offense on Coryell's principles. (The franchise had moved from Los Angeles to St. Louis before the 1995 season, seven years after the Cardinals had jilted the city and taken up with Phoenix, Arizona.) "When St. Louis won the Super Bowl, I could have stepped into the Rams huddle and run their plays," insisted Winslow. "It was the same offense." Around the same time, other teams around the league incorporated its basic concepts. "With the Chiefs and Redskins, we even used Ernie Zampese's name to identify some of our offensive packages, because the ideas were driven by concepts that he implemented," revealed Marty Schottenheimer, head coach for four teams. "Putting three receivers on one side and flooding that area is a concept that probably had its genesis with those Chargers teams."

The Coryell offense can reap major benefits for coaches willing to take full advantage of its many features. "Assistants coming to teams that run it have to get used to the volume available in these plays," said Saunders, who coached Don's system with the Chargers, Rams, Chiefs, and Redskins. "At first it can be intimidating to them. Because there is so much to it, the reaction by some coaches is to reduce what you do. But then you lose the effectiveness of the system, and a lot of its versatility is no longer there. Used to its maximum, it's pretty tough to stop."

Coryell's offense introduced both strategic innovation and a new vocabulary to the NFL. My *Monday Night Football* partner Jon Gruden learned the term "joker" when he was an assistant with the 49ers in the early nineties. "Winslow was a pure joker," says Gruden. "He could line up in a three-point stance next to the tackle and power block. On the next snap, he'd be in motion, then be out there in a two-point stance. He was comfortable in any formation. And you never knew where he was going to be. That's what a joker is.

"There's a potful of jokers in today's game, but they didn't exist until after Winslow did it. In San Francisco, we used running backs as jokers—Ricky Watters or Charlie Garner. The Eagles used Brian Westbrook that way. You can present a four-wide look in regular personnel because you line the back up as a receiver. These are the guys you're looking for today; the ones who create matchup problems. Everybody wants them."

According to Bill Belichick, Winslow ushered in the age of tight ends who were more pass catchers than blockers. "Go back to some of the great tight ends: Ditka, Mackey, Chester, Mark Bavaro, Keith Jackson. They were great players in both the passing game and the point of attack in the running game. Now you see guys who are just receivers playing tight end—people like Dallas Clark, Owen Daniels, Tony Gonzalez, and Antonio Gates. None of them are really blocking at the point of attack, and they don't *want* to block there either. They kind of do it because they're big and take up space, but that's not their thing. That position has evolved to the point where, each year in the draft, there are fewer athletes who are block-on-the-line tight ends. Those types are getting harder to find. The pass-receiving tight ends are the ones getting paid the big money—Jeremy Shockey, Gates, and those guys—catching passes and scoring touchdowns. They're all direct descendants of Kellen Winslow."

Winslow's overall accomplishments and impact on the game made him a first-ballot choice for the Pro Football Hall of Fame in 1995. His greatest hope was that his former head coach could join him in Canton, Ohio. Don made it as far as the finalists' level before missing the last cut in the 2010 balloting. Sadly, just five months later, Coryell passed away at the age of 85. "When voters for the Hall make their choices, they look at stats. If they look at impact and innovation, Don Coryell is a slam-dunk," Winslow argued. "I hear stuff like, 'He never won a Super Bowl.' But that's not what it's about. He was a great innovator with a huge impact on the game. How in the world can Joiner,

Fouts, Winslow, and Joe Gibbs be in the Hall and Coryell not be there? A lot of what Walsh did in San Francisco is a variation of what we did in San Diego. What Gibbs ran in Washington was a variation of what Air Coryell did. It's a shame they don't recognize the impact and innovation he's had on the game of football. He changed the way teams draft, how clubs have to stock their rosters. And if that's not enough, he was also the first coach to win a hundred games in both college and the NFL."

Joe Collier also recognizes the changes that Coryell's changes imposed on defenses. "By using multiple receivers, Don forced an evolution on both sides of the ball, because defenses now had to counter what he was doing by bringing in different packages to play against them. A lot of defensive backs should thank Coach Coryell for the fact that he forced teams to draft more of them. And scouts now had to look for linebackers who were 'in-between' guys, athletes who could run with that inside receiver."

Don Coryell's greatest impact may have been on the attitudes of offensive philosophies. Grind-it-out attacks would eventually give way to much more aggressive strategies, all because of him. "Don knew that if you had better players, you would win," explained Bass. "There are some coaches who feel they're the genius and the players are in a supporting role. Don did not believe in that; he felt his athletes were the most important. By the time he got to the Chargers, he realized he finally had the total package for talent—guys who could do *anything*. Previously he'd have to attack defenses. Now he believed that defenses had to stop what the Chargers were doing. That mind-set difference is really important."

Dan Fouts agrees emphatically: "I don't think there's ever been a coach who was more courageous about creating offense, especially with formations and his use of personnel. If you look at the way the game is played today, his influence is everywhere. You look at four- and five-receiver sets, then you look at the other side of the ball with five and six defensive backs. Before Coryell, who knew about nickel or dime backs or anything like that? He has contributed to this game. He has made the game better, more enjoyable."

Joe Gibbs owes much of his NFL success to Coryell. "My owner with the Redskins was Jack Kent Cooke, and Mr. Cooke used to say, 'There are no geniuses in football. There are probably only two in the whole world—and they're not in football.' I would disagree and say that one of the geniuses in football was Don Coryell."

I'll give *my* favorite coach, Dick Vermeil, the last word on this great innovator. "You look at the records he set—the route philosophies, the speed cuts, the vertical passing game, speed screens, quick screens. All these things stemmed from the founder, Don Coryell. No offense in the NFL, when applied and coached correctly with everyday good personnel, performs more efficiently or scores more points than the Coryell-influenced offense. He deserves to be in the Hall of Fame."

Bill Walsh's West Coast Offense

PHOTO BY MICHAEL ZAGARIS

1981 NFC DIVISIONAL PLAYOFF
NEW YORK GIANTS vs. SAN FRANCISCO 49ERS
Candlestick Park, San Francisco, California — January 3, 1982

During football season, NFL Films is my second home. I spend most of my work week at its Mount Laurel, New Jersey, facility, studying coaching tape in preparation for *Monday Night Football* telecasts and the *ESPN NFL Matchup* program. For a pigskin fanatic like myself, it's like being in Disney World every day. The walls and shelves are decorated with photographs of current and former players, vintage programs, magazines, and collectibles. It is as much a football museum as it is a production company, and its most famous asset is the largest football film library in existence. The NFL Films vaults contain game footage dating from the nineteenth century all the way up through the current season. Equally vast in scope is its collection of interviews recorded over the years with football's greatest players, coaches, writers, and historians. Here accounts and insights are catalogued, transcribed, and preserved for future generations of football fans.

The interview archives were especially valuable to me as I began my research on Bill Walsh. He, of course, was the legendary coach of the San Francisco 49ers, winner of three Super Bowls, a man who has influenced the game's strategic development as much as anyone in recent history. After a long battle with leukemia, Bill passed away in 2007, leaving a lasting legacy not only on the football field but also with the innovative ideas he so generously shared with others.

Many of those innovations are discussed in exacting detail in the numerous interviews he granted to NFL Films throughout his time in pro football. He also donated to it hundreds of hours in lectures, meetings, and practice footage—all insightful lessons in the art of offensive football. As I sat watching and listening to the man deservedly nicknamed "the Genius," I almost felt as if he were in the room with me. I feel privileged to present these pearls of wisdom anew in this chapter on the "West Coast offense"—a name he never really embraced but a strategy that is visible in every NFL game you see today.

You know Brian Billick as an NFL head coach and TV analyst, but you may not be aware that after finishing college, he served as Walsh's public relations assistant during Bill's first two years in San Francisco. Billick later coached under Walsh disciple Dennis Green and is himself a strong believer in the principles of the West Coast attack. Brian later collaborated on a book with Bill and author James Peterson entitled *Finding the Winning Edge*. It's a source I refer to often because it really explains the Walsh philosophy in its most basic terms.

At the beginning of this book, I stated that the key to any team's success in today's NFL is exploiting favorable personnel matchups. Walsh made this a foundation of his system long before almost anyone else, and Billick was there when it happened. "Bill Walsh was at the forefront of isolating such matchups as, Who do we go after? What is our most favorable matchup? Where is our strength, and how do we manipulate that? Bill was the protagonist for a lot of things in this league: the way you practice, the way you game-plan," added Billick. "He became a head coach right around the time there were profound rules changes that would open up NFL offenses, and Bill recognized his unique concepts could thrive under these conditions."

Al Saunders knew Bill for many years, going back to their shared college ties at San José State, and appreciated Walsh's unique view of the sport: "Bill approached football as an intellectual game; a game of strategy and execution. He saw it as an art form, a thing of beauty, something to be choreographed with everything working in harmony. He thought many other coaches were narrow-minded in their views. The prevailing philosophy when he first started was how to make your team 'tougher'—being able to pound your opponent into the ground. Walsh believed that everyone who made it to the NFL level was *already* tough. He wanted to magnify the *mental* aspects of football."

Former Giants quarterback Phil Simms recognized Bill's special qualities while he was still a college senior. "Walsh worked me out before the '79 draft," he recalled. "I'll never forget that session. He was different from any other coach I can remember. He was just so polished. He'd say things like, 'Try that a little softer,' or 'Make that throw a little more graceful.' I must have thrown more than two hundred fifty passes for him that day, and he told me that no matter who he went with at quarterback that season, the guy would win the NFL passing title—and it would be me if I were picked by the 49ers." Walsh actually had Simms rated higher than Joe Montana prior to that draft and had every intention of taking Phil in the second round. But when the Giants selected Simms as their first choice, the 49ers were forced to "settle" for Montana in the third round. I think we can safely say that everything worked out pretty well for both quarterbacks and both teams. And for what it's worth, Walsh's prediction wasn't far off the mark. In 1979, Bill's first year as an NFL head coach, he chose journeyman Steve DeBerg to be his quarterback. And although Steve wasn't the league's top-ranked passer, he did set an NFL record for passing attempts and completions.

Before Bill Walsh, the NFL was basically a pitch-and-catch game. Aerial attacks relied primarily on seven-step drops by the quarterback, followed by deep downfield passes. Star quarterbacks like Pittsburgh's Terry Bradshaw rarely thought about manipulating a defense. He'd just chuck it deep to Lynn Swann and didn't care what the coverage was, because they were both more talented than their opponents. Walsh changed all that. In *Finding the Winning Edge*, Bill boiled it down to the basics: "The West Coast offense is really more of a philosophy and a methodical approach to teaching than it is a set of plays or formations. While it certainly has come to mean a ball-control passing game based on timing, rhythm, and precision, it also describes an entire offensive structure from play schematics, preparation, installation, implementation, game planning, execution, and, perhaps most importantly, total attention to every detail."

Northern California's Silicon Valley was a center of discovery long before the hi-tech digital computer explosion. In the 1950s, it was the launch point for many future football geniuses, and their home base was the campus of San José State College. "Bill's coach at San José was a guy named Bob Bronzan," recalled Saunders. "Dick Vermeil and Tom Bass were Bill's teammates, and I also played for Bob a few years later. We all ended up coaching in the NFL. Bob was really ahead of his time. I don't think there was anyone else—certainly on the West Coast—who was doing some of the things he did on offense, and I'm sure this had a huge impact on Bill's own philosophy." Those innovations included sophisticated line blocking, running the option, wider end splits, and three-receiver sets. In another great book about Walsh, entitled *The Genius*, Bill told author David Harris that Bronzan was "a theorist and an excellent teacher who set a standard as to the detail of everything he coached and the organization skill he set up. He coached football like it was a science, a skilled sport instead of just head bashing."

Bronzan wasn't Bill's only college mentor. Another was Bud Winter, the Spartans' track-and-field coach. "His two star runners, Tommie Smith and John Carlos, won medals at the '68 Olympics in Mexico," said Saunders. "Winter's whole philosophy was about quickness; what he called the 'explosiveness of sport.' Practice session durations weren't as vital as what you did in a concentrated time period. Bill took note of that and was one of the first to vary the length and frequency of his practices. To Bill, his system was more than just its language. It was how you practiced, how you taught it, prioritizing what was important."

After graduation, Bill coached high school ball before future Buffalo Bills head coach Marv Levy hired him as an assistant at Cal-Berkeley. Eventually Walsh joined a Stanford staff that would include John Ralston, Jim Mora, Sr., Mike White, and my future Eagles coach, Dick Vermeil. "At an academically rigorous school like Stanford, they weren't able to get the quality athletes other Pac Eight schools could," explained Saunders. "So their feeling was, 'Let's commit to throwing the ball, then go find quarterbacks and receivers,' with the idea they'd outscheme and outdesign the better-talented opponents. They'd have to win by turning games into shoot-outs, which would force opponents like USC and UCLA to go out of character and pass more than they were really accustomed to doing."

Walsh's work at Stanford caught the eye of Oakland Raiders coach and general manager Al Davis, and he gave Bill his first pro coaching job in 1966. "Al was using Sid Gillman's offense," recalled Walsh. "It was the most complete and conceptually broad-based offense in the history of pro football. That same year, we were playing in San Diego. I was sitting in my hotel room and happened to catch Sid's coaching show on TV. He had Lance Alworth as his guest, and the two of them were discussing specific pass patterns. It hit me at that moment: I recognized this man's brilliance—he was explaining football as an art form. I was enthralled with this aspect of the game. From that point on, I always looked at football this way, and seeing that TV show was the inspiration for this way of thinking."

Later on, Sid was helpful to Walsh's career advancement in a more direct way. During the midsixties, coaching legend Paul Brown was residing in La Jolla, California, a coastal section of northern San Diego. Brown had been unceremoniously fired by the Cleveland Browns in 1963 and was living in exile, biding his time for a return to pro football. Sid and Paul were both Ohio State guys, former coaching rivals, and longtime friends, and they spent a great deal of time together in those days. In 1967, as Brown was formalizing his plans for the creation of the expansion Cincinnati Bengals, Sid told him about Walsh. He believed Bill would be a good fit for Brown's new team and encouraged Paul to contact him.

As Brown began assembling his staff, Walsh's name came up again. "I was the first coach Paul Brown hired when he started the Bengals," stated Tom Bass. "Bill and I knew each other from San José State, so we kept in touch. Cincinnati didn't have a quarterback coach, and I knew Bill was out of work. He'd been running a semipro team called the San José Apaches after leaving the Raiders. I told Paul that Bill would be a good guy for our quarterbacks, and Paul ended up hiring him."

Working with Paul Brown was the dream of every aspiring football coach in America. Perhaps no one has a better understanding of Brown's impact on the game than Bill Belichick, who knew Brown on both a personal and professional level. "My godfather, Bill Edwards, was with Paul Brown at Massillon High, Wittenberg College, Ohio State, and Cleveland, so I was going to Brown's training camps from the time I could walk," he explained. "I later went to the first few Bengals camps as well.

"The way Paul conducted those training sessions was so much more professional and meticulous than any other camps I visited. Essentially, everything that Paul Brown did with those teams is what we do today. Every film breakdown, meeting, walk-through, and practice is based on Brown's system. Every teaching progression, how plays complement each other—it all goes back to Brown. Ninety-five percent, if not more, of everything we do now comes from him. He is the father of professional football. What he did as a coach fifty years ago, everybody in the NFL is still basically doing the same thing."

Early on, Walsh absorbed as much knowledge from Brown as possible. "Bill just didn't come right in and take over," recalled Bass. "Those first few years, Paul ran the Cincinnati offense. Brown was a Hall of Fame coach and had a very successful passing game with Otto Graham at Cleveland, so he was used to throwing, and incorporated a lot of that in Cincinnati. Bill added some things, but it really wasn't till 1970 that he started to put his stamp on the Bengals' passing game."

Walsh got that opportunity in the midst of unfortunate circumstances. Cincinnati lost its star quarterback, a guy named Greg Cook, who Bill claimed had the most pure talent of any passer he ever coached. Considering that Walsh also had Montana and Steve Young, that's quite a statement. The year before, Cook averaged 17.5 yards per completion—a rookie record that still stands. "Greg Cook could have been one of the greatest quarterbacks in NFL history," stated Sam Wyche, who was Cook's backup with the '69 Bengals. "He had size, the quick forearm release, and could scramble as well as throw deep. Our receivers could now lengthen their routes, and we could split guys out wider because Greg's passes traveled so much faster and got to the target much quicker."

When Walsh was asked many years later what his Cincy offense would have looked like had Cook stayed healthy, Bill admitted, "It would have been totally different. Deep throws, all the time, down the field. Greg had so much confidence, and the players gravitated to him. He led the league in passing as a rookie on an expansion team, so that's an indicator of how great he could have been. But he tore his rotator cuff, and the conventional procedure for that injury back then was extremely severe. There was no arthroscopic surgery in those days, and he never completely recovered from the operation."

Cook's injury thrust a journeyman passer named Virgil Carter into the starting lineup. "Virgil was a smallish, weak-armed quarterback who really couldn't go deep, but he was mobile," said Billick. "He could throw quickly and made good decisions. Bill basically designed the three- and five-step quick-sprint offense around Carter." Cincy's running game wasn't very consistent either, so Walsh was forced to create an offense that could function despite the Bengals' talent limitations. "We were still essentially an expansion team," admitted Walsh. "We knew we couldn't score very many points. But we had to make as many first downs as possible to control the clock and get field position. We couldn't run the ball because we didn't have near the depth of offensive linemen or the talent in running backs. So consequently, a short passing game appeared to be the best way to control the ball."

What he ended up with was a short passing game that relied heavily on hooks, slants, screens, and underneath crossing routes. It achieved positive results almost immediately, as the Bengals enjoyed their first winning season in 1970, only their third season. The West Coast offense was up and running—although it certainly wasn't known by that name at the time. In fact, it didn't even have a name! Given its lineage, it really should be called the "Ohio River" or "Midwest" offense. As Bill wrote in *Finding the Winning Edge,* "We had no idea that we were creating a template for the future of offense in the NFL. We did what we did just to stay competitive, then expanded on it as we continued to have success."

With Carter under center, running this controlled passing scheme, the Bengals won the AFC Central. It ranks among Paul Brown's greatest coaching achievements. "It was a privilege to be around Paul," said Walsh. "He was a legend, an icon. He controlled everything initially, but in those later years he leaned more on his management skills and handling of people, leaving the strategy and tactics of the game to people like myself. It was a tremendous opportunity to develop my ideas."

Eventually Cincinnati's personnel improved, and so did its record, with the addition of weapons like quarterback Ken Anderson and receivers Charlie Joiner and Isaac Curtis. But when Brown retired at the end of the '75 season, his successor would not be Walsh. "We had an excellent offensive line coach named Bill 'Tiger' Johnson, who was strong and sturdy," Walsh remembered. "I think Paul thought that this was the form of command you needed to have to be an NFL head coach, so he picked Johnson over me." Brown may have believed that Walsh wasn't tough enough to run the team, an idea that would haunt Bill for years. Deeply hurt and disappointed, Walsh resigned from the Bengals and headed west.

B y the time I left Cincinnati, that offensive system had been really refined," said Walsh. "We were doing things that people hadn't seen since the days when Clark Shaughnessy was coaching those explosive Rams offenses of the fifties. So I signed on with the Chargers as offensive coordinator and installed it there with Dan Fouts. From there I became head coach at Stanford, which was a great place for me to be. The Stanford athlete could pick up my system so easily—much more readily than many pro athletes. And we did very well at that level. That was important, because had I not been successful there, I would never have gotten the opportunity to be an NFL head coach."

That opportunity came in 1979 from the San Francisco 49ers, arguably the NFL's worst franchise. With a roster of aging or untested players, and with few draft choices available, Walsh took a deep breath, dug out his old Bengals playbook, and put the same offense into practice in San Francisco. The immediate results weren't pretty. "After his first year in San Francisco, when he went 2-14, Bill had real misgivings about whether this was the right approach and was ready to get out of pro football," revealed Saunders. I actually remember sitting in Dick Vermeil's office one day after practice, overhearing a phone conversation he was having with Walsh. Because they were close friends, Bill was very candid with Vermeil about his problems. Dick really had to talk Bill off the cliff, and, of course, things did get better in San Francisco. One big reason for that improvement was the emergence of Joe Montana as the Niners' quarterback.

Joe didn't fit the NFL mold for star quarterbacks of that era, but that was fine with Walsh. "Bill didn't want the prototype passer that everyone was drafting in the seventies," explained Vermeil. "Big guys with strong arms wasn't what he was looking for. He felt that some of the prospects with those tools lacked the proper footwork. And he felt that the game never slowed down enough for them; that they had trouble reading defenses quickly enough."

Montana was different, and Bill recognized it almost immediately. "The quick, decisive movement of his feet, his agility and balance, and his rhythm in throwing the ball were something to see," Walsh recalled. "I'd never worked with anyone as quick and mobile as this man. He was very accurate with his arm, had an excellent passing touch, and his passes were thrown in areas where receivers could do something with them." Montana also proved to be a quick study, as his 49ers position coach Sam Wyche could attest: "When I taught Joe, he would lean in when you started talking to him—almost like he was going to eat the last word off your tongue if you didn't hurry up and finish the sentence."

The pairing of Walsh and Montana became a match made in football heaven, because Bill now had the quarterback that would allow him to redefine the NFL passing game. "Bill was absolutely meticulous in his precision at practice," recalled Billick. "Once Montana threw a little swing pass that the receiver caught right in stride—absolutely perfect. And Walsh scolded him! He said, 'Joe, you've got to get it about a yard in front of him; I want him going downhill.' And you're thinking, *Man, he's really being unrealistic here*. But it was just that attention to detail that points to his main strength."

Montana caught on quickly. "Learning the basics of the offense was really pretty simple," Joe stated. "Making the actual throws to the right person in a short time was a little more difficult. But that's why Bill had us practice these plays over and over, so that when it did happen in a game, you knew how to react. First of all, you were always attacking a specific area on the field, so you knew where to go right away. You also were aware where your receivers were. And there were always three potential targets, sometimes even four. Bill tried to get as many people out there for me as he could."

A critical element to the West Coast offense was the run after catch, or RAC: the ability of 49ers receivers to tack on additional yardage once they caught the ball. Bill made a statistical study of quarterbacks who'd thrown for 3,000 yards and found that half of those yards came from the flight of the ball—the rest was yardage made afterward. So he drilled constantly to make sure that 49ers receivers caught passes above the waist. This way, they'd be able to keep running after a completion. Bill understood that the RAC is as dependent upon a quarterback's passing accuracy as a receiver's ability to separate from defenders.

My *Monday Night Football* partner Jon Gruden is a West Coast offense disciple and understands the system's complexities, because he taught it to his quarterbacks in Philly, Green Bay, Oakland, and Tampa. "There's a lot of volume to it: runs, passes, protection schemes," he explained. "Many of its plays start out *looking* different but end up being the same. The offense has the illusion of complexity with all its different formations and personnel groupings, but it remains simple and basic in terms of the plays themselves. The core philosophy is that if the defense hasn't seen it, they can't prepare for it.

"You want to use all five eligible receivers, and the main object is to complete passes," he emphasized. "If your quarterback does this, he'll be successful, and if he's successful, your whole organization will be successful. One of the most important goals Walsh's offense accomplished was keeping the quarterback safe. The number one risk you have when you throw the football is your quarterback getting killed. One hit, and he's gone for the season, and it's amazing how inept some teams are once their top guy goes down. With the West Coast attack, you have what's called a progression passing system. You have the primary receiver, the companion receiver, and the outlet receiver. There's always someone to throw to. I never met any quarterback who didn't like this system."

Bill assisted everyone, not just the quarterback, by scripting the first twenty-five or so plays of every game. "It helped take a lot of the stress out of the initial stages of the game, especially with our offensive linemen," Walsh explained. "You can set up one play to another this way, set up your play passes, your reverses, when you go deep. And you can establish specific formations that you'd like to see your opponent adapt or adjust to." An additional benefit was that it made it hard for defenses to identify the 49ers' tendencies, especially in normal down-and-distance situations. Bill's play choices were often unorthodox and unpredictable, so defenders had to be ready for *anything*.

As he had done in Cincinnati, Walsh called more short passes instead of running plays. Some writers referred to them as "long handoffs," and by throwing so much, the Niners challenged slower linebackers to cover faster receivers in the underneath area. This heightened the chances for San Francisco to turn short catches into much longer gains. Bill had to do this during his first seasons with the Niners, because he didn't have a great back or a big line to block for him. In addition, it just wasn't what Bill wanted to do. "Teams that depended on their running game would usually get upset two or three times a year by an inferior opponent who would hit a couple of big plays, and then they couldn't overcome that unexpected deficit," he noted. "In a sixteen-game schedule, there's going to be a number of times that your running game just isn't going to get it done. That's why it was so important for me to develop our passing game."

My first reaction to the West Coast offense was one of exasperation. In Philadelphia, when we studied film of an upcoming opponent who'd just played the 49ers, I wanted to switch off the projector because I felt I was wasting my time. San Francisco's formations, splits, and motions were the very antithesis of our Eagles offense. What the Niners did was so different that opposing defenses were responding to stuff that had absolutely no relation to our offense. And the more I watched, the more irritated I became.

It seemed as if it didn't take much of a quarterback to run their offense. Nothing was going on downfield, there were no deep drops, just a lot of dinks and dunks. I just didn't buy into it. I felt like their re-

Base West Coast Offense Read Progression

The name of this play is Fake 97 Whip Naked Right Z Special Fullback Slide—and it's the most fundamental of progressions in the Walsh playbook. Quarterback Montana rolls to his right with three pass options at his disposal: a deep post route to Z receiver Solomon, a shorter crossing route from X receiver Clark and a check-down throw to halfback Patton in the right flat. In a worst-case scenario, Montana could keep the ball, run to his right and get out of bounds with at least a four- or five-yard pickup. Walsh's offense always provided his quarterbacks with plenty of options.

ceivers didn't run precise routes to get open. Instead they needed other players to help them get free with "picks" and "rubs," which are crossing routes by teammates that got in the way of defenders. I also got angry at what I perceived to be a lack of effort on certain pass routes. A lot of times, you'd simply see receivers eliminated from the play, and that burned me up. After the snap, the back-side receiver did little more than jog into his pattern, because the play simply wasn't designed to go to him. In the early years of Walsh's West Coast schemes, all the effort on each play went toward getting just one receiver open. Whereas most offenses were full-field reads—seeking to find voids throughout an *entire* defense—Walsh believed in half-field or area reads, spotting *individual* locations to exploit a defense. I didn't appreciate the effectiveness of this approach until much later. All I could think of in those days was that with the Gillman offense we ran with Philly, each receiver had better be busting his ass on every route, because he could be the primary target.

Gradually though, the West Coast offense began to grow on me. For one thing, the 49ers began winning big, and did it with average talent. They didn't have burners like Jerry Rice, John Taylor, or Roger Craig on their roster yet, so if people were going to get open, the offense's design was going to have to spring them loose. Something else caught my eye, too: Montana was completing almost 65 percent of his passes, a ridiculous number for that time. When I was league MVP in 1980, I made good on only 57 percent of my throws. And this wasn't simply because Joe was so good. His percentages improved because Walsh's system had reduced many of the risk factors in the passing game with shorter drops, quick releases, and high-percentage throws.

On-field success led to growing confidence for Bill's players. They also came to realize something Paul Brown never did: that this distinguished looking, white-haired guy could also bring the hammer down when it was called for. "You looked at him and think, 'He looks like a professor,'" receiver Dwight Clark observed. "Maybe that's how he appeared, but he was a hard-nosed guy, and when he needed to, he could be really tough on people. He could really chew you out when you made stupid mistakes. You couldn't be a 'dumb jock' in Bill's offense because of all the adjustments; all the plays that were installed in such a quick period of time. There was a lot of memorization. You really had to be on the ball."

The team tripled its previous win total in 1980 as Montana took over the offense, but San Francisco still wasn't considered a contender entering the '81 season. The 49ers had some solid players, including veteran receivers Clark, Freddie Solomon, and tight end Charle Young, and an undersized but athletic offensive line. Still, it didn't seem like that would be enough to make a difference, and most NFL people, myself included, were unconvinced there'd be much improvement. Walsh himself had only modest expectations. "At the start of the 1981 season," he said, "I just wanted our team to be competitive and start gaining some respect around the NFL, because we had lost for so long. People liked watching us play because we were interesting, but then we also began winning—a lot—because we played more fiercely than anyone in the league. We beat some of the best teams that year strictly on our intensity."

The 49ers rolled to a 13-3 record, the most regular-season wins in franchise history, earning their first trip to the playoffs since 1972. California football fans dreamed of a possible intrastate Super Bowl showdown between the two most pass-proficient teams in the league: San Francisco and the wildly explosive Air Coryell attack of the San Diego Chargers. "Both Walsh and Coryell lived by the pass, viewing the running game as a growth off the passing game," noted Al Saunders. "The biggest difference between the two was that Bill's offense was as much lateral as it was vertical. Hooks and slant patterns in the zones as the basis of a controlled passing game, occupying defenders. He liked big receivers catching the ball inside, looking for windows to sit in.

"Coryell was all about 'running through windows,' attacking vertically," he pointed out. "Walsh's receivers were physical guys like Dwight Clark. Coryell's receivers were little guys like Charlie Joiner and John Jefferson. For Coryell, the key word in his attack was *seams*. In Bill's, it was *angles:* short throws to get long gains. Bill was patient. Don was all about getting huge chunks, quick strikes." When later asked to compare his offense with San Diego's, Walsh said, "Coryell's offense had lower completion percentages but a much higher return if the play was successful. One main difference between us is that we managed to move the ball with less talent than our opponents. Air Coryell required more talented players, a passer who could get the ball there, and men who can really run—a lot of them. Our offense was devised and developed out of necessity until we could get the right players in place. Don already had the talent and used it brilliantly."

There was also a philosophical connection between Sid Gillman and Walsh. Both Bill's scheme and Sid's depended on timing and rhythm. There was also a great deal of emphasis placed on three essential quarterback attributes: (1) quick feet in gaining clearance from the center, (2) downfield focus in the face of pressure, and (3) touch and accuracy to deliver catchable balls. Both were creative men who saw football as an intellectual exercise. But they were also sticklers for practice and repetition, demanding that their players succeed thanks to what they were taught, as opposed to raw talent or improvisation. Walsh often said, "Coaches that depend on the athletic ability of the athletes are strictly at their mercy, because they can't be sure of any continuity or efficiency in what they do." That's why his West Coast offense was so successful no matter which players were in it—and why whichever team San Francisco was to face in the '81 postseason would certainly have its hands full.

Here's a quick trivia question: During his Hall of Fame career, what quarterback did Giants linebacker Lawrence Taylor sack more times than any other? Don't bother looking it up—I'm the poor soul who holds that dubious distinction. I literally have firsthand knowledge of how good a player L.T. was.

In an NFL Films career retrospective produced after his retirement, Taylor also let me have it verbally. "Of the twenty-eight quarterbacks who played at that time, Jaworski may have been the slowest," L.T. said with a chuckle. "Ron wasn't going to do a whole lot of running. He always liked to throw to his right, and I always came from the left, so whenever I hit him, it was a blindside shot. If I had another twenty-seven Ron Jaworskis in the league, I wouldn't have had to retire for fifty years! He sent me to my first couple of Pro Bowls."

And he went to a bunch of them, while also collecting a pair of Super Bowl rings and a bust in the Pro Football Hall of Fame. Dick Vermeil claimed, "Taylor and Reggie White are the two finest defensive players that ever played the game. Lawrence forced teams to change the way they blocked. You could never go back to the old ways after Taylor came to the NFL." Broadcaster and Cardinals Hall of Fame tackle Dan Dierdorf confessed, "In my entire career, Taylor was the only guy that, when we broke the huddle, we knew exactly where he was. You better believe we game-planned for Lawrence Taylor, every snap of every game."

L.T. was a terror from the day he signed his first professional contract in 1981. "I remember the first time I saw Lawrence in practice," said Phil Simms. "On the first six plays, Taylor sacked the quarterback six times. The coaches were all yelling at the offensive linemen—I'd never seen anything like it." Defensive teammate Harry Carson noted, "We changed to a 3-4 defense because of Taylor. Bill Parcells used him as an unconventional outside linebacker, pressuring the quarterback. If Lawrence had been a more traditional player, he would have dropped back into pass coverage and would have been good at that. But because they utilized him as they did, he made history."

Taylor's talent was simply too great to stay shackled within the defined parameters of the position. "When I got to New York, a linebacker was just a linebacker," Taylor remarked. "He played the run, dropped back into coverage, and that was it. Coach Parcells allowed me to do some new things. He did this because I made too many mistakes in pass defense, where I'd drop when I wasn't supposed to. My answer for all that was, if you forget what to do—or don't even know what to do—just rush the quarterback and see what happens." What happened was a first-year performance that got his team to the playoffs, earned him a trip to the Pro Bowl, and handed him the NFL Rookie of the Year Award.

The Giants liked to put Taylor in one-on-one situations, looking to create mismatches. There was no one else like L.T. at the time, a guy his size with 4.4 speed, and he revolutionized the game, altering the way quarterbacks had to think. He changed the way teams designed their protection. It was Taylor who forced Joe Gibbs to switch to a two-tight-end offense in Washington because Joe didn't want L.T. to have a shortened corner to rush from the blind side. In Philadelphia, I always asked for a tight end next to the tackle to move Taylor away from me. Judging by his sack numbers on ol' no. 7, that bright idea didn't always work.

Taylor wasn't "L.T." right away. That first year, he wasn't initially a force you had to build your game plan around. But he was a load even then. Our Eagles teams tried blocking him with running backs, and both Louie Giammona and Wilbert Montgomery gave it their best shot, but L.T. just tossed them aside. Lucky for me, in those early years, New York mistakenly put him in pass coverage, where he was only an average player. I was much happier seeing him out there in the middle zone, far away from me. The Giants finally realized that Lawrence was best suited to rushing the passer. They turned him loose the same way the Raiders did with their Hall of Fame linebacker Ted Hendricks. That meant letting Taylor line up all over the defense, with the freedom to read and go.

Taylor's arrival in '81 was a major reason why New York went 9-7, its first winning season in ten years. Up till then, the Eagles had beaten New York in a dozen straight, going back to 1975. As reigning NFC champions, we played Big Blue on opening day in '81 and won again. That was L.T.'s first NFL game, and it wasn't very memorable: a business-as-usual 24–10 victory for us. But in the rematch a few months later, the Giants beat Philadelphia, 20–10, then shocked the football world when they upset us at home in the wild-card playoff round. In this game, the Eagles' coaches made the decision to put our All-Pro left tackle, Stan Walters, on Lawrence instead of a back or tight end. Stan was one of the best linemen I ever played with—physical, tough, and tremendously bright. Stan tried his best that day to control him, but Taylor tore him apart. He sacked me once and must have hit or knocked me down at least another six or seven times. No doubt the coaching film from that loss was played in heavy rotation by the 49ers a day later, because the Giants' next playoff stop was Candlestick Park for a date with Bill Walsh's 49ers.

Despite posting the best regular-season record in football, the Niners were still looked upon as somewhat of a freak show—a team that had sneaked up on its opponents, winning with gimmicks rather than by the accepted strategies of power football. League traditionalists viewed Walsh's strategies as sissy stuff and were confident that its delicate design would be shredded in the pressure cooker of the postseason.

Walsh wasn't surprised at such smug opinions from the NFL establishment. But he was supremely confident in his young team—and the game plan he had drawn up. "We had forty-something runs and maybe a hundred pass plays available for the Giants game," recalled Randy Cross. "Walsh took the time to design and diagram them. You learned that they were very special to him, and that if he was taking this much time to go over them, you knew damn well we'd be running those plays in that game. At your job, did you ever go into a meeting when you knew something the other people didn't know? That was our attitude against the Giants. No matter how prepared they thought they were, there were things we were going to do that they had never seen; things they had no idea were coming."

Allow me to flash forward for a moment for an interesting sidebar connected to this game. The highest-grossing sports movie of all time is 2009's *The Blind Side,* which won Sandra Bullock an Oscar for Best Actress. It's the true story of a white southern family that adopts a homeless African American teen named Michael Oher. With their support, Oher is able to piece his life back together and go on to become the top draft choice of the Baltimore Ravens. The movie is based on Michael Lewis's best-selling book *The Blind Side: Evolution of a Game.* In the book, Lewis also devotes an entire chapter to the '81 Giants-49ers playoff and the unsung hero who was instrumental in neutralizing Lawrence Taylor.

Walsh realized that L.T. could not be blocked with tight ends or backs, and left tackle Dan Audick didn't match up well physically with Taylor. So Bill turned to left guard John Ayers to stop the rookie linebacker. Ayers was instructed by line coach Bobb McKittrick to

"Molly" block, a technique that asked the guard to pull, or pop up from his interior line position to ward off an outside pass rusher. Cross knew that Ayers was the right man for the job. "John was a guy who was country strong, had unbelievable strength in his legs, and was an extremely good pass blocker," he praised. "He was from West Texas and spent his off-seasons branding cattle, so wrestling with Taylor might not have seemed so tough by comparison. As the game wore on, Ayers turned out to be the kryptonite to L.T's Superman." Sam Wyche knew that if the Molly worked, then San Francisco's passing game would be operating at full strength: "The uncovered offensive lineman, usually Ayers, would do a double-read. First he'd read the linebacker over him, his primary responsibility, since he was the guy with the shortest route to the quarterback. If he didn't come, then the lineman could pull out and help somewhere else."

The '81 Giants played a standard Cover-Two behind a base 3-4 defense, which meant that inside linebackers Brian Kelley and Harry Carson rarely blitzed. Taylor was almost always the fourth pass rusher in what was predominantly a four-man rush concept. Whenever they

---

Molly Block

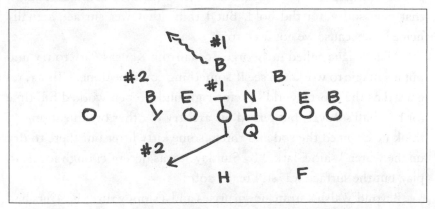

Left guard Ayers was the 49ers' strongest player and the man most responsible for slowing down blitz pressure from New York's Taylor. If Taylor blitzed, then Ayers would pop up and drift to his left to take him on. If inside linebacker Kelley was blitzing, then Ayers had to stop him and hope San Francisco's halfback could at least slow Taylor down until the pass was released. Bringing both weakside linebackers was uncommon for the Giants, which is why the Molly technique was effective against them. Note Walsh's use of the basic pro set of that era: a halfback, fullback, two wideouts and a tight end. You almost never see this formation used in today's NFL.

got solid pressure up front, this was an extremely effective design. But the defense itself was built on the talent of a great individual and solid supporting players, not a sophisticated and complex scheme. "Conceptually, the Giants weren't difficult to figure out," stated Redskins quarterback Joe Theismann, who faced New York twice a year in division games. "It was blocking Taylor that became an issue. And if you became overly concerned with him, you had Carson or George Martin to deal with. Their front seven was almost like playing against seven defensive linemen. They were big, active, and physical. There was no comparison between playing against them and the Cowboys. I could play Dallas, and then on Monday go out and do whatever I wanted. After playing the Giants, it wasn't until Thursday before I felt like doing anything."

The 49ers believed that field conditions would pose major footing problems for the big and physical New York defense. "That fall we had a lot of rain, and the field was miserable all year," recalled Dwight Clark. "The playing surface at Candlestick is under sea level to begin with, and when the tide comes in from the bay, the water just rises right up through the ground. We'd play our games and rip things up, so they constantly had to put new sod in. They had groundskeeper guys wearing special jackets that said 'Sod Squad' on them. Of course, that new sod never did hold. But I think that wet surface actually helped us because we got used to it.

"The league called in George Toma from Kansas City to try and put his magic to work and see if something could be done." Toma, regarded as the sports world's premier groundskeeper, worked full time for baseball's Royals but rented his artistry to other organizations. "I think he changed the sod and threw some kitty litter out there to dry up the water," said Clark. "By Sunday, it was decent enough for us to play, but the surface was still really soft."

Beyond Walsh's strategic surprises and a sloppy turf, the 49ers had one more advantage in their favor: the motivation to prove that their coach's innovative ideas were valid. "We knew we were different," snapped Cross. "We'd get people looking at what we did and ask, 'What is that?' But we made it work. To this day, there are people who still don't understand it. And they never will, because it's out of their box, out of their comfort zone. Damn it, in 1981 the NFL was 'smash-mouth.' *Real* football was the NFC East. It meant coming off the ball and beating people up. And if you didn't play to that style, it wasn't really football. Bill presented playing the Giants as a challenge. He reviewed what they did well, what they didn't do well, and where we were going to take advantage of them. He was almost like a surgeon in a preoperation meeting saying, 'Here's what we're going to cut out, and here's how we're going to do it.' "

1ST HALF

49ers Series No. 1
1st Quarter, 14:50 Remaining: San Francisco 0, New York 0

The Giants weren't all that disappointed when they lost the coin toss, because head coach Ray Perkins believed his team could more easily set the game's tempo with its defense. He was wrong. The 49ers' offense took control early, and it would be a long time before New York regained its equilibrium. San Francisco set the tone from the very first play with a three-step drop from Montana and a bullet throw to Dwight Clark for a 16-yard gain. Because Joe's drop was so short and he got rid of the ball quickly, it was feasible for fullback Johnny Davis to block Lawrence Taylor coming in off the edge, and Davis did. But Davis, in his first and only season in San Francisco, was just one of several 49ers in a "blocking by committee" corps that would be handling Taylor all afternoon.

After halfback Ricky Patton broke out of a Harry Carson tackle to pick up 5 yards, the Niners went back to the air. A play-action fake sent Patton and guard Randy Cross running right to simulate a sweep. Taylor followed the fake, then Patton blocked him, allowing Montana to make a full seven-step drop with minimal pressure. He threw it deep and within reach of Freddie Solomon, but Freddie was unable to hang on. No matter. Walsh had made an early statement. He was going to stretch the field vertically, and the Giants would have to respect that capability.

The next play was the first time John Ayers was called on to Molly block Taylor. L.T. beat him to the outside and moved toward the pocket but arrived too late. The ball was already out of Montana's hands and in the clutches of a wide-open Patton in the right flat. Ricky gathered it in and raced 64 yards for a touchdown. But beyond the Niners' lightning-quick execution, there was another reason why no Giants were nearby: Solomon had clipped New York corner Mark Haynes, which wiped out the score and put the ball back near midfield. The penalty allowed New York to collect itself, and the defense responded by shutting down a run and sacking Montana for a big loss after a fake reverse. On third-and-long, Montana looked and found Patton open again, but the pass caromed off his shoulder pad. It appeared that the Giants had weathered San Francisco's opening assault, but a disastrous holding penalty on Haynes during the punt gave the Niners an automatic first down.

Even at this early stage in Joe Montana's career, it was not a good idea to give him a second chance. From his own 41, Joe play-faked to Patton, freezing New York's linebackers. After a three-step drop, the QB hit receiver Mike Wilson for 15 yards. "One of the things Bill liked about Joe was that his passes had a 'nose up' flight of the ball," said Wyche. "This way the ball always arrived very soft; it was never a hard catch. A ball traveling nose down comes in heavily and can shoot right through you, down your chest, and near the ground if you don't get your fingers on it." Joe then lofted another beauty, a quick-out to Dwight Clark for 11 more. On the Clark play I saw Ayers pop out to block Taylor, but this time Lawrence wasn't rushing. If the Giants wanted L.T. in pass coverage, well, that was just fine with Walsh. In fact, Taylor rushed only twice on the opening series. It was Clark again on the next snap, a hook route between two defensive backs for 22.

San Francisco was now inside the 10, but was pushed back when center Fred Quillan was flagged for holding. Facing second-and-18, Montana play-faked, then ran a sprint-right option away from Taylor, who was blitzing from the other side. Solomon caught the pass to move the ball to the 8-yard line on third down. Anticipating a blitz from New York's 3-4 front, Walsh had tight end Charle Young align on the line of scrimmage. He then moved Solomon in as a wing tight end on Taylor's side of the field. But neither Taylor nor inside backer Brian Kelley blitzed—a huge break for San Francisco. If both had rushed, the Niners' protection schematically could not have handled it. When neither of the linebackers came, it allowed Ayers to help the left tackle, Audick, block end Gary Jeter. Montana completed his five-step drop, sliding to his left, then found Young in the back of the end zone for the touchdown.

This illustrated the high-quality pocket mobility that became a Montana trademark and the kind of movement we've come to expect from such current stars as Tom Brady and Peyton Manning. "Bill was so big on footwork, which got you into a rhythm when you passed," said Montana. "It all depended on how far you were going to throw the ball. He'd want you to make your drop, then push yourself back up into the pocket. This avoided a lot of sacks and took pressure away from the offensive line."

Because of the two San Francisco penalties, Joe's stats on the touchdown drive were seven of nine passes completed for 111 yards— not a bad feat considering the whole field is only 100 yards to begin with! Maybe the most impressed person was New York's sidelined quarterback Phil Simms, who couldn't play because of a separated shoulder. "I'm thinking, *God, they're making it look so easy, just moving right down the field,*" he recalled. "It seemed like they were throwing at will."

49ers Series No. 2
1st Quarter, 5:16 remaining: San Francisco 7, New York 0

During the bulk of the first quarter, the Giants exerted very little pressure on Montana. This allowed Joe to develop his rhythm and timing without much harassment. The Niners got their chance to pad the lead when they took over at their own 46 after a defensive takeaway. But they promptly put themselves in a hole when Solomon committed his second clipping penalty of the quarter. The Niners could not recover from the long-yardage deficit and punted, but the offense would be back on the field barely a minute later. Giants quarterback Scott Brunner, substituting for the injured Simms, drilled a bull's-eye on a slant pass to Earnest Gray, who slipped past free safety Dwight Hicks's tackle for a 72-yard touchdown. Even so, the shock of New York's sudden score eased a bit when 49ers special-teamer "Famous" Amos Lawrence ran the kickoff across midfield into Giants territory.

49ers Series No. 3
1st Quarter, 2:45 remaining: San Francisco 7, New York 7

Throughout the first half, the 49ers' offense came out on a variety of formations, rarely repeating any of these looks over consecutive plays. To start the drive, Clark lined up as a tight end across from Taylor. Bill did this to put bodies in front of L.T.; to get him thinking rather than allow him to play instinctively. "You use these different formations because you know they will force adjustments from your opponent," said Walsh. "This will help you for the remainder of the game, to see how they adjust to what you do."

Confusion with San Francisco's multiple formations was one Giants problem. Dealing with Candlestick's muddy turf was also troublesome, and Randy Cross couldn't have been happier about it. "That's why they call it 'home field advantage,'" he said with a laugh. "A lot of what we did was to capitalize on that kind of surface. We'd wear long cleats, and I guess they didn't. Well, that's *their* problem. If it takes you a quarter or a half to get the right shoes on, we just might score a bunch on you." The Giants were literally out of their element. "We were a team accustomed to playing on an artificial surface," admitted Carson. "Once you got on slow, wet natural turf, you get slower yourself. You feel bogged down and don't have the same kind of quickness you'd have on a dry or artificial field."

The slippery surface was also affecting how their secondary covered San Francisco's receivers. Even though the rain had tapered off by game time, the grass remained slick all day. The Giants didn't want to get burned for a cheap score, so they gave huge cushions to Niners receivers, coverage clearly evident on this first play. Solomon ran a short pattern largely undisturbed by Haynes, and Montana easily hit his wide-open target for 11 yards. On the next snap, most of that yardage was given right back, however, after Patton caught his spikes in the grass. Ricky pulled up a chunk of turf, losing his footing—and 7 yards to boot.

After an incomplete pass, San Francisco faced third-and-17. Anticipating pressure, the Niners kept Young and fullback Earl Cooper in to protect, but Taylor once again dropped into coverage. Against New York's Cover-Two, Montana made a seven-step drop, then avoided defenders by sliding up in the pocket. "A play like this is what made Montana so great," stated Walsh. "His focus is down the field— he doesn't see these pass rushers at all. He *feels* them. Guys like Joe, who have the nerve and focus, can do this. Other quarterbacks can't help but take their eye off the receivers and look at the men rushing him. A lot of people go through their entire career without mastering this. But Joe had this gift, plus he'd done this thousands of times in practice, so it came very naturally to him."

Having eluded the rush, Montana threw to Clark, who, surprisingly, was open on the right sideline. The third-year receiver out of Clemson had initially been bumped by Haynes, then broke free. Haynes wasn't too concerned at first, because he expected safety help from Larry Flowers. But here's another example of Walsh's creative design: He had Patton run a seam route in the middle of the field, and Montana looked briefly in his direction. Joe's body movement also indicated that he might be throwing over the middle. Flowers saw this, knew he had to respect Patton's route, and briefly hesitated. He was now too far away to come over and give Haynes deep help on Clark. Dwight made the easy catch and ran all the way down to the 5—a 39-yard gain. From there, the Giants held, and San Francisco came away with a Ray Wersching field goal.

49ers Series No. 4
2nd Quarter, 13:11 remaining: San Francisco 10, New York 7

San Francisco's defense forced its second turnover of the game when Brunner's deep pass was tipped by Dwight Hicks, who, during the regular season, had intercepted nine passes and returned them for an NFL-best 239 yards. This time, however, the ball landed in the hands of corner Ronnie Lott. The offense took over at its own 32, and once again Walsh lined up Clark as a tight end across from Taylor. Solomon ran a Go route down the sideline, but Haynes had him blanketed in man coverage, so the pass fell incomplete. On second down, Ayers displayed his run-blocking chops by turning Kelley inside, creating a hole for Cooper to pick up 10 yards. "These runs were all part of Walsh's scripted plays," explained Cross. "And here's why: They were there to help set up our play-action. We had to make these running plays work, because the play-actions looked really dumb without a decent ground game. Look, we weren't a running juggernaut. We didn't have any runners who gained a lot of yards. But we did run effectively. We were a 'movement' team; a team that relied on pulling guards and play-action. Bill always said we were going to hit harder than anybody and move quicker than anybody."

Following Cooper's run, Montana signaled for a time out and went over to Walsh to make sure he had the correct call for the next play. Not only was the play correct, it was the perfect call. The Niners broke the huddle in a balanced set with two backs and two tight ends. There'd be no Dwight Clark lining up close this time—it was legit tight ends Young and Eason Ramson aligned next to their tackles. Freddie Solomon was San Francisco's only wide receiver on the field. The Giants reacted by putting eight men in the box with a single high safety, which left Terry Jackson in man-to-man outside coverage against Solomon.

At first, it appeared that New York had guessed correctly. The initial look of the play was an inside run, with the line firing forward, as opposed to standing up to pass block. To the Giants, it clearly looked as if a running play was coming. I have to give special credit to Joe on this one, because he really sold the idea that he was going to hand off to Patton. This was even more misleading than his earlier play-fakes. Following the snap, Solomon ran in a straight line, with no variation on the pattern whatsoever. He simply blew past the much slower Jackson. Joe delivered the ball right on the money, and Solomon had himself a 58-yard touchdown. Freddie had clearly atoned for those two costly clipping penalties he'd committed in the first quarter. Later on, when I watched the CBS broadcast, I noticed that their cameraman was as badly fooled as the Giants. He too was convinced the play was a run, so he kept his camera trained on the line of scrimmage and nearly missed the action downfield. By the time he recovered, Solomon was gathering in the pass just a few yards away from the goal line. After the game, Montana told reporters, "We had to get respect from their defensive backs, and that's why we went long. They were playing a lot of zone defense, and we were guessing right."

This score was the payoff for all the time that Walsh's team had spent perfecting this play on the practice field. Even today, Clark still remembers his coach's classroom mantra: "He'd tell the receiver, 'This is the play we're going to run at this time against this defense. You'll be wide open.' Or 'we're going to use this in such-and-such a situation, because they'll be in man coverage and will leave this guy open here.' He just had such a great ability to look at tape and come up with the other team's holes and weaknesses, then just starting pounding on 'em."

49ers Series No. 5
2nd Quarter, 11:46 remaining: San Francisco 17, New York 7

Montana and his teammates barely had time to gulp down their Gatorade before they were back on the field. The Giants fumbled on their first play from scrimmage, and the Niners' defense recovered, giving the offense terrific field position at the New York 42. Taylor rushed the pocket, but Ayers pulled out and easily shoved him aside, giving Montana more than enough time to hit Young on a 14-yard slant pass. "If you look at a lot of the movement we were doing," noted Cross, "it was always the back-side guard who was pulling out. We went full speed, balls to the wall. And by the time we got a guy like L.T. on play-action, the Giants might have known it was 'pass,' but they believed it *could* be 'run' just long enough that we could deal with them."

Already tentative and confused, the Giants defenders could only scratch their heads in disbelief at Walsh's next formation. On the TV broadcast, announcer John Madden identified it as a four-wide-receiver set, but it certainly wasn't what we'd commonly recognize as a four-wide set in today's NFL. Walsh had Wilson and backup Mike

Shumann split out as conventional receivers, and put Solomon and Clark behind Montana in a two-back set! I can't imagine what must have been going through L.T.'s mind when he saw this. In the end, the play was only a 3-yard toss to Solomon out of the backfield. But it was yet another different look; one more exotic formation for New York to worry about.

Walsh had told Madden the night before the game, "I'm going to try to hide my players so it'll be tougher for the Giants to plan against them." That approach was working flawlessly during the first half. The Niners featured constant backfield movement on their running plays to create hesitation and indecision—exactly what Walsh wanted from a defense as reactive and quick flowing as that of the Giants. The next play provided a perfect example of this.

The Niners came out with Cooper aligned directly behind Montana, with Patton offset to the left, favoring Taylor's side. The play appeared as if it would be a counter, *away* from L.T.'s area. After the snap, left tackle Audick pulled completely across the formation, leading Patton to the right. What I found fascinating was that instead of pairing Audick with the fullback Cooper to lead the blocking—the conventional way you run the counter—Walsh had Cooper attack L.T. head-on to prevent him from running Patton down from behind. You just never saw that kind of scheme back then. This was clearly a tactic designed to account specifically for Taylor, to negate his unique ability to run down ballcarriers behind the line of scrimmage. Once the play started, Audick cleared out two Giants to spring Patton. Ricky had a clear path from there and sped the final 25 yards for the touchdown.

"Walsh went off of a script, and the thing about his scripts were that there's no rhyme or reason as to when they'd run particular plays," admitted a frustrated Carson. "They didn't show tendencies. Montana kept us off balance. We expected one thing, and he'd run another. You had to hold on to your hat and just do your best to defend it. If, by the end of their script, they're up a few touchdowns, then it may already be too late. It's tough to come back in a playoff game from that far back."

49ers Series No. 6
2nd Quarter, 5:32 remaining: San Francisco 24, New York 10

After coughing up the ball on successive possessions, the Giants were a little more careful on their series. Although they burned nearly five minutes off the clock on a solid drive, they weren't able to close the deal and had to be content with a 48-yard field goal from kicker Joe Danelo. San Francisco had more than enough time to tack on another score before halftime—and nearly did. On the second play from scrimmage, Ayers popped out, looking for Taylor again, but L.T. was in coverage. Montana ran a double-pump fake and then completed his pass to Solomon for 17 yards. Joe's fakes were confusing enough, but an additional weapon he used to torment the Giants was designed movement that continuously varied the launch point of his passes. They seemed to change on *every* play, and for a defense—even one as good as New York's—this had to be terribly frustrating. It kept their pass rush from generating any kind of rhythm or timing.

That wasn't the only variable tilting in Montana's favor. "I think the flexibility Joe had in '81 worked hand in hand with the West Coast offense," said Clark. "The play would be called to go against a certain coverage. If Joe saw that coverage was different before the snap, then he could change the play. Of the seventy-five to one hundred plays we'd have in a game, maybe thirty percent of those had audibles to them." Cross took it a step further: "From an improvisational stand-point, when you talk about Montana, it'd be like comparing your average comedian to Robin Williams. Joe could riff on the field and 'improv' amazingly. He could take a lot of what Bill wanted to do and sort of put his own spin on it while he was doing it."

A run by Cooper was stopped after just a couple of yards, and then Joe threw again. Ayers successfully Molly blocked the onrushing Taylor, and Solomon hauled in a 7-yard pass. Third-and-1 from the 46 suggested that the Niners would run, and they did—no trickery this time. From their two-back set, Ayers pulled out, and Patton provided the lead block. It was your garden-variety power running play. But it wouldn't have picked up big yardage without Ramson manhandling Taylor: He washed L.T. inside and eliminated him from the play.

Cooper found open space and ran for 20 before Flowers finally caught up to him. In 1981 the 49ers ranked near the bottom in yards-per-rush average, but in the playoffs, against one of the league's most physical defenses, they were running with surprising efficiency.

In the closing moments, the Giants kept the Niners from going any farther, forcing a 50-yard field goal attempt. It would have been a challenge even on a dry field, but on Candlestick's slippery surface Wersching was unable to maintain his footing and slipped as he approached the football. The kick was both wide and short, keeping San Francisco's two-touchdown lead unchanged at halftime. Even with the missed scoring opportunity, the Niners had to be extremely pleased with what they'd done in the first thirty minutes. Anyone who'd thought that the glare of the playoffs would expose the "Finesse 49ers" to a trampling by Big Blue had just received a rude awakening. Walsh's offense was making one of the league's most feared defenses look tentative. Both Clark and Solomon had already accumulated over 100 receiving yards each. San Francisco's running game was averaging nearly 5 yards a carry with its emphasis on sweeps and toss plays. Joe Montana was playing a mistake-free game, and his three- and five-step drops had all but neutralized New York's ferocious pass rush.

The key, of course, was shutting down Lawrence Taylor. "We slid the offensive line to him on one snap, then on the next we'd keep a back in to help the left tackle," explained Wyche. "Then we lined up in a formation so that the tight end was on Taylor's side. He'd either stay in to block or would run through Taylor, chip him, then let the tackle pick him up. We had about three or four different ways to block him that day. The mistake we'd seen other teams make was settling on just one way to account for him, then work hard on that in practice. Well, if that approach didn't work on Sunday, you were out of luck. That's why we had so many schemes to block him that day."

It wasn't simply the multiplicity of methods: The 49ers' success stemmed from what they *didn't* have to sacrifice in order to keep Montana on his feet. Brian Billick put it best: "You can always stop one guy, but at what price? Walsh wanted to contain Taylor, and he also wanted to leave his quarterback with enough options to make plays.

When the Niners accounted for L.T. in that game without sacrificing any eligible receivers, it forced the Giants' defense to have to cover people they normally didn't cover, and that created doubt in their minds. Handling five receivers in the pattern made their job much tougher."

2ND HALF

49ers Series No. 1
3rd Quarter, 12:49 remaining: San Francisco 24, New York 10

The Giants had the ball to start the third quarter, but failed to pick up a first down. With one more score, the 49ers would put a stranglehold on the game. They started strongly from their own 36 when Cooper faked a run inside but broke it back around right end for 14 yards. Then New York's defense made its most important play of the game. Montana dropped to pass but couldn't escape either Jeter or rookie linebacker Byron Hunt. With both in hot pursuit, he forced a throw that was picked off by strong safety Bill Currier. It was Joe's only significant mistake in the entire game.

On New York's first play following the turnover, Brunner threw a laser between two 49ers defenders. It ended up in the hands of Giants receiver Johnny Perkins, who quickly broke away and sprinted 59 yards for the touchdown. As poorly as New York had played up to this moment, it was back in the game.

49ers Series No. 2
3rd Quarter, 11:13 remaining: San Francisco 24, New York 17

For the first time all afternoon, the Candlestick crowd was uneasy. Its team had dominated play, but now a rare Montana turnover had allowed the Giants to draw within a touchdown. Ideally, the 49ers wanted to mount a clock-consuming drive that would shift momentum and end with points, but that didn't happen right away. Although it had taken a while, defensive coordinator Parcells finally got his athletes to start playing up to their reputation. San Francisco began well enough when Montana play-faked, then hit Ricky Patton in the flat. Patton got clocked by Terry Jackson, but bounced off and staggered to a first down at the Niners' 46. On the next play, center Fred Quillan was whistled for holding, and conditions for San Francisco quickly deteriorated from there.

With a first-and-20, Taylor finally had the opportunity to pin his ears back and rush the pocket with abandon. Ayers, sensing that L.T. was coming full tilt, moved to his left and stood up the rookie in his tracks. It was muscle on muscle, and Ayers won this battle. Unfortunately for the Niners, while great blocks can earn film-session props from your position coach, they don't always translate into yardage. That's what happened here, because Haynes had Solomon blanketed, so Montana was forced to throw it away.

L.T. turned the tables on the next snap. Ayers tried to block him high, but L.T. slid to his left as Montana moved up in the pocket. Taylor turned, found Joe virtually in his lap, and dragged him down for the sack. It was only L.T.'s second tackle of the day, but the wait was brief to get number three. On third-and-23, Taylor initially dropped into coverage. Then he rotated back to the flat, shoving Audick to the side to get the drop on running back Lenvil Elliott. San Francisco was forced to punt, and the Giants took over at their own 29, with the wind at their backs and momentum on their side.

I believe this was the drive that decided the game. New York maintained possession for over five minutes, running off a dozen plays to get inside San Francisco's 5-yard line. But there the 49ers' defense held fast, and on fourth-and-3, the Giants resigned themselves to settling for a field goal. New York's bench then groaned in disbelief when Danelo badly shanked his 21-yarder wide to the left. Two great Giants defensive stands and an efficient offensive drive had amounted to nothing.

49ers Series No. 3
3rd Quarter, 4:12 remaining: San Francisco 24, New York 17

The 49ers were clearly elated to maintain their one-touchdown lead, but the Giants kept playing solid defense and got off the field quickly. They gave up an early first down when tight end Eason Ramson slipped past Taylor off a Montana play-fake for an 11-yard reception. The next play was also a pass, and Ayers moved to his left to find Taylor. In another display of sheer strength, the six-foot-five left guard blocked L.T. so effectively that he almost appeared to swallow him up. But New York's pass coverage was airtight, and Joe had nowhere to go, so he took off. Showing the foot speed that I became painfully familiar with, Taylor wriggled away from Ayers, moved to his left, and ran Montana down from behind to hold him to just a couple of yards.

After a Cooper run that gained almost nothing and another incomplete pass, the Niners punted. But a special-teams penalty pushed the Giants back inside their own 10-yard line. It was early in the fourth quarter and still only a one-possession game, but the Giants needed to march over 90 yards for the tying score. When New York couldn't convert on third-and-1, it was forced to punt within the shadow of its own goalposts. Dave Jennings got off a decent enough kick, driving Solomon back to his own 42, but New York's coverage was poor, and Freddie weaved his way for a solid return to the Giants' 36.

49ers Series No. 4
4th Quarter, 14:07 remaining: San Francisco 24, New York 17

It seemed as if San Francisco was going to squander its excellent field position when a flat pass to rookie running back Bill Ring lost 4 yards and a holding call on Young pushed them back another 10. But the Giants gave it all back on the next snap, when Jeter was penalized for unnecessary roughness. With a fresh set of downs on the Giants' 26, the Niners weren't going to blow it again. Walsh called a double reverse, with Elliott taking the initial handoff and then pitching it to Solomon, who cut back for a dozen yards.

From the 14, Ring swept left end and escaped Taylor's tackle for 7 more yards, a clear sign that L.T.'s competitive fire was fading. After another Niners run set up first-and-goal from the 3, Ring followed a lead block from Johnny Davis into the end zone for the touchdown. There were two times during this drive when Ayers moved out of his guard spot and successfully walled off Taylor: one on a play where the 49ers lost yardage, the other on a Giants penalty. Although the blocks had little to do with the end results, they evidenced Ayers's ongoing mastery over the rookie linebacker—a dominance that was clearly sapping Taylor's spirit.

49ers Series No. 5
4th Quarter, 9:46 remaining: San Francisco 31, New York 17

By now Walsh was content to sacrifice scoring for clock burning, so he called mostly running plays. After two rushes netted 7 yards, Bill Ring took Montana's pitch and followed Cross to the right side. On the tape of the telecast, what I heard was almost as incredible as what I saw. Randy leveled Currier on his first block, then wiped out veteran linebacker Brad Van Pelt a moment later. Even with the hometown crowd in a frenzy, you could still hear the explosion off Cross's collision and an audible groan from Currier as he crumpled to the ground. Then Ring added to my surprise by showing an uncharacteristic burst, cutting back across the middle of the field for a 40-yard gain. One of his pursuers was Taylor, who not only couldn't catch up but also hurt himself when he was kicked in the shin at the end of the play. A dejected L.T. limped off the field, and although he would eventually return, the leg injury was a fitting last straw to his thoroughly frustrating afternoon.

Unfortunately for Ring, an illegal crackback block by teammate Mike Wilson wiped out the entire run, which would have been the longest of Bill's career. On third-and-long, Montana was content to dodge a sack from Van Pelt and throw incomplete to avoid an interception. Even with eight minutes remaining, this would be the last pass Joe needed to throw the rest of the game. San Francisco's unheralded but steady runners would take it from here and drain the clock. Then Ronnie Lott sealed the win with a play indirectly inspired by Taylor himself. "He was a rookie, and I was a rookie. I didn't know him that well then, but I really respected him," Lott explained. "For me, playing against the Giants was all about saying to the world, 'I know L.T. is good, but there's somebody like me with the same type of demeanor, the same type of attitude. Let me see what I can do, to show people I'm just as good and maybe even better.'"

With three minutes remaining, Lott read Brunner's eyes perfectly, picked off his pass, and ran 20 yards to the end zone for the Niners' final touchdown. It was Ronnie's second interception of the game, giving San Francisco a three-touchdown lead. It made a last-minute Johnny Perkins touchdown catch nothing more than a consolation prize, as the Niners decisively outclassed the "Beast from the East" Giants, 38–24. It was the most points New York's defense had allowed in a game all season. And if the 49ers had eliminated just a few of their penalties, the margin of victory would likely have been even more decisive.

A week later, in the NFC championship before a home crowd, Dwight Clark's iconic leaping touchdown catch in the final minute lifted the 49ers to a 28–27 upset over the Cowboys, sending them to the world championship. In Super Bowl XVI, Walsh earned some payback by beating Paul Brown's Bengals, the team and owner that had passed him over for its head coaching job six years earlier. That 26–21 win capped a remarkable season for a franchise that would go on to change the NFL both historically and strategically. In a 2002 interview with Steve Sabol, Walsh displayed real emotion when speaking of the '81 season. "Looking back on it, that was Camelot," he said. "That was the greatest experience for everyone involved that they'll ever have in their life. Because the 49ers had been embarrassed and humiliated for a number of years by virtually everyone in football, each of our games became a sort of vendetta: 'We're gonna show these guys.' Every game, we came out with so much intensity. I never had another season like it."

Randy Cross had suffered through all the losing prior to Walsh's arrival and was there for much of the glory that followed. Nineteen eighty-one was also Randy's favorite season, and he recognized how much its success sprang from the Niners having won that first playoff game against a team like the New York Giants. "Walsh's way challenged those who thought size and strength was what made the NFL what it was," he maintained. "What Bill did in the early eighties was not yet looked upon with high regard. But it made sense. If you're smaller going against bigger, what should you do? Try to flatten your forehead? Or will you trap 'em, make 'em move around, and do things they don't do well?

"The answer is obvious, and when you succeed, you end up pissing them off even more. That's probably what pissed the Giants off more than anything else: that they gave up so many yards to us. This game proved to everyone—and ourselves—that what we did worked. Against the smashmouth New York Giants, we showed we belonged. We'd only won ten games the previous three years, and there was no rich tradition of winning, so it meant a lot to get that first one."

Walsh later acknowledged, "We won our first Super Bowl with a less-than-great football team, even though at the time people thought it was outstanding. But as you look back, you now realize it couldn't compete with today's teams. Joe was dependent on the system for survival—in fact, all of us were—and we believed in it."

Montana was just as beholden to John Ayers, whose Molly-block protection kept Joe out of L.T's crosshairs. As Taylor admitted to Michael Lewis in *The Blind Side,* "It was the first time I'd seen it. It was the first time they'd brought the guard back to meet me. I couldn't figure out what to do with him. There was nothing I could do but try to run him over." Lawrence tried, all right, but was continuously frustrated by San Francisco's protection scheme.

Bill Parcells believed that Taylor's troubles were due in no small measure to the muddy playing surface. "Their tactic of using a guard to block is one that would not work on a dry field against Lawrence," he insisted. "It could be used in bad weather. We couldn't get any pressure that day because of the field conditions. They had a good design and were a better team than us at the time. But as time went on, it became more difficult for them to do that to us." Parcells pointed out in *The Blind Side* that when he studied the game film later, he saw that whenever Ayers dropped back, he left a hole in the middle of the line. Had the Giants blitzed either Hunt or Kelley from the inside, they would have had a clear path to Montana, but on that day they never did.

"You look at Giants-Niners games from then on, and you'll see they didn't do a whole lot against us," stated Bill Belichick, who was on New York's coaching staff throughout the eighties. "Pulling the guard out was effective in that game, but part of it was that we hadn't really seen it and didn't have a good answer for it. The field slowed Lawrence down, plus the ball was coming out so fast. Their receivers never really stopped because they were always in motion routes. We just didn't match these things quickly enough, didn't pressure the quarterback with a quick pass rush. We were still playing a more traditional game. They were better than us, had better players, and—I'll admit it—they outcoached us. But by the time it got to the end of the decade, we beat them a number of times, and they didn't have anything near the offensive success against us that they did in those first few games."

"The Giants gave us the most trouble," admitted Walsh. "From then on, we were pretty even with them. Their great talent and coaching really crowded Joe. They got in his face, and he didn't have as much time to throw those precision passes. There were times we just couldn't get it done. Our games with New York were slugfests, and they took away a lot of what we had. Parcells and Belichick figured out better ways to defense us."

Bill was being gracious when he said this. There were some notable Giants victories, especially in '86 when they won the Super Bowl. But for the record, the Niners beat New York seven out of ten times between 1981 and '89. The Giants shouldn't feel too bad, though, because during that same stretch, San Francisco was so good that it had a better overall regular-season *road* record than any team's *home* record. The 49ers won three more Super Bowls as they expanded their explosive repertoire with better offensive players.

None of this would have happened without the events of the '81 Giants-49ers playoff game. I know the Niners-Cowboys game played the following week—highlighted by Clark's amazing catch—is part of NFL mythology, but it wasn't as far reaching as the Giants game. Here's why:

- *This game made clear the potential dominance of a pass-rushing outside linebacker in the 3-4 defense.* Now every team was on the lookout for someone like Lawrence Taylor, a force that could disrupt an opponent's passing game.

- *This game made clear that left tackles are critical.* Bill Walsh had gotten away with using John Ayers to stop Taylor, but that was only a short-term solution. If the Niners were going to prosper, they'd have to get a better athlete on Montana's blind side—and did in '83, drafting Bubba Paris. Today the offensive left tackle is one of the highest-paid positions in the NFL, and it all started because coaches could now see how critical a good one was to keeping their quarterback healthy.
- *This game expanded defensive pressure concepts out of the 3-4.* Coaches now understood that they were going to have to broaden their repertoire with more variety and disguise if they were going to compete against teams that ran West Coast systems. Otherwise they would be picked apart. Defenses would also have to become faster, especially at the linebacker position.
- *This game inspired innovation from offensive minds . . .* Taylor's arrival forced Redskins coach Joe Gibbs to modify his Air Coryell–oriented offense into a new system that relied upon the H-back position to neutralize L.T. Joe's breakthrough made Washington a dominant team over the next decade, earning three Super Bowl championships.
- *. . . as well as defensive ones.* As timing and precision offenses became more widespread, people like Buddy Ryan and Dick LeBeau were forced to come up with new and better ways to apply pocket pressure.
- *This game formally introduced football fans not only to a new offense but also to a new philosophy.* Walsh's West Coast attack changed everything: how offenses were called, how they were coached, how teams were built. Standards for higher pass completion percentages jumped dramatically.

After I retired from the Eagles, I was an NFL analyst with CBS," recalled Dick Vermeil. "I was doing a Niners game early in the 1986 season. That summer, Jack Kemp's son Jeff was really struggling at quarterback for the Rams, and they let him go. Walsh signed Jeff, and it's a good thing he did. Montana hurt his back and missed a lot of playing time, so Kemp replaced him. I don't think Jeff had been there more than a few weeks when he was pressed into the lineup, but he did very well. He actually did better than that—he was putting up big passing numbers and eating people alive. Why? Because of Bill Walsh's system. It was so quarterback friendly."

Bill followed his old friend Vermeil into sportscasting shortly after retiring from the 49ers in '89. But the competitive fires still burned, and Walsh went back to coach Stanford in the early nineties. He later returned to the 49ers as their general manager and then came full circle by returning to where it all began: San José State. In 2005 he served as a consultant to his alma mater, even as he bravely battled the leukemia that would eventually end his life.

As the NFL enters its second decade of the twenty-first century, there are many differences between today's game and what it was like when Bill Walsh began tinkering with his West Coast philosophies. "When Walsh started this approach, it really wasn't a complex system," observed Bill Parcells. "He had a tight end, two wides, and two backs almost all the time. You didn't see much motion, because he wanted to see what the defense would be before the snap. Mike Holmgren and Andy Reid have since changed the West Coast offense to be something quite different from what Bill originally designed." Al Saunders acknowledged those profound differences, but also noted, "The language Walsh created for his offense is still prevalent in the NFL today. If you see Reid's offense in Philadelphia, it may look more like a Gillman or Coryell attack, but he uses Bill's terminology."

I asked Jon Gruden about the Walsh lineage, and he offered some additional examples: "A lot of Walsh disciples have taken the West Coast offense in new directions. What Holmgren did with the screen game in Green Bay was sensational, and Mike Shanahan's ability to add his own touches with the Steve Young teams of the nineties might have been the most exciting shit I ever saw. Just look at footage from their Super Bowl win over the Chargers. They absolutely shredded them—stuff with Brent Jones and Ricky Watters—it was a full-court press. And they ended up doing it to everybody."

There are still occasional flashes of Walsh's original precepts. In

Green Bay, Mike McCarthy has quality receivers who run those familiar slants, hitches, and comeback patterns, and his quarterback Aaron Rodgers is a quick thinker who reads defenses rapidly. The slant-pass foundation is still a big part of what Brad Childress does with the Vikings' passing game. In Houston, Gary Kubiak likes to run inside slants with Andre Johnson, throw to his backs out of the backfield, and use tight end Owen Daniels in classic West Coast style. But the reality is that Bill's original offense has been modified so much and by so many that, in its purest form, it no longer exists. Two-back sets are rare because of multiple-receiver spreads. The fullback was a key component in Walsh's original offense, and some teams don't even carry one on their roster anymore! Zone blitz schemes and defensive exchanges have totally altered protection packages, all but banishing the pro set package of the early eighties.

Timing and rhythm were really what Bill was all about, and that's what has most endured of the West Coast offense. The synchronization of the quarterback's drop and the depth of the receiver's route, spot-on pass location so that the receiver can make the catch without breaking stride, the harmony between the receivers and the offensive line—this is Walsh football. When you look at today's precision offenses, like those of the Colts and the Saints, you are witnessing skilled, cerebral quarterbacks who understand and live by Walsh's principles. Peyton Manning and Drew Brees honor the memory of Bill Walsh every time they put the ball in flight.

Buddy Ryan's 46 Defense

COURTESY OF THE CHICAGO BEARS

CHICAGO BEARS vs. DALLAS COWBOYS
Texas Stadium, Irving, Texas — November 17, 1985

One of the best experiences in my sports career happened well after my playing days had ended. Along with rock legend Jon Bon Jovi and several other partners, I became co-owner of the Arena Football League team the Philadelphia Soul. My favorite moment came in 2008, when we won the Arena Bowl, the AFL's version of the Super Bowl, to become league champions.

That '08 Soul team started out 9-0, then hit a few speed bumps before we bounced back to win the title. After suffering our first loss of the season to the Cleveland Gladiators, we appeared to have regained our footing the following week against the Georgia Force. We were ahead by 21 with barely three minutes remaining in the fourth quarter, but the Force staged a furious rally and beat us in the final seconds. This was easily our most painful loss of the year. And Georgia's head coach was Doug Plank, a guy who'd inflicted considerable pain on me in the past. You may recall that it was Plank who put me out of that 1980 Bears-Eagles game after Mike Hartenstine had first blindsided me. Like a lot of safeties, Plank wasn't a great cover guy, but he could really whack people around. Battering opponents until they didn't want to get up anymore is a longtime Chicago Bears trademark, and Plank did it as well as anybody. He became such a destructive force that Chicago's defensive coordinator eventually named his signature scheme in Plank's honor, calling it the "46," which happened to be Doug's jersey number.

That coach was James David "Buddy" Ryan, and the philosophy behind the 46 has, in my opinion, been the single most influential factor in shaping modern NFL blitz pressure packages. I view Buddy's defenses the same way that I came to regard Bill Walsh's revolutionary offenses: something radically different from what everyone else was doing. You could look at Buddy's designs on film, and there'd be stuff you'd never seen before. He went so far with it that, at times, his schemes were fundamentally unsound, and they often looked disorganized. As a quarterback, I could glance at any other defense and have a general idea where the holes were, where I could throw. Against Buddy's defenses, I was never sure *what* I was going to see.

As far as I know, Buddy was the first guy who blitzed regardless of down and distance. He blitzed anytime and anywhere. One of the craziest things he did was to blitz during the final two minutes of the half; no other defense dared do that. He'd call a base defense on the first play, and, as a quarterback, you'd feel pretty safe. Then he'd cross you up with a full-house blitz, and all hell would break loose.

The 46 propelled the Bears to a world championship in Super Bowl XX and then got Buddy a head coaching job with the Philadelphia Eagles. His first year in Philly, 1986, was my last, and that was no coincidence. From day one, I was persona non grata. Buddy came in with a "Let's clean house" attitude, and one of the things he wanted to do was to replace the guy who'd been Philadelphia's starting quarterback for nine straight seasons. He traded for veteran Matt Cavanaugh and also had a young Randall Cunningham waiting in the wings. But to Buddy's extreme disappointment, I beat them both out for the starter's job at training camp. From there, our strained relationship only got worse.

Philadelphia went 5-10-1, but the numbers were even more embarrassing when it came to our pass protection. The '86 Eagles set an NFL record by allowing 104 quarterback sacks in sixteen games! All these hits took their toll, and I missed six games because of injuries. With so many breakdowns, you can imagine the problems we had on offense. Even so, I'm not sure Buddy really cared all that much. His heart was with the defense. I think that's why he preferred Cunningham at quarterback over me: He didn't want a disciplined system in Philadelphia because he didn't think Randall would do well in it. I was there for a speech Buddy made at Philadelphia's Maxwell Football Club dinner in which he told a stunned audience, "I hear all this about the three-step drop and the five-step drop. I tell Randall, 'Forget all that bullshit, go out there, make two or three big plays, and we'll win.'"

I remember, during one game, coming to the sideline to get the next play from offensive coordinator Ted Plumb. In the middle of our conversation, Buddy stuck his head in and screamed, "Run the goddamn ball!" I asked him what he wanted, a "power-O" or one of our other standard calls in the Eagles playbook. He spat back, "I don't give a shit! Just run the goddamn ball!" Buddy simply did not know the plays. He had no real understanding of our offensive scheme. The one thing he *did* know was how to stop one.

If Buddy comes off sounding like a master sergeant, it's probably because that's exactly what he was. When he was barely eighteen, Ryan left his small farming town of Frederick, Oklahoma, to join the army, later serving two years in the Korean War. After being discharged from the army, he returned home to play football at Oklahoma A&M. Buddy coached at a number of southwest high schools in the late fifties before making the jump to the college level. My former *ESPN Matchup* colleague Sam Rutigliano knew him in the mid-1960s when Buddy was coaching at the University of Buffalo. "Even then, Buddy Ryan was the kind of guy who'd pull the trigger before the target was up," said Sam. "He'd say and do whatever he wanted. Buddy didn't give a crap about anyone's feelings. He always did things his way, but he was also a smart and very funny guy whom his players loved."

Buddy's first job in pro football could not have come at a better moment. He was hired by the New York Jets in the winter of 1968, in time to be part of their Super Bowl championship season. He remained on their staff for eight years, which is why Buddy must have been a proud pop when his son Rex was named Jets head coach in 2009. Rex later stated, "My dad is most famous for what he did with the '85 Bears, coaching maybe the best defense of all time and winning the Super Bowl. But to this day, his Jets Super Bowl III ring is the only one he wears."

The most influential concept of Buddy's football life came from the guy who gave him his first job in the pros: Jets head coach Weeb Ewbank. Weeb put a lot of emphasis on protecting his "meal ticket," quarterback Joe Namath, whose knees were in bad shape even before his rookie season as a Jet in 1965. Ewbank spent hours refining and teaching intricate pass blocking schemes, including a technique he'd developed with Paul Brown called "cup" protection (in which a semicircle formed around the quarterback, with the linemen interlocking their hands to avoid both holding calls and arm slaps from pass rushers). This clearly made an impression on Buddy. He figured that if Weeb thought it was so important to keep Namath from getting hit, then, as a defensive coach, Buddy needed to come up with whatever he could to hit the quarterbacks of other teams. More than anything else, pocket pressure became the most significant principle of his entire defensive philosophy. This was a truly groundbreaking idea when pro football, especially as played back then in the NFL, was totally defined by the running game.

I got my first exposure to "Buddy Ball" while I was still in college. I had just completed the last game of my senior season at Youngstown State when I got a call from Bills coach Lou Saban. Lou was in charge of the North squad at the Senior Bowl, and he needed another quarterback to replace Oregon's injured Dan Fouts. Naturally, I said yes and flew to Mobile, Alabama, to join the team. It proved to be one of the luckiest breaks of my life. I got into the game in the second half with our side trailing, 30–13, then threw two long touchdown passes and nearly rallied the team to victory. Even though we lost, 33–30, that performance greatly improved my status in the NFL draft. Before that game, I was probably going to be only a fifth- or sixth-round pick, but because of what I did in Mobile, the Rams ended up selecting me in the second round.

You're thinking, *Nice story, Jaws, but what does it have to do with Buddy Ryan?* Well, the South team was coached by Weeb Ewbank and his Jets staff, which included Mr. Ryan. College all-star games have different rules than what you have in the regular season, mostly restrictions to protect players from getting hurt. The last thing bowl executives wanted was for some highly touted prospect to suffer a career-ending injury in their game, so blitzing was strictly prohibited. Well, Buddy really didn't care about any old sissy rules and decided that he was going to pressure us with extra defenders anyway. All game long, you could hear Saban screaming on our sideline, "That son of a bitch Ryan is blitzing my quarterbacks! He can't do that! Doesn't he know the goddamn rules?" I know I had to hurry a lot of my throws when I was out there, but the refs never said a word to Buddy all day.

Buddy continued to spread his "gospel of aggression" when he coached one of the great front fours in history, the Purple People Eaters of the 1970s Minnesota Vikings, which included future Hall of Famers Carl Eller and Alan Page. When Vikings assistant Neill Armstrong was hired to be head coach of the Bears in 1978, he asked Ryan to come with him as his defensive coordinator, and Buddy jumped at the opportunity. Now he could run a defense *his* way, experimenting with ideas that those once above him had found too radical. It didn't happen overnight. Chicago was a mediocre team, and Buddy's early Bears defenses didn't have the best talent. But they did like to hurt people—which made them just the kind of players he liked. The NFC Central was still known as the "Black-and-Blue division," and Buddy's boys lived up to that name every Sunday. But blood and broken bones didn't translate into many wins, and in 1981, a 1-6 start put the Bears at the bottom of the standings.

"We weren't very good that year," recalled safety Gary Fencik, a former Ivy Leaguer from Yale who played in Ryan defenses for eight

seasons. "We seemed to make a lot of untested quarterbacks successful in those days, and Eric Hipple of the Lions was one of them." Hipple's very first pro start came in a Monday night game against
Chicago, and all he did was throw four touchdown passes and run for
two more scores as Detroit crushed the Bears, 48–17. Buddy was
pissed and knew he had to do *something.* "Our pass rush wasn't worth
a shit," he said. "We had to find a way to create more pocket pressure
because we were getting beat up by every quarterback in the league."
Chicago's next game would be against one of the league's best quarterbacks: the Chargers' Dan Fouts. He and the rest of the Air Coryell
juggernaut were the NFL's top-ranked offense, and they came into
Soldier Field that Sunday as two-touchdown favorites.

"I still remember Neill Armstrong's speech he made at the hotel
the night before we played the Chargers," Fencik recalled. "Neill basically said we didn't have any chance of winning the game. But Buddy
had some new defensive schemes to try and put added pressure on
Fouts, force him to hurry his decisions."

Another change came at the middle linebacker position when
Ryan gave rookie Mike Singletary the first start of what would eventually be a Hall of Fame career. Back then, Mike and Buddy weren't
yet friendly. "He had lots of irritating ways of pushing my buttons,"
Singletary recalled. "For that first year and a half, I hated him and
thought he hated me." But at that moment, the young linebacker was
so excited that he called his friends and family to let them know. After
the euphoria died down, Buddy looked him in the eye and said,
"You're startin', but whatever happens, you do exactly what I tell you
to do. Do anything else, and we're gonna have problems."

Singletary's debut was so brief, so disastrous, that it's easy for him
to remember exactly what happened: "I make the tackle on the first
play of the game. Now I'm really jacked up. So on the next play, Buddy
signals in, 'four-three, three-V.' I call that play in the huddle, and Fencik says, 'No, no! You mean *two*-V.' He and I are arguing, here come
the Chargers out of the huddle, so I call time out. I *know* I'm right. So
I go over to the bench, and before I can even say a word, Buddy's
screaming at me, 'How stupid can you be? No rookie ever calls time
out! Go over and sit on the bench.' So I was on the sidelines the rest of
the game and was pretty burned up."

With Singletary out, Ryan switched gears, abandoning his standard alignments and, for the first time, leaning heavily on strategies deployed from the 46. "Using my jersey number to identify that defense wasn't unusual," Plank explained. "There were a lot of coverages and blitzes Buddy labeled by a specific player's number, and in this defense I had a lot to do, so that's where the name came from."

Against the Chargers, Ryan unveiled the first permutation of the 46: a nickel package with a 5-1-5 personnel grouping the Bears had not previously shown that season. It looked like this: Buddy moved Plank from his safety position into the box, as if he were a linebacker. The other two safeties, Fencik and future Tennessee Titans head coach Jeff Fisher, were also sent in at key moments to apply additional pressure. "We ran that game from the secondary," said Plank. "We were able to communicate Buddy's calls with code words, expressions, and hand signals."

At the same time, something was different with the Bears' down linemen. The weakside defensive end lined up outside of the offensive tackle in a wider pass rush position, while the other defensive end and the defensive tackles set up directly over the guards and the center. This became known as a "reduced front," and it forced the interior offensive linemen into awkward and difficult one-on-one matchups. *It became the defining feature of the 46.* This alignment must have looked like something from outer space to the Chargers, and with good reason. In those days, nobody else was playing with eight men in the box. Buddy wanted opponents to throw against the alignment. Heck, he was *daring* them to do it.

The only true linebacker on the field was second-year player Otis Wilson, whose main responsibility was to cover tight end Kellen Winslow. Wilson held Winslow to just four receptions. "I don't want to be bragging," Wilson told reporters afterward, "but I'd seen film on them, and I don't think anyone covered Winslow as well as I did. They didn't go much to him until late in the third quarter."

With eight men crowding the front, the Chargers weren't sure *what* was going on. If I had been the quarterback that day, I'd have been thinking to myself, *How many of these guys are actually going to rush? From which direction are they coming? What kind of protection should I choose?* And I'd have to come up with answers for all these questions in the blink of an eye. Plank recognized immediately that this new "Buddy system" could work. "Perceived pressure was a key concept of the 46," he pointed out. "The anticipation of what *might* be coming was just as important as what then actually *did* happen. Against the Chargers, we created a sense of urgency for their entire offense, forcing them to play at a more hurried pace than what they usually did. It changed their whole mind-set."

One way the befuddled Chargers responded was to frequently keep their running backs in to protect Fouts. But with Wilson blanketing Winslow, that left only two other available receivers to run intermediate patterns: Wes Chandler and Charlie Joiner. They struggled all day to get open, while Fouts was under constant siege from the Bears' rush. "Their guys were coming at us from a myriad of stunts and blitzes," recalled Chargers running back Hank Bauer. "They were pressuring and hitting Dan by pushing the pocket inside. Even after he

Bears Zero Coverage

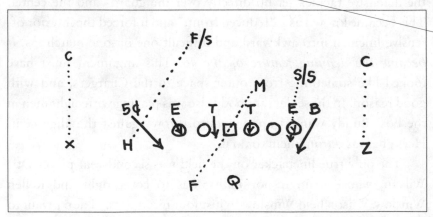

Buddy gave this formation its name because there is no safety help for either cornerback. Both corners must cover the X and Z receivers one-on-one. That's because one of the linebackers has been replaced by a nickel back who blitzes from the left side. The remaining outside linebacker, Wilson, blitzes from the right. Middle backer Singletary is also coming straight up to the quarterback. Free safety Fencik must cover the half back if he comes out of the backfield, while strong safety Duerson handles the tight end. Here's another variation on this play: if Duerson also blitzes to bring more heat, then Wilson has to pick up the tight end. But if Wilson is the blitzer, then left end Hampton has tight end responsibilities. With so many variations, Bears defenders had to be smart and athletic to play in this scheme. When it clicked, it was devastating and almost unstoppable.

got rid of the ball, Dan was still getting hit. The Bears' main goal was to create negative plays, but also to create doubt in the quarterback's mind." In essence, Ryan was making the *threat* of the 46 just as important as its execution.

It worked even better than Buddy had hoped. Fouts suffered the worst statistical day of his career, completing only 13 of 43 passes while throwing 2 interceptions. One of those picks came in overtime from Fencik, which set up the winning field goal for a 20–17 Bears win. "We'd never seen this defense before and weren't prepared to deal with it," said Bauer. "When that happens, it's pretty tough to change the game plan you came in with. And they whacked us around pretty hard."

The most pleasantly surprised people that day may have been the Bears defenders. "You wouldn't think these blitzes would work against a quarterback like Dan Fouts," said Fencik. "But we did pretty well that game and felt that if the 46 could succeed against a Hall of Fame passer, well, then it would probably do just fine against a lot of other, less talented quarterbacks."

Despite their surprising win over San Diego and a few other strong defensive performances, the '81 Bears never got out of the Central Division cellar. By late December, it appeared that Ryan's time in Chicago was coming to an end. After a 6-10 finish, Neill Armstrong was going to be fired, and the rest of the coaching staff assumed that it would be canned along with him. But Buddy's defensive stars went on the offensive. The charge was spearheaded by Alan Page, Buddy's favorite player with the Vikings, who was now finishing his NFL career in Chicago. Page would eventually go on to become a state supreme court justice in Minnesota, and he pleaded a strong case for retaining Buddy in a letter he wrote to team owner George Halas. The note was then signed by the rest of the defensive players. "We did that to cover our butts," confessed Fencik. "The letter basically said we thought Buddy and his staff had done a good job with us, and no matter who was hired as head coach, Buddy and his people should stay on.

"So one snowy day at practice, Halas shows up—which he rarely did at this point in his life because he was eighty-six years old. We were all terrified that he was going to be angry about our petition. He told all the assistants to 'take a walk,' because he wanted to speak to the defensive players privately. He pointed to us and said, 'I got your letter, and I want you to know that in all my years in football, I've never received one like it. I came here to tell you personally that your [position] coaches will be back next year.'"

The players were overjoyed. Halas's new head coach, Mike Ditka, was not. Ditka had been a Hall of Fame tight end with the Bears in the 1960s and was a Halas favorite. But this was Mike's first head coaching job at any level, and he'd have no say in picking the defensive staff. It was the NFL version of a shotgun wedding, and neither Ditka nor Ryan was thrilled with their marriage. "I always described them as two people who were so similar that they just could not get along," said Singletary. "They had big egos and were strong willed and had so much pride. Neither one of them were going to say they were sorry for anything. So they just stayed away from each other." Buddy put it even more bluntly: "No 'getting along' was necessary. There was no relationship between us. Not much communication, either. He coached the offense, I coached the defense. That's what Mr. Halas hired me for. That's what I did, and it worked."

Bears quarterback Jim McMahon viewed the Ditka-Ryan feud as a source of entertainment. "Just watching them argue every game was hilarious," he recalled, laughing. "The other team would get a big play or maybe a score, and Ditka would blow up. 'Damn it, Buddy, run some zone once in a while.' Buddy would just say, 'Fuck you. I run the defense. Get out of here!' The players would just sit there and go, 'Can you believe this? These are our leaders right here.'"

Following Ditka's arrival, the personnel department began its search for more athletes who'd fit into Ryan's system. Dave McGinnis coached with the Bears for ten years and understood the skill set this defense demanded. "First you needed defensive linemen who could win individual matchups against the guy blocking him," he explained. "Then you needed linebackers who could run—people with lateral range and explosiveness. And the 46 had to have a smart middle linebacker and strong safety to make the defensive calls."

Chicago already had a good foundation in Dan Hampton, Leslie Frazier, Fencik, Wilson, and Singletary. It had also gotten lucky in '81
when Steve McMichael was plucked off waivers from the Patriots.
"We were gonna make him a center but didn't have enough defensive
linemen," Buddy remembered. "We really needed help there because
Hampton was about the only thing we had at the time. So we switched
McMichael to defense." Subsequent drafts brought in defensive backs
Dave Duerson and Mike Richardson, linebackers Wilber Marshall
and Ron Rivera, and defensive end Richard Dent, a steal in the eighth
round.

Leslie Frazier was with the Bears at the birth of the 46 and saw it
improve season by season. "What gave Buddy the impetus to create
this whole system was that better players were added to the team," he
said. "Once he got Dent and some of the others, then Buddy could
create situations to capitalize on these mismatches. If we hadn't had
that talent, I don't know if the 46 would have become the force it came
to be." McGinnis believed that the arrival of Marshall from the University of Florida allowed Buddy to finally do everything he wanted.
"Marshall was essential," he stressed. "He could physically play over
the tight end at the line of scrimmage and had the lateral agility to stay
with those tight ends in the passing game. He was just as good in confined areas as he was in space." Fencik called Marshall "the best athlete on our defense, hands down."

Whenever anybody asks me what the finest defense in NFL history
was, I always answer with the '85 Bears. It was the single most talented
defensive unit I've ever seen. But what also made them great was the
system in which they played. Buddy Ryan got absolutely everything he
could out of his players because they understood that his conceptual
design would take full advantage of their outstanding abilities.

"We didn't have just one leader, we had a bunch of them," recalls
Rivera. "Dan Hampton was the blood and guts of the line. He played
with a broken arm, a broken leg, broken fingers, and wobbly knees.
Fencik was the guy in the secondary. He was so bright and could
change things right in the middle of the game. It was like having a
coach on the field. And Singletary may have been the smartest of them
all."

"The 46 needs a traffic cop who can make all the adjustments, and

Singletary was our traffic cop," said Plank. "There are some sets where there could be three different defenses out of one specific play. You have to have a leader who spots when an offense makes changes before the snap and can make the right adjustments." For a unit that earned its reputation primarily for its smashmouth style, the Bears' defense mastered concepts that were highly complex and considerably more sophisticated than any other defensive scheme of its time.

In Fencik's opinion, "Buddy was the most unique coach I ever had, because he would reach a point with his players where he trusted you to make decisions. This was a totally different dynamic from any other coordinator I ever had." But first that trust had to be earned— which was why rookies never got much playing time under Ryan. According to Richard Dent, "Buddy used only two words with them: *horseshit* and *asshole*. Every now and then they *might* hear 'good play.'" Rex Ryan laughed as he remembered how "Dad called players only by their numbers until they did something he liked. 'Hey, 51, get your ass in gear!' That kind of stuff. If you played hard for him and bled for him, he'd suddenly remember your name just fine.

"Everybody knows about when my dad punched another coach on the sidelines [Buddy took a swing at Kevin Gilbride when both were on the Oilers staff in 1993], so they think of him as this wild guy. But I've coached with my dad and watched how he ran a game. He's as calm and in control as anybody I've ever seen. He was always thinking, always one step ahead of his opponent."

Our Eagles team met Chicago twice in 1983 as the 46 was evolving, and we were defeated both times. The first game was especially frustrating. It was played in a steady downpour, and our sputtering offense made the afternoon even gloomier for the rain-soaked Philly fans that bothered to show up. Even if the weather had been dry, I don't think it would have made a difference. In the first half, we gained a grand total of 24 yards. The Bears were in our backfield all day, sacking me four times. My passing stats stunk: 11 of 30 for 136 yards. I just never had time to throw, and we lost, 7–6. I did slightly better in the rematch about a month or so later at Soldier Field, but still only threw for 150 yards, was sacked four more times, and the Eagles got beat again, 17–14. We just never figured out how to handle their pressure.

Clearly Ryan was on to something, and the improving Bears finished at 8-8. By '84 Chicago was a complete team, including an offense run by Jim McMahon and a pretty decent runner you may have heard of named Walter Payton. And Buddy's defense was beginning to look downright scary, setting an NFL single-season record with 72 quarterback sacks. The Bears won their division and made it all the way to the conference championship before losing to the eventual Super Bowl champion 49ers. A year later, it was the Bears who'd be world champions.

I want to take some time to examine the essential features of the 46 and show you how it was more than just a defense that beat up people. It may have often looked unruly, but, believe me, everything was calibrated to work a specific way. The 46 was the perfect defense for its era. At that time, offenses were frequently run out of two-back/single-tight-end personnel sets, which bunched a large number of players near the line of scrimmage. Consequently, Buddy could bring more people closer to the ball, often in eight-man fronts. It became a simple function of spacing. The Bears' defenders had less ground to cover and a shorter distance between them and the quarterback.

One crucial element of the 46 was a concept known as the "automatic front and coverage" (AFC). This meant that the Bears could, before the snap, change the angles from which their rushers came and flip what kind of coverage their defensive backs and linebackers were employing. This was virtually unheard of back in the eighties. "We gave lots of different looks to quarterbacks," explained Fencik. "We were big on shifting around, because defenses on other teams gave simplistic pre-reads, which I thought made it too easy for quarterbacks to figure out. We never wanted that to happen with us. When we moved around in our AFC, it looked like a jailbreak at times, because we'd swap out a 4-3 for a 3-4. Guys would be coming or dropping back—it looked like chaos. But I assure you it was all coordinated. The offensive line saw this and wasn't sure who to block, and the quarterback wasn't sure what coverage he was seeing."

Singletary can best explain the other staple of Chicago's proactive/reactive approach, which the Bears referred to as "blitz to formation" (BTF): "When Buddy clapped his hands, there were about thirty or forty different things that could happen, depending on what our opponent's formation was, where their receivers lined up, the backfield set, down and distance. We'd factor all that in and make an on-the-spot choice as to where we were going to go with the best blitz for that situation. We're going to run certain fronts. Our corners would do things in tandem with our safety. A number of things could happen, but there had to be a lot of communication within that clap Buddy conveyed to our defense."

See what I mean when I say you had to be smart to play in the 46?

"With most coordinators, their players didn't know what was going to be called, but not us," Fencik bragged. "Buddy told us everything we needed. You could run the defense off a cheat sheet. Our calls were dependent on game situations. We ran our BTFs and AFCs so seamlessly that you never felt like you were in a bad spot. Buddy put us in the best position to beat a specific offense with a specific play in a specific formation."

Rex Ryan often uses a chess analogy to explain his father's strategies: "Dad basically had the black piece on the chess board. The white piece always moves first. Dad's piece gets the second—and then the last move. When the offense moved its piece, Dad had what he thought was the perfect blitz against your protection—and the perfect coverage to stop whatever routes you ran out of that formation."

Because the 46 calls for eight men in the box, it was very effective against the run. There would always be one extra defender for which the offensive team simply could not account, so rushing lanes closed down in a hurry. But Buddy's primary goal was to apply pressure on the quarterback. Here's what he did: He put both of his outside linebackers (Marshall and Wilson) on the strong side of the field, where the opponent's tight end lined up. On the weak side, he lined his pass-rushing defensive end (Dent) out much wider than normal from the offensive tackle assigned to block him. The other defensive end (Hampton) and the two interior tackles (McMichael and either Hartenstine or William "the Refrigerator" Perry) aligned head-up over the center and guards. Then Buddy put the middle linebacker and strong safety in stacked positions just behind his down linemen. Buddy called this his "Bear front."

It's hard to overstate how much confusion this caused for offensive lines of that era. They didn't know who they were supposed to block, because none of the defenders was where he was supposed to be. The Bears didn't always rush the same guys, and they didn't always rush in the same numbers. And if Chicago's two interior tackles and defensive end each aligned head-up against an offensive lineman, that guard or tackle *had* to block the man directly across from him, as no one else would even have a shot at blocking those guys. That left both the middle linebacker (Singletary) and the strong safety (Duerson) with unblocked paths to the football. That was the basic premise of the 46: attack, break down blocking schemes and pass protections, not individual players. Let's be clear, though: The 46 could not be an everydown defense. The better NFL offenses could still make big plays if it was used too much, so its risk-versus-reward ratio was deemed too detrimental for Chicago to run it for an entire game. But Buddy dialed it up frequently enough (often 30 to 35 percent and sometimes more) to keep quarterbacks guessing.

Base Bear Front

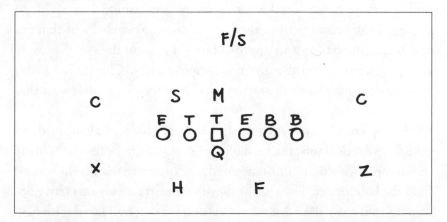

Ryan slides his customary four defensive linemen so that they overload to the offense's left side. Two linebackers then align themselves directly over the right tackle and tight end. Strong safety Duerson steps up into the box, alongside middle backer Singletary. Offensive lines of the era weren't used to blocking against this alignment and it took a long time to figure out their actual assignments. This eight-man front puts so much pressure on the quarterback that he has virtually no time to get rid of the football. Corners Frazier and Richardson are in man coverage against the wide receivers, with over-the-top help from free safety Fencik.

Joe Theismann understood as well as anyone how difficult it was to play against this defense, having lost twice to the Bears while quarterbacking Washington in 1984 and '85. "What Buddy Ryan did by covering the center and two guards was him saying, 'Your interior linemen will not be able to help anybody,'" he observed. "Their ends and linebackers went one-on-one with offensive tackles and backs. If you're asking your tackle to block exceptional athletes like Dent or Marshall, that isn't good. Indecision is the worst thing that can happen to you on a football field. The 46 made it tough for quarterbacks and linemen to figure out who was coming. Once you were in an obvious passing situation, you were at a distinct disadvantage. The Bears would give you the *illusion* of pressure, then drop seven into coverage. So if you'd checked off to a man route, you were in big trouble."

You're probably wondering about the vulnerabilities in Chicago's pass coverage if all eight players in the Bears front rushed the quarterback. Couldn't the offense burn those three remaining defenders if it got the ball out quickly? Well, sure, that did happen sometimes, but not often enough to hurt the Bears that badly. Here's why: You've got the two corners (Frazier and Richardson) playing man coverage on the opponent's wideouts, with Fencik as the single high safety in the middle of the field to make sure nobody gets behind him. With so much pressure coming from the front eight, quarterbacks of that era had to get the ball out in approximately 1.8 seconds—or they were going to wind up on the ground. In most cases, Chicago's corners were more than capable of staying with their receivers for at least that long.

Buddy could also switch up and have his corners align inside to take away quick slants, the kind of throw a QB under pressure is likely to attempt. With that option negated, the quarterback would have to hold the ball longer, and against the 46, that isn't a very attractive option! Even if the passer does avoid getting sacked, he's faced with having to complete a fade pass, a much tougher throw than a slant. A third coverage Buddy liked with the 46 was known as the "stalk." That's when one of the box defenders (either the middle linebacker or the strong safety) runs underneath the widest outside receiver to his side of the field. If either of these defenders gets there quickly enough, then that passing lane is denied, and the quarterback is likely going to have to eat the ball or throw it away.

Ryan figured that some teams would try to help protect their passer by keeping a back in the pocket to block an outside linebacker or the pass-rushing defensive end. Well, Buddy had an answer for that too: something called the "green dog" or "Frisco," a rush scheme that Bud Carson had also used with Pittsburgh's Steel Curtain. As soon as Singletary recognized that his back was staying home, he'd head straight for the quarterback because "Samurai Mike" (as he was nicknamed) would not be accounted for in the opponent's pass-protection scheme.

Buddy also came up with what is now known as the "peel" technique, which Doug Plank insists never existed until the Bears ran it. "If a running back free-released to the outside," he said, "Chicago's nearest defensive end would peel out from his three-point stance and cover the back man-to-man. Once the linebackers saw this, they could totally change what they were doing. They could pressure blitz, look for a running lane to go through, or drop back into coverage to take away slant or curl routes. Those guys on offense didn't realize that having their running backs checked went on to trigger other functions of our defense." The peel did more than add to an offense's confusion. It was also a coverage that camouflaged and compensated for what first appeared to be a speed mismatch between a back and a slower defensive end.

The 1985 Chicago Bears were virtually unstoppable, winning fifteen of their sixteen regular season games. In the playoffs, the defense pitched shutouts against the Giants and Rams, then crushed the Patriots, 46–10, in Super Bowl XX. Because it's among the most widely viewed Super Bowls ever, fans probably remember that Bears performance more than any other. To me, though, the one game that best exemplifies the awesome force of Buddy's defense was its week-eleven demolition of the Dallas Cowboys. The images I saw on the coaching tape of that day were shocking. My study of the game feels more like an autopsy than a film breakdown; that's how violent Chicago's performance was. Seen twenty-five years later, it's still a frightening thing to watch.

In 1985 Dallas was still a ranking power in the NFC and hadn't lost to the Bears in fourteen years. Head coach Tom Landry was a brilliant innovator in his own right. He'd pioneered both the 4-3 and "Flex" defenses, popularized the concept of men in motion, and been among the first to computerize his team's scouting system. Landry won Super Bowl VI with Mike Ditka catching the final Dallas touchdown, and Super Bowl XII with Ditka on the Cowboys' sideline as a staff assistant. Landry had taken a chance and given "Iron Mike" his first coaching job. Now the student was looking for his first win against his teacher. Singletary remembered what Ditka said to his Bears squad the night before the '85 game. "He told us how much he loved being with the Cowboys when he was there as a player and coach, and they'd always be an important part of his life. But that in order for us to get to where we wanted to go, we had to not just win but dominate the Cowboys, in Dallas. We needed to make a statement against 'America's Team.' And then the rest of the league would hear that statement too."

The 10-0 Bears achieved all that and more in one terrifying afternoon. Chicago mauled both Dallas quarterbacks, forcing turnovers and scoring a pair of defensive touchdowns. Starter Danny White was knocked out of the game *twice*. Deep into the fourth quarter, with the outcome long since decided, Buddy was still blitzing, just in case the Cowboys weren't getting the message. It wasn't a football game, it was a massacre. And when the final gun sounded, the Cowboys limped off the field having suffered their first shutout in twenty-five years.

1ST HALF

Cowboys Series No. 1
1st Quarter, 13:47 remaining: Chicago 0, Dallas 0

Chicago was missing injured starting quarterback Jim McMahon, and it showed. Backup Steve Fuller failed to move the Bears following the opening kickoff, and the Cowboys quickly took over at their own 30. The game did not begin well for Chicago's defense, either. On the first play, Richard Dent was slow to move after the snap, giving Cowboys fullback Timmy Newsome the opportunity to make a textbook-perfect lead block. Dent went down and it sprung running back Tony Dorsett for a 22-yard gain. Two plays later, Danny White scrambled to his right, avoided a pursuing Dan Hampton, and hit receiver Tony Hill for another first down. On the next snap, White took a seven-step drop-off play-action and threw deep downfield to Hill on a post route. Hill's defender, cornerback Mike Richardson, had missed the previous three games with a hamstring pull, and Dallas wanted to find out early if he might still be gimpy. The Bears' corner stayed with Hill stride for stride and had him well covered, but White made a perfect throw. It probably would have been a touchdown—except that the ball went through Hill's hands.

On second-and-10, the Bears went into the 46 for the first time. Hampton hovered over the center as the nose tackle, while Perry and McMichael aligned over the guards. Wilson and Marshall rotated to the strong side of the offense, with Marshall inside, across from the tight end, and Wilson directly outside. Singletary crept up to the strong side, while Duerson crouched between Dent and Perry. Dorsett took the handoff, looking to go wide, but this time Dent overpowered lead blocker Newsome, forcing future Hall of Fame running back Dorsett back inside, where he was held to no gain. (On the play, Refrigerator Perry physically drove Dallas guard Glenn Titensor back into the pile—a stunning display of strength that would be repeated numerous times.)

Facing third-and-10, the Cowboys broke the huddle, still in their base offensive personnel: two backs, a tight end, and two wide receivers. It struck me that if you had the same situation in today's NFL you'd *never* see an offense go with base formation on third-and-long, but back in the 1980s, this was conventional strategy. It didn't work for Dallas on this play, either. White dropped back to pass, hoping to throw to his left, but the play wasn't there. So he worked back to the middle toward tight end Doug Cosbie. Dent was practically draped on White when he threw, and it was nearly intercepted by Fencik. Dallas

punted but soon had the ball back after yet another unproductive
Bears possession.

Cowboys Series No. 2
1st Quarter, 9:29 remaining: Chicago 0, Dallas 0

I couldn't help noticing, even this early in the game, how good Hampton and Singletary were at recognizing and diagnosing Dallas plays.
They both seemed to rapidly process what they saw and react accordingly. A great example came on the Cowboys' first play of this series,
where both defenders were quick to stop a Dorsett run for no gain. But
on second down, Chicago's secondary got caught in a mismatch. Wide
receiver Mike Renfro started in motion to the weak side, then quickly
reversed to the strong side toward Cosbie and Newsome, forming
what's known as a "bunch" concept. This cluster of Cowboys played
havoc with the Bears' man coverage, and strong safety Dave Duerson
was forced to pick up Renfro on a short crossing route. White hit Renfro, who had room to run after the reception, picking up 20 yards and
a first down.

After a short pass to Newsome gained 4 yards, the Cowboys
dipped into their playbook for a call that had worked well against
Chicago in their last meeting. It was to be a left-side screen to Dorsett,
which Tony had taken 68 yards for a score the year before at Soldier
Field. Nothing doing this time—the Bears were ready for it. Lining up
in the 46, Wilson blitzed from the left, but when Cosbie moved to
block Wilson instead of run into the pattern, it freed Wilber Marshall
to blitz as well. Wilson easily shed Cosbie's blocking attempt, and the
two Bears linebackers converged. Meanwhile, Singletary alertly diagnosed the play as a screen to Dorsett and went right to him. Even if
White had completed the pass, Singletary had his man covered. But
White's toss traveled only a few inches, as the converging Wilson and
Marshall batted it into the turf.

Cosbie made up for his blocking whiff with a 12-yard reception
that gave Dallas a first down at midfield. This would be the high-water
mark of field position for the Cowboys; in the first half, they would
not even get into Bears territory until late in the second quarter, and
by then, they'd be trailing by more than three touchdowns.

The beginning of the end for the Dallas Cowboys started with a draw to Dorsett, which Singletary easily diagnosed and shut down for a 1-yard loss. A second-down pass attempt by White was swatted down in the backfield by the long arms of Richard Dent. On third-and-10, the Cowboys swallowed hard because they knew the Bears would be coming in full force. So Dallas went to the shotgun, with both backs staying in the pocket for White's protection. It made no difference whatsoever. Newsome ended up trying to block Otis Wilson one-on-one, a mismatch if ever there was one. Meanwhile, McMichael showed surprising lateral quickness and not-so-surprising hand strength to shove aside guard Kurt Petersen. Wilson and McMichael pressured White into leaving the pocket and throwing the ball away. Once again the Cowboys were forced to punt, but once again the McMahon-less Chicago offense was off the field in short order. Buddy's defenders got barely a minute to rest before returning to action. Clearly they weren't happy to be back on the field so quickly and saw to it that their next stay would be brief.

Cowboys Series No. 3
1st Quarter, 5:23 remaining: Chicago 0, Dallas 0

Fridge Perry, the six foot two, 325-pound rookie, gobbled up Dorsett on the first play, dropping the Dallas runner for a 2-yard loss. And although the Cowboys picked up a first down right afterward, you could see the Bears' front line beginning to take control. White spotted a favorable matchup with Cosbie against Singletary and completed a 13-yard pass. But, I noticed a terrific move by Dent, away from the play, to beat tackle Chris Schultz. Although White got the throw off successfully, he took a brutal (but legal) shot in the back from Dent as he released. Schultz was in the game only because starting left tackle Phil Pozderac had been injured on the first series. Dent was simply too strong and fast for anybody, let alone a seldom-used backup, and the Bears would exploit this mismatch again and again.

The drive ended on the next play, even though White made another terrific throw on the run to avoid Chicago's pocket pressure. Danny gunned it to Renfro, who picked up 13 yards before colliding with Mike Richardson, the left cornerback. Richardson stripped the ball free from Renfro's hands, then recovered the fumble himself to give the Bears possession at the Dallas 45. Surely a takeaway would spark the previously lifeless Bears offense. Unfortunately for Chicago, it did not. But after another three-and-out, a Maury Buford punt pinned the Cowboys back on their own 2-yard line. The Bears' defense figured, *Okay, if our offense isn't going to score we'll just have to do it ourselves.*

Cowboys Series No. 4
1st Quarter, 1:54 remaining: Chicago 0, Dallas 0

This Dallas possession lasted just one play, but it was the play that permanently changed the direction of the game. Its featured performer was Dan Hampton, who's in the Pro Football Hall of Fame precisely because of moments like this. The man nicknamed "Danimal" had already made contributions lining up as a nose tackle, but with the Cowboys operating in the shadows of their own goalpost, Buddy had Hampton line up at left defensive end. Here's how good the Bears were: They were in a conventional four-man rush with nobody blitzing, and still put incredible pressure on the pass pocket. In one motion, Hampton clubbed right tackle Jim Cooper and rushed in toward White, who tried to get rid of the ball. With both arms extended, Hampton's long reach deflected the pass straight up in the air. The six-foot-five Dent leaped, plucked it away from the crowd and spun into the end zone. It was the game's first touchdown, and the first score of Dent's NFL career.

Cowboys Series No. 5
1st Quarter, 1:38 remaining: Chicago 7, Dallas 0

The play by Hampton and Dent galvanized the Bears' defense. So what if they'd been on the field for two-thirds of the first quarter? They were jacked up after their touchdown and really teed off on Dallas the next series. On first down, Chicago sent only its down linemen to rush as the linebackers dropped back, but the front four created more than enough pressure to ruin the play. Perry muscled past Titensor, and Dent swept past Schultz. The pocket collapsed, and Dent pulled down White for the sack.

"To me, Richard Dent was the talent who put the Bears defense over the top," stated Phil Simms, who had the misfortune of facing him numerous times while quarterbacking the New York Giants. "He was simply unblockable. That was always the first thing on your mind when you played them: How are we going to block him on every play? And because the Bears were the only team at the time running the 46, you never really saw this stuff anywhere else. Their coverages were different, everything they did was different. It was very hard to prepare for them."

On second-and-16, the Bears returned to their 46 front, with Hampton moving back inside as the nose tackle. Incidentally, I noticed in my film study that Hampton played at *every* defensive line position at least once in this game. Now, *that's* versatility! The snap was botched, and White was lucky to regain control, but it upset the Cowboys' timing. To compound their troubles, Hampton ran a line stunt, looping behind McMichael. Kurt Peterson moved laterally to stop Hampton, but over on the left, Chris Schultz's rough day was getting worse. The six-foot-eight tackle came down inside to try to help Titensor block Perry, but it seemed to me that Schultz may have blown his assignment. He probably should have fanned out and tried to block Otis Wilson. I say this because Wilson blew in untouched to make the sack.

On third-and-21, the Bears were quite content to give up a pass over the middle to Newsome that fell short of the first down. It was the last play of the quarter, but just the start of Chicago's defensive dominance. Danny White admitted, "We needed to stop the game at the end of the first quarter, go take a week off, prepare for what we'd just seen, then come back, and play the remaining three quarters. You're always looking to find a solution, and we never did find it. We didn't have a clue."

Cowboys Series No. 6
2nd Quarter, 9:37 remaining: Chicago 10, Dallas 0

The Bears' offense was finally able to get on track at the beginning of the second quarter, and although its scoring drive resulted in only a field goal, it did eat up more than five minutes of game clock, giving the defense a badly needed rest. Chicago's defenders returned to action refreshed and just as ferocious. White began with a screen pass to Newsome that picked up 6 yards but came at a cost. As soon as the quarterback released, he was clobbered by Perry. Danny managed to get to his feet and return to the huddle, but moments later he probably wished he hadn't. On second-and-4, the Bears went back to a 46 front. This time both Wilson and Marshall blitzed, but only Marshall got picked up. Once again Wilson came barreling in and drilled White in the back as he fired, incomplete, toward Cosbie. The Cowboys tight end was actually wide open and could have gone a long way if White had gotten the ball to him in time, but Danny never had a chance because the pressure was on him too quickly. Dallas had given Wilson an easy path also known as a "short corner," since it had no tight end or back on Wilson's and Marshall's side when Chicago was in the 46. This was a disastrous offensive design and a flawed pass protection concept to use against a team like the Bears.

In a postgame interview, Wilson told reporters, "When we shifted into our 'over-under' defense, their line could see who they needed to block. But then we would change our fronts while they were calling blitz protection, so now they've got to change *their* blocking scheme all over again. That's when them boys have to think. You know, linemen don't think a lot."

After the play ended, it was clear that White had been hurt by Wilson's hit, and he had to be helped to the sidelines. "Our multiple protection packages worked fine against conventional defenses but not against the 46," the quarterback confessed. "We needed a simpler blocking scheme in 1985, and we just didn't have it. Otis Wilson was in the right place at the right time that day. When we slid right, he was coming from the left. He never seemed to have anyone blocking him. We made him an All-Pro that day for sure. I still have knots on my body today from all those hits." Wilson was indeed named an All-Pro in 1985, for the only time in his nine-year career.

With White on the bench, the Cowboys handed the controls to backup Gary Hogeboom, who was rushed into the game with no time to get loose. Small wonder, then, that his first play was a poorly thrown third-down pass that Duerson nearly picked off. Dallas punted but would be back on the field just a few minutes later after another Bears offensive series went nowhere. Although the quick drive had given Hogeboom time to throw some warm-up tosses on the bench, they didn't help.

Cowboys Series No. 7
2nd Quarter, 5:49 remaining: Chicago 10, Dallas 0

Hogeboom had watched most of the first half from the bench and seen the Bears' stunning variety of looks and schemes. But on his first and only play of this possession he found himself staring at yet *another* different front—a 3-4—with Dent standing up as a linebacker on the weak side. This time Buddy sent five rushers, with Wilson blitzing from Dent's side, and again Dallas did not account for Otis. Under normal circumstances, the right tackle Cooper would have tried to block the Bears linebacker, but he was aligned across from Hampton and followed Dan as he went inside. Both Cosbie and Newsome took off on pass routes, so *they* weren't available to block Wilson either. Dorsett couldn't help because he was on the other side of the formation. So here comes an unblocked Wilson—again! Hogeboom saw that now familiar number 55 heading his way and quickly got rid of the ball, thinking that the intended target, Renfro, would be breaking inside. Unfortunately for Dallas, Renfro broke the other way, and the pass went right into the hands of Mike Richardson. Not a Cowboy was in sight as Richardson chugged 36 yards for the touchdown, the second defensive score of the half.

Cowboys Series No. 8
2nd Quarter, 5:31 remaining: Chicago 17, Dallas 0

Poor Gary Hogeboom. The guy gets thrown ice-cold into the game, nearly gets his first pass picked off, then has his next pass intercepted for a touchdown. Things couldn't get much worse, could they?

On the first play of his next series, Hogeboom threw a deep post route pass to Tony Hill. But Leslie Frazier was right there with Hill and intercepted the overthrow, returning it 33 yards. The injured Jim McMahon saw the play unfold from the bench and wasn't the least bit surprised. "I thought Leslie Frazier was the best corner I'd ever seen," he said. "I played against him every day in practice and watched him in games. He was just incredibly smooth, could run, and had really long arms to snatch the ball away from receivers." CBS analyst John Madden was equally impressed. Watching the tape of the TV broadcast, I heard John say, "To make the 46 work, you need two corners who can be out there on an island and cover the receiver. The Bears have that with Frazier and Richardson. Because they play man-to-man so well, it allows Buddy Ryan to send more guys in to rush the quarterback."

From midfield, it took the Bears only five plays to score against a now dispirited Dallas defense. A Steve Fuller quarterback sneak from the 1 earned Chicago's offense its first touchdown of the game.

Cowboys Series No. 9
2nd Quarter, 2:52 remaining: Chicago 24, Dallas 0

Hogeboom finally executed a positive play on the first snap of this series, rolling to his right to avoid McMichael, then hitting reserve tight end Fred Cornwell for a 32-yard completion. On the following play, however, the Bears' pressure forced Hogeboom to throw into double coverage, and the pass went incomplete. It was confusion, not pressure, that ruined Hogeboom's next pass. The Cowboys' backup quarterback, obviously still shell-shocked from the Bears' blitzes, dropped back frantically, expecting quick pressure. But Buddy was playing mind games once again, and this one probably gave him a good chuckle. After the snap, there was virtually no pressure, as most of Chicago's defenders dropped off into coverage. But Hogeboom was so psyched out at this point that he hurried needlessly, then threw off balance and incomplete to rookie wide receiver Leon Gonzalez. After a nervous Newsome juggled and dropped a third-down pass that would have been good enough to sustain the drive, Dallas punted away.

Cowboys Series No. 10
2nd Quarter, 0:29 remaining: Chicago 24, Dallas 0

Chicago took over with little more than two minutes remaining, but following two solid gains that got them into Dallas territory, Fuller was intercepted, and the Cowboys were granted one final possession with a half minute to play. After Richardson broke up a throw to Gonzalez, Hogeboom completed a screen pass to Dorsett for 16 yards. On the CBS telecast, John Madden was appalled. "It's really bad heading into halftime and the only thing Dallas has going is a screen pass. You need a bigger grocery list than this." The half finally ended with a McMichael sack on Hogeboom and a harmless Hail Mary pass that, like the Dallas offense, went nowhere.

The embarrassed Cowboys left the field knowing they were finished, even though an entire half remained to be played. "We were a ball-control, move-the-chains kind of team—and when they knocked us out of that mode, we were done," admitted White. "We kept trying to go with the short stuff, and that wasn't going to work. We would have been better off throwing jump balls downfield, hoping to hit one out of every three. We couldn't have done any worse than what we actually tried that game."

The man with the best seat in the house to witness Chicago's carnage was Gary Fencik. "As the free safety that day, I didn't have a whole lot to do," he recalled. "Neither Duerson nor myself had to roll up, because the rest of our defense had nullified their inside running attack. I watched a good game and had a great view of everything. Gaps were opening wide, and it wasn't like we were always knocking people down to create them. The Cowboys' whole protection scheme just collapsed. Usually teams can say, 'Wait until halftime, and we'll correct things with blocking adjustments.' They never did. And then the fun really began in the second half. I'd never been on a Bears team that had beaten Dallas, and we wanted to let them know, 'You're not America's Team anymore—at least not this year.'"

2ND HALF

Cowboys Series No. 1
3rd Quarter, 14:52 remaining: Chicago 24, Dallas 0

For the first time since early in the first quarter, Cowboys fans let out a hearty roar—but it had nothing to do with any action on the field. Gary Hogeboom had performed so poorly that Dallas fans cheered when Danny White trotted onto the field to start the second half, despite his injury. Unfortunately, his return would be short—and painful.

After running the ball only six times the entire first half, the Cowboys handed off to Dorsett on their first three plays and picked up good yardage. Dallas was trying anything to slow down Chicago's overpowering pass rush, but the Bears could afford to be patient. With their sizeable lead, they knew that White would have to put it up eventually, and when he finally did, the demolition derby picked up right where it left off. On the fourth play of the drive, White ran a play-fake to Dorsett. Tony was so focused on executing the fake that he ignored his blitz-pickup responsibilities, allowing the ever-present Otis Wilson to charge in untouched. White had the presence of mind to get rid of the ball, but it landed well behind the intended receiver.

The next play was a clear-cut example of the blocking blind spots in the Cowboys' system against the Bears' defense. Chicago's linemen completely tied up the left side of the Dallas offensive line, leaving only Dorsett in the backfield to protect. Everyone else had run out into the pattern. The Bears called a BTF that sent both Duerson and Singletary on inside blitzes. Dorsett now faced the football equivalent of choosing death by hanging or firing squad. He could block *one* of the blitzers, but not both. Hoping for a miracle, Tony tied up Singletary. However, White could not escape Duerson, who leveled the

Dallas quarterback for a 14-yard loss. The Cowboys punted but quickly returned to action after their defense held on three downs. Any hint of satisfaction quickly evaporated after another coffin-corner punt from Buford wedged Dallas inside its own 5-yard line. Master sergeant Buddy Ryan smelled blood and sent his shock troops in for the kill.

Cowboys Series No. 2
3rd Quarter, 11:40 remaining: Chicago 24, Dallas 0

Dorsett opened with a run that barely avoided disaster. Singletary shot the gap between two Dallas linemen, nearly tackling the running back in the end zone. Somehow Dorsett escaped to pick up 3 yards, and then another run put White in a manageable third-and-short situation. Danny completed a quick toss to Renfro to earn a fresh set of downs, but White's next play would be his last.

The Bears once again came out in the 46, with Duerson aligned in the gap between center Tom Rafferty and left guard Titensor. Following the snap, Titensor was forced to react to Duerson, whose pre-snap proximity put him closer to White than tackle William Perry. The Refrigerator rushed directly at White, forcing Danny to step up in the pocket. The good news for Dallas was that the motion receiver, Renfro, inadvertently found himself in position to block Otis Wilson, a rare event in this game. The bad news was that Renfro's block did little to slow Wilson down. Otis quickly got to his feet and found himself in perfect position to sack White from the blind side for an 8-yard loss.

Danny was on the turf, and it would be a while before he got up. A cart was brought onto the field, but White refused to get on it, eventually rising on his own and limping to the sideline. "On that play, I thought Wilson had broken my neck," White recalled painfully. In a way, he must have been relieved that his day was finally over. "I hate to admit this, but this was the only time in my career where my thought process was to get rid of the ball as quickly as I could. I wasn't even trying to read anything by that point. I was just looking for someplace to throw. When you can get a quarterback to watch the rush and not look at the secondary, then you've got him. I knew on virtually every play someone was going to be unblocked, but I never knew where he was, and my linemen didn't know where he was either. The Bears just completely destroyed the rhythm of our offense."

In 1985 Rex Ryan was in his senior year at Southwestern Oklahoma State, and had made the four-hour-plus drive from college to watch his father's team play in Dallas. "I got back to campus the next day, and one of the comments I overheard was, 'From now on, whenever Danny White drives down the highway, he'll be flinching, because every time he sees that number 55, he'll be thinking it's Otis Wilson instead of the speed limit sign.' Once Danny was gone, Dad's defense was gonna be just as rough on Hogeboom."

I'm sure Hogeboom was nervous when he came back on the field and was probably looking for help anywhere he could find it. Early in the drive, it turned out that his best offensive weapon was a penalty flag. On a deep throw, Richardson drew a questionable 44-yard pass interference call, putting Dallas in Chicago territory. But even that failed to spark the Cowboys' attack. The Bears continued to apply pressure, while also preventing Dallas backs from releasing cleanly into their receiving routes. During those rare moments when a Cowboys play was properly executed, it still ended disastrously, thanks to Chicago's superior talent.

A perfect example came on the last play of the drive, a deep third-and-10 throw from Hogeboom to Hill. The pass, well timed down the left sideline, was within Hill's reach, and he had Frazier one-on-one. But Frazier blanketed his man perfectly, and the pass fell incomplete. All game long, both Bears cornerbacks were outstanding in single coverage. At the time, neither Frazier nor Richardson was viewed as a shut-down corner. But the nature of the 46 dictated that both of these guys would be put on an island, and against Dallas they won virtually every battle.

By early in the final quarter, the Bears had tacked on two field goals, extending their lead to 30–0. At this point, all the numbers were bad for Dallas, and they were only getting worse: The Cowboys ran fifteen plays during the third quarter for a grand total of 9 yards. Their futility extended into the final fifteen minutes, with their last three possessions netting a mere 24 yards. And in the remaining twenty min-utes of the second half, the Cowboys made just one first down.

"Over by our bench, I was standing next to Dave Duerson," re-called Otis Wilson. "I told Dave that we were like a pack of wild dogs, killing each other to be the first guy to the football. Then I began bark-ing, and Dave did the same. Before you knew it, some of the other guys picked it up, and the fans started doing it at the rest of our home games." For the balance of the season, the chorus of dog barks be-came the signature battle cry of the Bears' defense.

Two reserve running backs scored Chicago's last two touchdowns, swelling the final score to 44–0. By early in the fourth quarter, Ditka had removed his offensive starters out of respect for his coach-ing mentor Landry. Buddy Ryan did not. His regulars remained on the field until late in the game, and whoever *did* line up on defense was still blitzing to the end. Leslie Frazier was not surprised, saying, "Buddy realized they had no answer for what we were doing and was the kind of guy who'd sense this and ramp up the pressure even more—show no mercy." Singletary said later, "There are lots of words to describe the '85 Bears. *Bullies* is one word I hate to use, because I've never liked bullies. But I guess when you look back at us, that's what we were."

Mike Ditka was deeply embarrassed for his former team. "I never felt worse at the end of a game than I did that day in Dallas," he re-vealed. "I tried to tell Buddy to call off the dogs, because you come to a point where the thing's out of hand and you should just pull back. We had broken their spirit—their offense could do nothing against our defense. Nothing. But our guys wanted to have their fun. Maybe if the shoe had been on the other foot, they'd have done the same to us." Rex Ryan had watched his father's teams lose to the Cowboys many times and understood what was going on. "Dad never could stand Dallas. He wanted a beat-down. He wanted to kick their ass."

Years later, Cowboys defensive back Dennis Thurman still couldn't believe what had happened. "I played eight seasons there, and

I have never seen a Dallas team get taken apart the way we were that day." The 44–0 wipeout marked the beginning of the end of the Landry era. The Cowboys staggered through their remaining games, barely making the playoffs. They were easily dispatched in the opening round and did not have another winning season until 1991, two years after Landry had been replaced by Jimmy Johnson—only the second head coach since the franchise's inception in 1960.

The destruction continued for another week as the Bears skunked Atlanta, 36–0. During this stretch of their schedule, the defense actually *scored* more points than it allowed! At this point many believed the 12-0 Bears were on their way to a perfect season. Leave it to my former coach Don Shula to figure out a way to beat the 46. I played for Don in 1987 and '88 and learned first-hand why he has won more games than any coach in league history. His '72 Dolphins remain the only NFL team to complete a perfect season, and his '85 Miami team made sure that Chicago didn't duplicate that accomplishment. In front of the biggest TV audience in the history of *Monday Night Football,* quarterback Dan Marino and the Dolphins did what nobody else could do that year: They moved the ball at will and beat Chicago decisively.

"When we scouted the Bears, we noticed that everybody else brought in extra people to block that defense," Shula explained. "But in the 46, there would always be one free blitzer unaccounted for. So instead of bringing everybody *in,* we spread everybody *out.* That way, we knew from their alignment where the free blitzer was going to be coming from. Marino recognized that the receiver would make a route adjustment, and Dan would get the ball to that receiver before the free blitzer got to him. There'd be times where Marshall or Fencik had to cover a fast receiver like Nat Moore, and that was a mismatch in our favor.

"The Bears did not go with any nickel defense against our three-wide-receiver set until very late in the third quarter. They played what they'd always played, because it had killed everybody else. Of course, everybody else didn't have Marino at quarterback. And Moore was great catching the ball against one-on-one coverage. Whenever I'm at a speaking engagement, I tell the audience that the best half of football I ever saw was what we did against the Bears that night."

"They rolled Marino away from Dent and pinned us in," explained Ditka. "And as good as Marshall was, him playing man-to-man on Nat Moore wasn't going to work. So you should put in a nickel back, but we didn't do that. At halftime I said to Buddy, 'Put the nickel in and stop being so goddamn stubborn,' and then we almost got into a fight—some pushing and shoving. A few players got between Buddy and me, and that was about it. I haven't gotten a Christmas card from him since."

Years later Ryan still refused to admit playing his base 46 personnel was the problem. "We get a punt blocked before the half, and they end up scoring. Another time we had 'em third-and-long, Hampton's rushing the passer, and the ball hits Dan in the helmet. It goes up in the air about forty feet, and one of their guys catches it for a touchdown. But mostly it was us screwing ourselves. Guys who were supposed to be containing were back inside, looking for Pro Bowl votes, playing by the seat of their pants, trying to be heroes rather than just doing their job."

In evaluating the footage from the Dolphins game, I counted a total of just seventeen snaps where the Bears were in the 46 alignment. They actually didn't do so badly in that defense. But they got killed whenever Nat Moore lined up as a third receiver. In the first half alone, Miami gained 163 yards and scored two touchdowns on eleven plays with Moore in the slot. Shula also had two backs line up on every first half snap, making it much tougher for Chicago's rushers to get in clean. Most important was Marino's pocket instincts and his quick release. He's in the Pro Football Hall of Fame for games like this one, which has to be regarded as one of the finest moments in Dan's career.

Chicago lost, 38–24—the only blemish on an otherwise perfect season that ended with the Bears' demolition of the Patriots in the Super Bowl. Final score? Fittingly, 46–10. "I think we came into that [Dolphins] game cocky and overconfident," Fencik admitted. "Dan got hot and caught us in some bad formations. But our losing that game was the best thing that could have happened to us." Singletary agreed. "I think that loss helped us get back our focus. It made us understand we had to be ready every week if we were going to be world champions."

Just moments after the final gun sounded at Super Bowl XX, I saw something I'd never seen before on a pro football field. As expected, a group of Bears lifted Ditka onto their shoulders and carried their head coach off on a victory ride. But just a few feet away, several members of the defense did the same thing for Ryan. That was unheard of: carrying off an *assistant* coach. But that's how much Buddy's players loved and respected him. They also understood this would be a farewell tribute. Within hours, Buddy Ryan became the new head coach of the Philadelphia Eagles.

I was curious to find out what inspired that kind of devotion, and I didn't have to wait long once Buddy arrived in Philly. From the start, he embraced the defensive players, while keeping his distance from us guys on the offense. One of my teammates, six-time Pro Bowl cornerback Eric Allen, explained to me why the defensive players became so loyal to their new coach. In the past, the offense had always been the "glamour" side of the ball, but Buddy made the Eagles' defense the star unit. That summer at training camp, I couldn't help but notice how much emphasis was put on forcing defensive turnovers—then having those guys score off them. Ryan devoted more time and energy to this than any coach I'd seen in all my years in the NFL. He wanted his defense to become the offense. Buddy's defenses in Philadelphia were always aggressive, trying to punch the ball out, gambling on turnovers. I think this mind-set was both Buddy's strength and his ultimate failing. And even though he basically kicked me out of Philadelphia after that one season, I was eventually able to be more objective and appreciate Buddy Ryan's impact on the evolution of defensive football.

Doug Plank, the man who whacked me around as a player, who beat my Arena League team more times than I would have liked, and whose jersey number gave the 46 its name, raised an interesting point when I spoke with him for this book. "If someone like Buddy Ryan hadn't come along—someone who totally disrupted offenses— I wonder if there would have been the wholesale transition to spread offenses we see today," he reflected. "The tightly packed eight man fronts from our day just can't succeed as a base defense against spread formations. Offensive coordinators came to the conclusion fairly quickly that unless they spread defenses out, their quarterbacks were going to get hit again and again. That isn't acceptable today, because more than ever, the NFL is a quarterback's league."

Another change the 46 brought about was how teams drafted. More and more personnel directors now pick receivers specifically to beat press coverage. Cornerbacks who cover wider field areas are also popular draft choices. And offenses have had to put in greater numbers of deception plays, such as quick screens where the quarterback gets the ball out fast to a receiver with linemen blocking in front of him.

As defensive coordinator of the Minnesota Vikings, Leslie Frazier knows that the original version of the 46 simply won't work in the NFL of the twenty-first century. "It was a different time in the 1980s," he explained. "With two-back sets, offenses operated in a more confined space, giving Buddy's players shorter distances to rush, less ground to cover, and greater ability to disguise their blitzes. Other than Don Coryell and the Chargers, offenses didn't go with three or four wide receivers back then. Coaches were afraid that if they spread things out too much, the quarterback wouldn't be protected, and he'd get hit. The 46 can't serve as a base defense today because offenses are spread so far it would be tough for defenses to pressure the same way we did with the Bears. But the 46 can and should still be part of an overall package in today's NFL. There are times during a game when a pure 46 can be devastating."

Former Baltimore Ravens coach and current broadcaster Brian

Billick has identified another significant change. "Defenses can no longer apply so much pressure that put their corners at risk. When people finally caught up with the 46, it was coaches like Jeff Fisher, who took its basics and added wrinkles to keep it effective. Fisher was the first to adapt it to the modern game. He came up with zone concepts that appeared to give the same look as the original 46—but weren't—and that created a new set of problems for offenses."

Plank, Fisher, and Frazier are but three of the branches extending from Buddy Ryan's coaching tree. You can also include current NFL coaches Mike Singletary with the 49ers and Ron Rivera at San Diego. Others with a direct Ryan lineage are his twin sons Rex and Rob, plus Fisher disciples Jim Schwartz in Detroit and Gregg Williams with the Saints.

The late Jim Johnson, Philadelphia's longtime defensive coordinator, also sported a Ryan connection. After Buddy left Chicago to join the Eagles in '86, the Bears selected Vince Tobin as his replacement. Dave McGinnis, who coached the linebackers for Tobin, recalled, "Vince adapted these principles after Buddy was gone and began running the same schemes with zone coverage behind it. He then shared all this stuff with Jim Johnson, because they had played together in college at Missouri and were close friends. You could see Buddy's fingerprints all over what Jim did during his many years as Eagles coordinator."

Having watched the Eagles as much as I have, I'd have to say that Johnson was the closest to Buddy as far as scheme aggressiveness and a gambling style. Jim would always bring one more guy than you could block—and that was risky. Jim was most interested in protection-scheme breakdown and was a true believer in the philosophy of the 46. By contrast, Jeff Fisher, at Tennessee, has dialed down much of the risk that was inherent in Ryan's original defense. In Buddy's scheme, you'd see unsound coverage principles at times, with potential receiving targets wide open, or in favorable one-on-one matchups. With the Titans, Jeff runs similar looks, but you don't always get the same rush patterns after the ball is snapped. Fisher can start with something resembling 46 pressure and then will suddenly switch to a zone defense with people dropping back. It's a more conservative 46, and over the long haul, it's been very successful in Tennessee.

Fisher has since taught his version to Gregg Williams, who's had a terrific track record at many places, including his present position as defensive coordinator for New Orleans. Gregg gives you disguised pressure with the green dog. You'll recall that's when a back or a tight end will initially be accounted for in man coverage. But the minute that one or both of them show that they'll be blocking, Gregg will send his defenders after the quarterback. This tactic surfaced many times in 2009 during the Saints' Super Bowl run.

There are pass coverage components of the original 46 that have become staples in every team's defensive playbook. Most evident is Buddy's "swipe" scheme, when a linebacker or safety can trade assignments in underneath coverage. But not all of Buddy's disciples have embraced other aspects of the 46. As much as I believe Ron Rivera would like to use it, he has to take into account what players he has in San Diego and whether they're best suited to succeed with the 46. At Minnesota, Frazier has never been an advocate of the blitz. In part, that's because he's had the great front four that included Jared Allen and the two Williamses (perennial Pro Bowl tackles Kevin and Pat), but I think there's more to it than that. Leslie has developed his own system and doesn't gamble much in pressure situations. He does, however, tap in heavily to the coverage principles of the 46. Maybe Frazier still remembers what it was like to be that cornerback on an island; the anxiety of being isolated on a receiver and the uncertainty as to whether the pass rush has done its job.

As far as Singletary is concerned, it's simply a matter of available talent. "With my team in San Francisco, we don't quite have all the pieces yet to run the 46, and you have to have those pieces or you can't run it," he said candidly. "The 46 is all about pressure, and if you don't have the right guys at the key positions, it's going to hurt more than help."

Singletary was once asked if the '85 Bears defense is the greatest of all time. "You can come up with comparative stats or the names of the players," Mike replied. "But the best way to tell is to take out the film of any team you want to compare us with: the Steel Curtain, the

Vikings' Purple People Eaters, the 2000 Ravens, Dallas's 'Doomsday Defense.' They're all tremendous. Watch them. Then put Bears film on and don't say a word. Our film will talk to you. What will it say? You'll know when you see it, because the film does not lie."

Rex Ryan agrees: "I was the D-line coach at Baltimore with the 2000 Ravens defense that set league records for fewest points and rushing yardage. The difference between that Ravens team and the '85 Bears was simple. Opponents who played Baltimore thought they had a chance to beat us right up until the game began. Then they'd start playing and realize our speed and size was too much to overcome. Before teams played the Bears, they weren't even *thinking* about winning. They were just hoping to survive—they didn't want to get the crap kicked out of 'em. The '85 Bears had teams beat before they even played."

As a defensive assistant with the Jets in 2009, Doug Plank had an insider's view of the newest schemes from the current generation of Ryan family coaches. "Rex has taken his father's ideas and improved on them," he observed. "He's created more new looks, more opportunities for his defenders to make plays. It's still all about creating confusion in the quarterback's mind, not just hitting people hard. Rex looks for favorable matchups. He'll give players multiple responsibilities on each play, so when he moves people around, he has the capability of making it look like a totally different defense. The number of men he uses up front is constantly changing. He'll get more movement from hybrid players rushing from a variety of different angles. Rex's schemes rely on the *threat* of pressure coming, but that pressure isn't always geared to overpowering the opponent each play."

I think Rex has expanded the scope of the 46 in ways his father could not have envisioned. Rex will take a linebacker from one side of the field and move him to cover a wide receiver—and rotate his down linemen in unconventional ways—with coverage concepts I've never seen before. Rex is vigorously responding to the many new looks he sees from offenses, figuring that he needs to be aggressive in order to stay ahead. In that respect, he's a chip off the old block. Mike Singletary has noticed the resemblance, saying, "It's obvious Rex is carrying on his father's legacy. He's so much like Buddy, it's frightening."

Buddy Ryan and I were hardly the best of friends. He didn't always treat me with respect. I thought his behavior was often unprofessional, and I *still* don't think he has a clue about offensive football. But I know a genius when I see one. Defensively, Buddy was exactly that. And I recognize his influence every Sunday, in every game, with every team. Ryan intuitively understood where pro football was headed, almost before anyone else. At a time when the running game was still king, Buddy could see the future: a future where passing would become the league's dominant offensive weapon. That is the world in which the NFL now exists. Buddy Ryan's 46 defense was a response to that developing trend, and it has had a wide-reaching and permanent impact on the tactics and psychological mind-set of today's NFL defenses.

Dick LeBeau's Zone Blitz

1992 AFC DIVISIONAL PLAYOFF
BUFFALO BILLS vs. PITTSBURGH STEELERS
Three Rivers Stadium, Pittsburgh, Pennsylvania — January 9, 1993

The first decade of the twenty-first century may not have been an especially robust time for America's economy, but it was clearly the best sustained period ever for exciting Super Bowls. You can begin in 2000 with the St. Louis Rams' goal-line stop of the Titans to win Super Bowl XXXIV. There was New England's shocking last-second upset of those same Rams in Super Bowl XXXVI (covered in the next chapter). Follow those up with back-to-back 3-point thrillers by the Patriots over the Carolina Panthers and the Eagles. Then it was Bill Belichick's crew feeling the sting of defeat when its dream of a perfect 19–0 season was shattered by the Giants in Super Bowl XLII.

The Arizona Cardinals–Pittsburgh Steelers classic in Super Bowl XLIII closed out the decade and may have been the best of them all. The signature moment of that game is arguably the greatest defensive play in Super Bowl history: an astonishing effort from linebacker James Harrison. Everything about it speaks to the toughness and mental awareness that has characterized the Steelers defenses coached by Dick LeBeau over the past twenty-five years.

With eighteen seconds remaining in the first half, the Steelers were clinging to a 10–7 lead, but the Cardinals had the ball on Pittsburgh's 1-yard line. There was still time for one more pass, and maybe even two before Arizona would need to kick a field goal. Steelers head coach Mike Tomlin will remember the next play until the day he dies. "With so little time left, the Cardinals couldn't run the risk of running the football, so we dialed up an all-out blitz," he said. "One of our linebackers, Lawrence Timmons, hit a gap at the line of scrimmage and got through there clean. And as he went by, Harrison knew there was a guy responsible for blocking him, so he simply backed out of the blitz and ended up in the throwing lane."

Five years in LeBeau's system had prepared Harrison for this moment. "I figured they had to do a quick slant in or out, and it seemed like we'd been a step late in getting to them all day," he explained. "If I just stepped at the tackle and got him to step out at me, that would free Timmons to get inside on his blitz. I figured that as long as I did my job and didn't hurt anybody else from doing what they were supposed to do, it was worth the gamble."

Arizona quarterback Kurt Warner never saw Harrison. *He was in a place Warner did not expect him to be.* The pass was intended for Cardinals receiver Anquan Boldin, but Harrison grabbed it instead. He took off in the opposite direction, preserving the Steelers lead— and much more. "I was hoping we'd get the ball to midfield for a shot at a field goal," admitted Tomlin. "Under no circumstances did I think James was going to take the thing back a hundred yards!" Harrison's touchdown was more than the longest play of any kind in a Super Bowl. It was a literal reversal of fortune, a defining moment in Pittsburgh's eventual 27–23 win. It helped earn LeBeau and his players their second Super Bowl ring in four years.

While writing this book, I've spent considerable time studying my selected games and the coaches whose innovations made those games so important. And it's clear to me that the common thread binding these coaches is that each one had both the brains and the guts to move in a different direction. Their creations stood in stark contrast to existing and accepted strategies.

In one fundamental way, Dick LeBeau is different from all the others: He is the only one who actually *played* in the NFL. And he was a damn good player. Dick lasted fourteen years as a pro cornerback, which is a remarkable achievement all by itself. He played every one of those years with the Detroit Lions, alongside Hall of Fame defensive backs Dick "Night Train" Lane, Yale Lary, and Lem Barney. He went to three straight Pro Bowls in the mid-1960s and picked off 62 career interceptions. Only three true cornerbacks in league history have more. He also holds the record for consecutive games started by a corner, with 171. It took longer than it should have, but Dick was finally voted into the Pro Football Hall of Fame in 2010.

I never competed against LeBeau when he was a player, because he retired just before my rookie season. But we squared off a number of times when I was at quarterback and he was either an assistant coach or a defensive coordinator. The last time I faced him was in 1989, my seventeenth and final year in the NFL. I was with Kansas City as Steve DeBerg's backup, but when Steve hit a rough patch in the first month, head coach Marty Schottenheimer decided to go with me. Our week-four game against the defending AFC champion Cincinnati Bengals was my first starting assignment in nearly three years, but just before halftime, I had the Chiefs ahead by 10. Even so, we ended up losing, 21–17, and I have to shoulder much of the blame. I threw four interceptions, including three to safety David Fulcher, about whom you'll learn more later. I don't recall many of the details from that game, but I do remember having difficulty making my reads against their defense, and I checked the stats to find that I also got sacked four times. The defensive coach who made my life miserable that day? Dick LeBeau.

You know from my work on *Monday Night Football* and *ESPN NFL Matchup* that I'm a dyed-in-the-wool football wonk. Here's more evidence: I've saved just about every game plan from my pro career, storing them in the basement of my home. As I was researching this book, I wondered if there was any mention of exotic LeBeau blitzes in the Chiefs' '89 week-four Bengals game plan. One night after dinner, I dug through my files to find out. Sure enough, our offensive coordinator, Joe Pendry, had diagrammed progressions for a dozen Cincinnati pressure schemes. Joe's first drawing depicted a blitz out of a nickel package. Another sketch showed a blitz that rushed a nickel back, an inside linebacker, and three of the four down linemen, with a defensive tackle dropping into coverage. Joe also included one blitz with a defensive end standing up behind the nose tackle, who then rushed the pass pocket. The most bizarre Bengals scheme showcased a pre-snap set of three linemen, one linebacker, and seven defensive backs. I don't think any other teams were running stuff like this back then. No wonder my stats were so lousy!

That was more than twenty years ago, and Dick's still at it today. Now in his seventh decade in the NFL, he remains one of the league's most respected coaches. Even as a kid growing up in tiny London, Ohio, LeBeau loved to compete. "I've been a game player all my life," he reflected. "When I was a young man, I'd try to figure out ways to beat pinball machines. In high school, I'd draw up plays for our team to run during PE classes." Dick was good enough to earn a scholarship and play for Woody Hayes at Ohio State, where he made friends with a basketball player named Bobby Knight. "Bobby always had a 'football' mentality, and I think that's the way he coached his basketball teams," said LeBeau. "We both agreed that pressure on the ball is a good thing—don't let the other guy breathe."

It looked as if LeBeau's pro career would continue in his home state after he was drafted by the Cleveland Browns in 1959, but Paul Brown eventually cut him. Ironically, Dick later served nearly two decades under Brown with the Bengals' coaching staff. The Lions claimed LeBeau off waivers, and for the next fourteen years, he was the primary cover guy for Detroit, a team that lived and died by the blitz. "I grew up in a pressure system—the Lions blitzed all the time with man-on-man coverage—and I saw what could happen; how it could dramatically affect the game," he said. Sometimes the results weren't pretty, and his days in Motown left a lasting impression about what could go wrong when a team blitzed too often without giving its secondary a safety net.

At the end of his playing days, Dick considered his options. "I had a background in business and considered becoming an accountant," he said, "because my dad, my cousin, and his son were all account-ants. I've always loved golf and thought I might do something there." Ultimately, LeBeau stayed in football. "I had gleaned quite a few tid-bits by the time I was thirty-five and had studied pretty hard. I felt if I just retired, all that knowledge would be wasted. So it seemed like a good idea to pass some of that on to the players coming after me. That's what got me into coaching. Coaching is just teaching. I think if you talk to any teacher in any line of work, the joy of their profession is to see your people improve, to reach certain goals that you set to-gether."

Dick spent his first seven years in coaching with the Eagles and the Packers before coming to Cincinnati in 1980. "He was always the coolest guy in the room, kind of like 'the Fonz,'" laughed Bengals receiver-turned-broadcaster Cris Collinsworth. "He knew stuff about everything, always looked sharp, and could destroy you on the golf course. He loved everything about football: calisthenics, meetings, watching film. And he genuinely cared about his players, truly wanting their lives outside of football to be great.

"I remember one time in practice these two big linemen got into it—swinging away, hitting each other in the helmet, doing all the stu-pid things you typically see when players in full pads try to duke it out. LeBeau took off, ran and jumped on the back of one of the guys, and started riding around on him, whoopin' and hollerin' like he was in a rodeo or something. It was the perfect way to break up a football fight. We all began laughing so hard—even the two guys who started it were cracking up. We'd never seen Dick do anything like it."

This outburst wouldn't have been such a shock to the players if they'd known about some of LeBeau's outside interests. "I was a stunt man for a while in Hollywood and worked with Robert Aldrich, who'd directed *Whatever Happened to Baby Jane?* and *The Dirty Dozen*," he explained. "Aldrich was a quite a football fan and was looking for doubles who could run a lot without getting tired. It was for a picture he was making in the tropics called *Too Late the Hero*."

Never let it be said that LeBeau doesn't have a little ham in him. He desperately wanted a few lines in the picture, but Aldrich explained that there was only one American character in the film. If Dick wanted a speaking part, he'd need to acquire an English accent—fast. So LeBeau sought out the cast member for whom he was stunt doubling: British actor Michael Caine. "We were playing pool after finishing the day's shoot, and I begged him for help. 'Michael, you've gotta teach me an English accent so I can get on camera. I want my buddies to see me on screen.' Michael replied, 'Oh, there's nothing to it. We'll do a little Cockney.' So we practiced that whole night while playing pool. The next day, I see Bob Aldrich and tell him, 'I think I can do it.' Bob told me to recite the line, and it was something like, 'There's a light out on the billiard table.' Aldrich wasn't impressed. 'You sound like a hillbilly trying to do a Cockney accent. Get the hell out of here.' That was pretty much the end of my acting career."

Well, not quite. With the Bengals, he gave two different pep talks, one dressed up as Superman and one dressed as Elvis Presley. "It was only at minicamp, so it was a more relaxed atmosphere, and I was trying to make a point—Super-*man*, Super *Bowl*—you get the idea. I guess I had this thing for capes. I was going to try Batman next." And it's a tradition every holiday season for all the defensive players to assemble for LeBeau's command performance of *The Night Before Christmas*.

LeBeau has many other talents. He can repair wristwatches, play guitar, and has a photographic memory. Dick can recite verbatim all the dialogue from his favorite film, *The Wizard of Oz*. "That movie was made at the same time Technicolor was coming in," LeBeau noted. "The picture begins in black and white, but when Dorothy goes 'over the rainbow' and her house falls in Munchkin Land, she steps outside, and suddenly she's in this beautiful color. Right there you're seeing the evolution of Hollywood technology. It's a great moment."

A similar moment occurred in Dick LeBeau's life when he first developed what I believe is the most important and long-lasting defensive concept the NFL has seen in the past two decades: the Zone blitz. And I'm in good company because Patriots coach Bill Belichick feels the same way: "To me, LeBeau's place in history is secure as creator of the Zone blitz. The fact that he not only created it but hasn't really ever had to modify it is incredible. I can't find anything else in football to compare it with."

In its simplest terms, the Zone blitz is a flexible defensive set designed to bewilder quarterbacks and their blockers. Its main premise is to create doubt for the offense in identifying who's rushing and who's in coverage. It's executed by trading off the conventional rush and coverage responsibilities of the defense. On any play, there is the potential for one defender to swap his role with another. This is often called "personnel exchange," and here's how it works: When the ball is snapped, designated defensive linemen can drop into coverage instead of rushing the passer, while selected linebackers or defensive backs switch from their traditional coverage responsibilities to apply pocket pressure. The hoped-for result is mass confusion for the offensive linemen.

Ultimately, the main goal is to impact the quarterback's progressions and delay what he's reading across the line. Obviously, defenses can vary who they send and drop off on every snap. A nose tackle could rush on one play, then slip into coverage on the next. Safeties can blitz two times in a row and then play a deep zone. The combinations are limitless, making it extremely tough for offenses to sort through all the possibilities as to who is rushing and who is covering. Just think about it: If defensive linemen are dropping into coverage, then it's a sure thing they're not going to be playing man-to-man. They can't. Those guys are simply too big and slow to stay with NFL-caliber receivers. So the coverage of this defense *must* be zone based. In the mid- to late 1980s, this was a real departure from the prevailing pressure concepts of that era.

Elements of the Zone blitz have been around for a long time. It's difficult to find examples from coaching film dating back to the 1930s and 1940s, but I'd imagine that college and pro teams through the years have tried variations of this concept. I do know that while breaking down game film of the Patriots-Chargers '63 AFL Championship, I was startled to find two distinct instances featuring zone blitz principles. On one play, Boston blitzed two linebackers while defensive end Larry Eisenhauer stood up to play the pass. Later in the game, the Patriots red-dogged two inside linebackers while *both* of their defensive ends initially faked the rush, then dropped into coverage. I shouldn't have been surprised, though, because as a Buffalo season ticket holder in the 1960s, I frequently saw something similar with the Bills defense. Their defensive coordinator, Joe Collier, was far ahead of his time. "We dropped off either of our defensive ends, Ron McDole or Tom Day, because both were agile enough to cover a clearly defined area," he recalled. "Day was about two hundred sixty pounds, but had terrific foot speed. What amazed our coaching staff was that we could also ask this of McDole. He was over three hundred pounds—the biggest lineman in the AFL—and his mobility in pass coverage was where he got his nickname, 'the Dancing Bear.'"

Base Zone Blitz

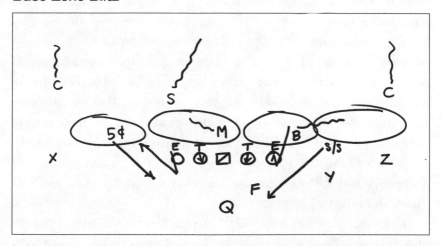

In this particular package, Pittsburgh's interior defensive tackles rush normally, but both defensive ends drop into coverage after making an initial step to the passer. The pressure instead comes from a nickel back on the left and the strong safety from the right. Meanwhile the free safety drops into coverage to provide help for the corners who are playing in man coverage. The middle linebacker also drops, but since the strong side safety blitzes, the left defensive end has coverage responsibility.

Al Saunders told me of another early example, this one from college ball. In 1970 the University of Tennessee promoted twenty-eight-year-old assistant Bill Battle, making him the youngest head coach in the country. "Battle would have his nose guard drop off and cover like a linebacker," said Saunders. "He'd also drop off his more athletic defensive ends on third-and-long." And then there was Bill Arnsparger, the genius of Miami's defenses during the seventies and eighties. Dolphins head coach Don Shula was thrilled when "Bill came up with the 53 defense, something truly revolutionary at the time. We had this guy Bob Matheson, number 53, who was a very bright and unique talent with the ability to rush the passer as a lineman or linebacker. Arnsparger figured out ways to have him do both by plugging him into a lot of different spots. When Bob got in the game, this rotation turned our 4-3 set into a 3-4 defense."

Arnsparger went almost exclusively to the 3-4 by the midseventies, after most of his best players from the Super Bowl No-Name Defense retired. The Dolphins drafted to that scheme by selecting hybrids such as A. J. Duhe and Kim Bokamper, athletes who could excel at a number of defensive positions. Duhe quickly learned the contrasts between the old 53 and Arnsparger's new approaches. "The 53 wasn't a Zone blitz, it was a conventional 3-4," he explained. "In a 53, the offense had a pretty good idea who was going to be rushing. So now Bill's got interchangeable parts like Bokamper and myself, and the wheels start turning. Let's put some doubt in the quarterback's mind. Bill begins by rotating *who* would blitz on a given play. The offense had to worry about as many as six or seven rushing, but we didn't always come with that number. They end up with not enough receivers out in the pass pattern, which causes hesitation—and the play breaks down. I loved this concept because it gave us an edge and more confidence. We had something the other guys didn't. Our toy bag was deeper than theirs."

Dolphins defenders also had to be smart, with an aptitude for adjusting prior to and after the snap. One of the brightest was safety Glenn Blackwood. "Bill gave me the responsibility that when I saw a formation or setup, I could switch blitzing responsibility with the Sam [strong-side] linebacker, who was originally supposed to rush," he noted. "He could then occupy the tight end so that when I blitzed, that tight end had no way to break through—and that created more pressure in the pocket by having me rush. O-linemen weren't prepared to block me because they weren't expecting a safety to be coming in. There were plays where I just blew in scot-free."

Blackwood remembered what took place when Arnsparger moved Bokamper to end and put Duhe at linebacker: "After the snap, Bokamper would take one step toward the tackle, occupy him, then back up into the inside zone. We'd roll the weak safety to that side, the strong safety then goes deep middle. To the quarterback, it feels like there's a five-man rush after him. When we ran this, there were a lot of times where the outside linebacker came in untouched. The offensive tackle is focusing on Bokamper, the guy he's *supposed* to block. But then Kim backs away, and the tackle is just standing there, watching as other people are sacking his quarterback! To me, this was the real beginning of the Zone blitz."

LeBeau had always admired Arnsparger's work. After being promoted to Bengals defensive coordinator, Dick traveled down south to pick his brain. "Arnsparger took a concept that reacted to basic protection schemes of the time and found a good way of attacking them," LeBeau recalled. "He'd blitz three people at the start, but really ended up rushing just two of the three. This was Bill's innovation, and he was the first guy I ever saw do it. The light really went on when he said to me, 'I was just looking for a *safer* way to pressure.' And that's when I started looking for my own ways to do that." In LeBeau's lexicon, "safer" meant fewer rushers and more defenders in coverage. The brilliance of the whole concept was creating ways to break down pass protections and pressure the passer with a lot fewer guys crashing the pass pocket. Sam Rutigliano probably put it best: "If Dick LeBeau is the father of the Zone blitz, then Bill Arnsparger is its *grandfather*."

The original Zone blitz concepts stemmed primarily from a 3-4 alignment, and at the time that LeBeau was formulating his ideas in Cincinnati, it was the NFL's most widely used defensive front. The Bengals had switched to the 3-4 in 1980 when Hank Bullough was defensive coordinator, and a year later, that system helped get Cincinnati to Super Bowl XVI. But in those days, the Dolphins and the Broncos were regarded as the most consistently successful AFC teams playing in the 3-4 system. Joe Collier spent two decades running Denver's defense and was its major advocate. In his opinion, "The 3-4 offers you more variety in schemes than a 4-3. You can shift into different fronts and stunt in different ways because you have more people off the line of scrimmage. I'll bet we had more than fifty front variations with the Broncos, which you would never have in a 4-3. It made it much harder for offenses to prepare for us. I'd hear from opposing coaches all the time, bitching to me about how late they had to stay up trying to get their teams ready for the Broncos." Arnsparger was causing similar headaches with his defenses in Miami. Now LeBeau wanted to expand on these principles in Cincinnati.

On a flight home, Dick began doodling like crazy on airline cocktail napkins, scribbling down every exotic blitz scheme that came to mind. The brainstorms were brewing faster than he could write. Fortunately Sam Wyche, Cincinnati's new head coach, was receptive to fresh ideas, no matter how bizarre they might have seemed at first. You may remember that Wyche was the first one to run the "No-Huddle" offense back in the mid-eighties. "I was one of those guys whose theory was: The more things you did outside the box, the better your chances of getting an edge on your opponent. When Dick first brought the basics of the Zone blitz to my attention, I wanted to hear them."

Even so, Sam wasn't sold on all of LeBeau's suggestions, at least not right away. "I can remember our initial discussions taking place in the hallway at Spinney Field, where we practiced. We were debating the merits of Dick's scheme in a confined area next to a secretary's desk. We started arguing in this cramped space, literally leaning over her workspace while she was typing, and it got pretty heated. I finally said, 'Let's take this conversation outside right now.' You have to remember that Spinney Field was located in the bowels of Cincinnati. It was right next to a garbage can manufacturer along the Mill Creek—which, by the way, was a polluted creek where we drew the water to hose down our practice field." It was in this glamorous setting that LeBeau's Zone blitz was born.

After another year of continuous discussion and planning, LeBeau had his new system drawn up and ready to present to the

I played ten of my seventeen pro
seasons with the Eagles, and set an
NFL record for consecutive starts by a
quarterback (116 games). That mark
has since been shattered by both
Brett Favre and Peyton Manning.
COURTESY OF THE PHILADELPHIA EAGLES

Dick Vermeil is unquestionably
the most influential person in
my playing career. He taught me
how to compete and how to lead.
I just wish I could have won a Super
Bowl for him in 1980. No one was
happier than I when Dick finally did
take home a Lombardi Trophy with
the Rams in Super Bowl XXXIV.
COURTESY OF THE PHILADELPHIA EAGLES

During one stretch in the 1970s and
'80s, the Eagles beat the Giants twelve
straight times. That streak ended the
year #56 Lawrence Taylor came to
New York. L.T. loved playing against
us; he sacked me more than any other
quarterback he ever played against.
COURTESY OF THE PHILADELPHIA EAGLES

Keith Lincoln takes the
handoff on the second play
of the '63 AFL title game
and explodes for 56 yards
against the Patriots.
Although he began the
afternoon with flu-like
symptoms, Keith set a pro
record with 329 yards in
total offense.
*COURTESY OF THE SAN DIEGO
CHARGERS ARCHIVES*

Chargers offensive tackle Ron Mix was nicknamed "The IntellectualAssassin." For a bright guy he was also plenty tough—the first AFL offensive lineman to be enshrined in the Pro Football Hall of Fame. On Paul Lowe's touchdown run in the '63 title game, Ron blocked one of Boston's defenders twice. *COURTESY OF THE SAN DIEGO CHARGERS ARCHIVES*

Future Hall of Fame receiver Lance Alworth leaps over Boston's Bob Suci in the third quarter. Forty-eight yards later Lance was in the end zone to put the Chargers ahead by four touchdowns. San Diego's 51–10 victory was the most lopsided blowout of any championship game in the AFL's ten-year history. *COURTESY OF THE SAN DIEGO CHARGERS ARCHIVES*

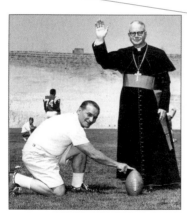

Bud Carson going over defensive sets with rookie middle linebacker Jack Lambert, whose amazing mobility allowed the Cover Two scheme to flourish. "Everything changed for Bud with the arrival of Jack Lambert," claimed Steelers safety Mike Wagner. "He was the salvation, the messiah." *COURTESY OF THE PITTSBURGH STEELERS*

Sid Gillman could be a tough SOB at times, but he also had a terrific sense of humor. Sid was a showman at heart and enjoyed posing for gag photos like this. He was also a football genius. Having him as my position coach with the Eagles in 1979 and '80 was like being a physics student tutored by Albert Einstein. *COURTESY OF SAN DIEGO CHARGERS ARCHIVES*

Ernie "Fats" Holmes sporting his trademark "arrowhead" haircut. Against the Raiders in the '74 AFC Championship Ernie played the best game of his career, continually overpowering future Hall of Fame guard Gene Upshaw. Holmes and the Steel Curtain held Oakland running backs to only 29 rushing yards. *COURTESY OF THE PITTSBURGH STEELERS*

Mel Blount is the Steelers all-time interception leader and a member of the Pro Football Hall of Fame, but was constantly victimized by Raiders receivers in the '74 AFC championship. By the fourth quarter Bud Carson was forced to bench him, but Mel recovered two weeks later with a brilliant performance against the Vikings in Super Bowl IX.
COURTESY OF THE PITTSBURGH STEELERS

Jack Lambert gets ready to lower the boom on Raiders quarterback Kenny Stabler, with L.C. Greenwood also in pursuit. Pittsburgh's Steel Curtain rush kept constant pressure on Stabler throughout the '74 title game, and even though "The Snake" put up respectable passing yardage he got the Raiders into the end zone only once.
COURTESY OF THE PITTSBURGH STEELERS

Dan Fouts was the perfect triggerman for Air Coryell, but he'd be the first to tell you it was only possible because of fantastic protection from his offensive line: Billy Shields #66, Doug Wilkerson #63, Don Macek #62, Ed White #67, and Russ Washington #70. After every win Dan dropped a ton of loot treating his linemen to elaborate steak dinners.
COURTESY OF THE SAN DIEGO CHARGERS ARCHIVES

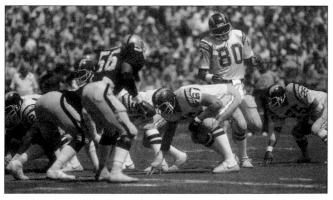

The Week Two game against the Raiders in 1980 was Kellen Winslow's "coming out party." For the first time, Don Coryell and his coaches put Winslow in motion all over the field prior to the snap, causing mismatches and confusion for Oakland defenders.
COURTESY OF THE SAN DIEGO CHARGERS ARCHIVES

No San Diego receiver ran his routes more precisely than Charlie Joiner. Charlie flourished in the Air Coryell system longer than any other Charger, and when he retired at the end of his 18-year career, Joiner was the NFL's all-time leader in pass receptions. *COURTESY OF THE SAN DIEGO CHARGERS ARCHIVES*

John Jefferson's leaping one-handed catch in the first half gave the Chargers their first touchdown of the game. It came against Oakland's Lester Hayes, the NFL's best cornerback at that time. JJ would eventually score the winning touchdown in overtime—and Hayes would be the victim on that score as well. *COURTESY OF THE SAN DIEGO CHARGERS ARCHIVES*

Winslow carved up the Raiders for 9 catches, 132 yards and a touchdown. Kellen was simply too quick for linebackers to cover and too strong for defensive backs to drag down without a fight. *COURTESY OF THE SAN DIEGO CHARGERS ARCHIVES*

Bill Walsh's pregame speeches were never "rah-rah" pep talks. They were pointed, analytical messages that reinforced the week's work at practice. In his matter-of-fact delivery, the man known as "The Genius" emphasized the strategies that would coolly and precisely carve an opponent up into little pieces. *PHOTO BY MICHAEL ZAGARIS*

The 49ers guard tandem of John
Ayers #68 and Randy Cross #51
just before taking the field against the
Giants in the 1981 Divisional playoff
game. Their success against New
York's pass rush played a critical part
in earning Bill Walsh his first postseason victory as an NFL head coach.
PHOTO BY MICHAEL ZAGARIS

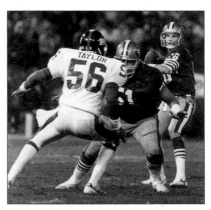

Randy Cross hunkering down to
keep the hard-charging Lawrence
Taylor from getting his mitts on
49ers quarterback Joe Montana.
San Francisco's entire line took
turns keeping L.T. from wreaking
havoc in the '81 playoffs. The NFL
defensive rookie of the year never
was a factor, as the Niners overwhelmed the Giants 38–24.
PHOTO BY MICHAEL ZAGARIS

One of my favorite football photographs—
a "meeting of the minds" between quarterback
legend Joe Montana and Bill Walsh, master of
the West Coast offense—beneath the burning
light towers of Candlestick Park. To me it
looks almost surreal—like a scene from a
Hollywood movie. *PHOTO BY MICHAEL ZAGARIS*

Safety Doug Plank hit people like a ton of bricks, making tackles his opponents wouldn't easily forget. But Doug's true claim to fame is his jersey number—the number that gave Buddy Ryan's devastating 46 Defense its name.
COURTESY OF THE CHICAGO BEARS

For the 46 Defense to perform at its peak, Buddy Ryan needed a "coach on the field"—a middle line-backer bright enough to make strategic changes split seconds before the snap. These adjustments would put the other defenders in the best position to shut down the play. With eventual Hall of Famer Mike Singletary #50, Buddy had the perfect guy for the job.
COURTESY OF THE CHICAGO BEARS

Dan Hampton #99 and Wilber Marshall #58 were just two of the Bears defenders who made life miserable for the Cowboys in their 1985 regular-season shellacking of Dallas. The 44–0 rout marked the first time Tom Landry's team had been shut out in 25 years.
COURTESY OF THE CHICAGO BEARS

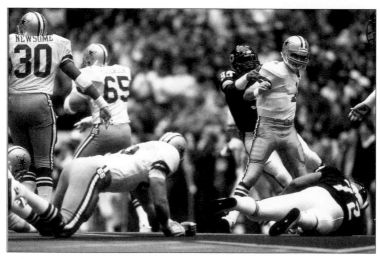

Richard Dent #95 and William "Refrigerator" Perry #72 have Dallas quarterback Danny White covered from head to toe, with one of the six sacks rung up by Chicago in its '85 massacre of the Cowboys. Poor Danny got knocked out of the game twice, and later admitted the Bears were unstoppable that day. "You're always looking to find a solution and we never did find it. We didn't have a clue."
COURTESY OF THE CHICAGO BEARS

Dick LeBeau going over Zone blitz variations with defensive team leaders Greg Lloyd #95, Rod Woodson #26, and Carnell Lake #37. For LeBeau, the basics of the Zone blitz could be boiled down to one question: How can we put pressure on the quarterback yet still remain fundamentally sound against the pass? *PHOTO COPYRIGHT © GETTY IMAGES / ALLEN KEE*

Don't let those flowing blond locks fool you. Kevin Greene was a lethal component of LeBeau's Zone blitz. Kevin was equally skilled either rushing the passer or dropping into coverage, although Greene clearly preferred knocking the quarterback on his butt. He half-kiddingly complained to Dick, "Hey man, you're dropping me too much, come on!" *PHOTO COPYRIGHT © GETTY IMAGES / JOSEPH PATRONITE*

Rod Woodson played for seventeen seasons with four different teams in his Hall of Fame career. He ranks third in all-time interceptions (71) and holds the league record for most interceptions returned for touchdowns (12). And it all developed in Pittsburgh under the coaching of Dick LeBeau. "Dick helped me understand the angles of the game. I don't know how I would have played later on in my career without his knowledge." *PHOTO COPYRIGHT © GETTY IMAGES / AL MESSERSCHMIDT*

Carnell Lake zeroes in on Bills running back Thurman Thomas. Lake's surprising speed and keen intelligence allowed him to attack Buffalo's offense from a variety of launch points, reducing Marv Levy's K-Gun attack to a pop gun. Lake believed in LeBeau's system because, "Dick thinks about his defenses from the secondary's point of view. He knows how crucial their role is because he played there himself." *PHOTO COPYRIGHT © GETTY IMAGES / JOSEPH PATRONITE*

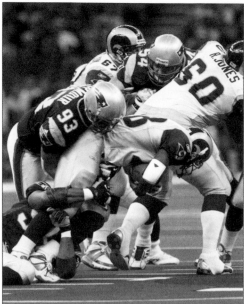

Richard Seymour putting the clamps on the Rams' Marshall Faulk—the very essence of New England's "Bull's-eye" strategy. Bill Belichick believed it was Faulk, not quarterback Kurt Warner who was the crucial player in the St. Louis offense. If Faulk could be neutralized, then their entire offense could be controlled. It was all part of what I believe was the most creative game plan I've ever seen in the NFL. *COURTESY OF THE NEW ENGLAND PATRIOTS*

Ty Law's second quarter interception turned Super Bowl XXXVI on its head. His return for a touchdown gave New England a lead it would keep for most of the game, and sent a message to anyone watching that the underdog Patriots were going to give the mighty Rams all they could handle. *COURTESY OF THE NEW ENGLAND PATRIOTS*

Mike Vrabel was the quintessential Bill Belichick defender: tough, smart, versatile and hungry. After evaluating his performance in film study, I had to admit that for a guy who had no sacks, no interceptions, and was in on only four tackles, Vrabel played as good a game as you'll ever see in a Super Bowl. What Mike accomplished away from the football was instrumental to the Patriots' upset win. *COURTESY OF THE NEW ENGLAND PATRIOTS*

Willie McGinest celebrates after dropping Kurt Warner for a loss of sixteen yards late in the fourth quarter of Super Bowl XXXVI. Trailing by only a touchdown, the Rams mounted a drive well into New England territory, but McGinest's sack ultimately forced St. Louis to punt. *COURTESY OF THE NEW ENGLAND PATRIOTS*

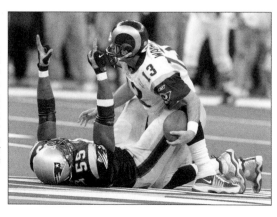

team. "These concepts were hard," said Wyche. "You were asking players to do things at their position they'd never done before." But after more than a decade as an NFL assistant, LeBeau had finally gotten a coordinator's job, and he didn't want to blow his chance. "I will always be grateful to Sam for what he did," he said. "I came to him with these ideas, and a lot of other people would have shown me the door. I don't think there were many coaches who would have agreed to devote significant practice time to prepare our defense in this new style of attack. We took some wrong turns and had some pretty ugly-looking defenses sometimes. But it was all part of the process to try and decide how far off the diving board we could go."

Cris Collinsworth watched the scheme develop from the beginning. "We were dumb, young ballplayers back then and didn't really know what was going on; kind of wrapped up in just what we were doing," he said. "At practices we'd watch defensive linemen dropping into coverage but were too clueless to understand what we were seeing was so revolutionary. Three-hundred-pound guys don't go backward very well to begin with!"

As I've already mentioned, innovations come about as a reaction to what people on the other side of the ball are trying. The creative timing and rhythm-based pass offenses of Don Coryell and Bill Walsh mandated a response from thinkers like Dick LeBeau. "We had to do something," said Dick. "They changed the pass protection rules to help offensive linemen. And they moved the hash marks into the middle of the field. That meant the sideline was now a long way away, opening the passing game even more. I've always said that the sideline is a defender's best friend—it's never missed a tackle yet. That 'friend' wasn't there much to help my people anymore."

With so many of the game's elements tilted in the offense's favor, LeBeau believed that his best chance to stop opponents lay in emphasizing deception. Since defenses weren't rushing more than the offense could block, LeBeau had to create the *illusion* of pressure. He wanted to force offensive linemen and quarterbacks to react to things that weren't actually going to happen. "With the old pressures, quarterbacks kind of knew where to go with the ball," Dick explained. "As soon as a defense would show one particular guy rushing, a receiver would break off his route accordingly, and the quarterback would get the ball out to him. So I'm thinking it would be nice to trap the quarterback and make him think a certain kind of pressure is coming *early* in the down. Then as things progress *later* in the down, we actually have an entirely different look. We want to trick them with a guy they're not figuring on coming, or somebody who shows up in a place you'd never expect him to be. That's the concept in a nutshell: You hold them by the nose, then sneak around and kick them in the tail— just like General Patton used to say."

Back in the eighties, Cincy's Zone blitz was mostly a third-and-long package. Unlike Buddy Ryan's 46 alignment, which brought more rushers than the offense could block, the Zone blitz rarely sent more than five people after the quarterback. Because of the *perceived* pressure, quarterbacks were taken out of their rhythm and hurried their passes. NFL Network analyst Solomon Wilcots, who played four years in LeBeau's system in the Bengals' secondary, can explain it as well as anyone. According to him, "LeBeau's concepts are much more effective in the 3-4. The fewer linemen you have, the more you can create the illusion of pressure. It's the defense's version of a Rubik's Cube, trying to make quarterbacks figure out what they're seeing. And they haven't got all day!"

Remember when I mentioned earlier how Sid Gillman asked a college math professor to help him apply geometry to determine where his receivers needed to be in San Diego's pass offense? Dick LeBeau is so intelligent that he calculated his defenders' angles all by himself! "It just dawned on me that there's a geometric concept to football," he explained. "The game is played on a rectangle, and within that rectangle, the offensive players fit into multiple levels that force opponents to defend the whole field. Offenses were literally creating squares and triangles with their routes. I thought it might be a good idea to match those shapes with squares and triangles of my own. I wanted to put my people in areas where the offense was sending its players."

That produced the second component that made LeBeau's strategy so brilliant: the aggressiveness of its coverage. The Bengals, and later the Steelers, didn't just sit back passively, as in traditional zones. Theirs was a proactive matchup zone incorporating man-to-man concepts. It was tailor-made to compete against an offense's combination routes. You'll recall those from Air Coryell: routes determined by both the location and distribution of receivers; how many receivers are aligned on each side of the formation; and whether they're wideouts, tight ends, or running backs.

Wilcots was able to grasp the LeBeau system and its complexities partly because of what he had learned years before from *my* mentor, Sid Gillman. "When I was in high school, I went to one of Sid's football camps in San Diego," Wilcots recalled. "He let us sit in during night sessions he held with people like Brian Billick and John Fox. And all Sid would talk about was combination routes and how they stretched zone defenses.

"Combination routes are the backbone to every passing scheme, then and now," he continued. "It depended on the combination read and where you were in coverage. That's what Dick was referring to when he talked about 'triangles.' You've got three people working: the safety, the outside corner, and the inside linebacker, or nickel back. The nickel or even the dime backs become more like linebackers. The points of LeBeau's 'triangle' are based on those three players."

LeBeau didn't school his players to defend specific areas. They did cover a receiver coming into their space, but they had to know which one it was before it happened. And they needed to know what route was coming, then try to break it up. As the defender moved to the ball, he had to take what LeBeau called the "intercept angle." Everything with Dick is mathematical in nature. The proper angles allow leverage on the route so that the defender is in the best position to make the play.

"That's what makes players love this defense so much," said Wilcots. "We'd come in Tuesday morning and ask, 'Hey, Coach, what have you got for us this week?' We couldn't wait to hear, because we knew we were going to get sacks, picks, and turnovers with his scheme. And the truly fun part of the defense is underneath, because that's the spot in the defense a quarterback can't read. He can read the deep safety, who'll provide a clue about single or double coverage. But the quarterback can't pre-read the underneath coverage. That's where the illusion takes place. When a quarterback is intercepted, it's to people he can't see; people whose locations he can't determine."

It was here where LeBeau was especially unpredictable. Dick has always believed that you had to have one wild card in your defense—one guy who acts purely on his own instincts. This makes the Zone blitz even harder to contain, because the improvising player can pop up anywhere at anytime. In Cincinnati, it was David Fulcher, the 240-pound safety who killed me with those three picks in the '89 Chiefs-Bengals game. He was violating the tendencies of LeBeau's defense, which is exactly what Dick wanted from him. Fulcher's massive size kept him from being a top cover guy, but that same bulk was a real asset when he played near the line of scrimmage as a run stopper or blitzer. And that flexibility allowed LeBeau to blitz other players from odd angles or to crowd the middle against quick slants and hook patterns.

Sam Wyche was especially appreciative of LeBeau's schemes in 1988 when the Bengals made it to the Super Bowl. "The Zone blitz was what won the game that gave us home field advantage," he said. "We were playing in the final week of the regular season against the defending world champion Redskins. Our blitzes were a problem for them all day. The score was tied at the end of regulation, and in overtime we won it because Dick called the right play at the right time."

The call was a blitz up the middle from defensive back Barney Bussey, nicknamed the "little backer" by LeBeau because he was so tough inside the box. "Bussey was a helluva hitter; a safety as talented as our starters," said Wilcots. "Because of Barney, Dick was able to make that call. The Redskins never saw it coming, and Barney forced their quarterback Doug Williams to fumble. We recovered, kicked the winning field goal, and secured home field for the playoffs."

Rushers breaking through faster disrupted the timing so critical to Coryell- or Walsh-influenced offenses. And for Cincinnati, the Zone blitz's finest moment came in Super Bowl XXIII. Through three quarters, the Bengals had held Bill Walsh's powerful 49ers offense to a pair of field goals and still led 16–13 in the final minutes. "Up till then, we'd played pretty aggressively against them," Wyche bragged. "The main reason we were ahead late in that game was LeBeau's defense. The one thing I think we could have done differently was not go to the prevent defense so much on the last drive."

Wilcots shakes his head when he thinks about how close the Bengals came to winning a world championship. "We were kicking their ass," he said. "They couldn't run on us, couldn't throw. And on that final drive, we had them in a second-and-twenty. This was the pivotal play of the game. We had Jerry Rice doubled from the outside corner, with the safety rotating down. If we'd played it right, we would have had a pick. But after the snap, Ray Horton collided with Fulcher and Eric Thomas. Three Bengals got tangled up. Rice makes the catch and goes streaking down the field for twenty-seven yards. At that point, I knew we weren't going to win. And what hurts most is that LeBeau called the perfect play! We had them right where we wanted them! Dick's call was on the money; we should have picked it off and maybe even run it in for a score. Instead John Taylor catches the winning touchdown pass two plays later. If we'd just done what we were supposed to do, I'd have a Super Bowl ring on my finger right now."

The Bengals won another division title in 1990, but after a disastrous 3-13 season in '91, Wyche and his staff were fired, including LeBeau. Dick didn't have to wait long for a job offer, though. After more than twenty years in Pittsburgh, Hall of Fame coach Chuck Noll was retiring, and successor Bill Cowher needed a new secondary coach. Dick soon joined a defensive staff that included future head coaches Dom Capers (Carolina Panthers, Houston Texans) and Marvin Lewis (Cincinnati Bengals).

LeBeau could not have teamed up with a more like-minded group of coaching colleagues. At one time, Cowher had been Cleveland's defensive-backs coach, and Capers had served in the same capacity for New Orleans. Cowher trusted his assistants to put the unit together while he acclimated himself to head coaching responsibilities. "I probably wasn't as involved in the off-season with the defense, trying to keep my hand in everything else, so I left matters to Dom, Dick, Marvin, and the others," he said. "I could do this because of the stability of our staff."

Cowher's coaches inherited a defensive squad receptive to their new ideas. "Before LeBeau and Capers got to Pittsburgh, we'd run a fairly complicated defense ourselves with Rod Rust as coordinator," said Hall of Fame cornerback Rod Woodson. "Rust had a matchup zone where you really had to understand football and change on the fly in game situations. We had the same responsibilities with the Zone blitz. What Rod did for us was give us a baseline for how to think on our feet. So when LeBeau introduced this new defense to us in mini-camp, we said to ourselves, 'We can handle this,' because of what Rod Rust had already taught us. Even though these concepts were Dick's ideas, he understood his role within Dom Capers's defense. Dom was the coordinator. Dick deferred to him on all decisions, and whenever anything new was put in, it was Dom who installed them."

Capers had been tinkering with various blitz packages, going all the way back to 1984 when he was defensive coordinator for the Philadelphia Stars in the now-defunct United States Football League, which played three seasons (1983 through 1985) before folding. "I then took these ideas with me when I went to New Orleans, because we had the best defense in the USFL," he stated. "In '91 the Saints had the top-ranked defensive unit in the NFL, so I knew it could work anywhere. Dick had been doing his thing in Cincinnati, so when we came to-gether with Pittsburgh in '92, we combined our ideas. We both were steeped in the 3-4, so that made it easier. Linebackers are just more flexible than linemen. They're more used to dropping into coverage. It really is the best defense for these types of pressure schemes."

LeBeau quickly bonded with his defensive backs, and it's easy to see why. He was one of them; a kindred spirit. "Dick thinks about his defenses from the secondary's point of view," noted safety Carnell Lake. "He knows how crucial their role is because he played there himself. I think that's why defensive backs relate to him. A lot of co-ordinators coach defense by building their foundation on the defensive line first. But I always felt LeBeau made sure he had the secondary's re-sponsibilities in place, then would work his way to the front."

Dick was well aware of the heightened stress and strain put on all defensive backs. "Secondary positions carry added responsibility," he maintained. "If a lineman gets trapped or makes a false step, he's still got linebackers or DBs who can atone for his error with a good tackle.

If a linebacker misreads a play, the ballcarrier can find the gap and break one, but there's still a secondary guy behind him to make a saving tackle. But if a defensive back falls down or goes the wrong way, there's no one behind him to bail him out. The ramifications of the secondary's mistake is always greater."

I've known Bill Cowher a long time. He and I were teammates with the Eagles in the early eighties. He had his own beliefs, his own system, and for him to put complete trust in new coaches with their unconventional methods was a gutsy move. "You talk about Bill Cowher, who was a real good defensive coach in his own right," remarked Bill Belichick. "He basically turned that defense over to LeBeau and bought into Dick's system. And that's hard for a defensive coach to do, but it's also hard to argue with what they've done with it since."

Cowher's decision was made easier because he saw how quickly Dick built rapport with his players. Retired running back Merril Hoge, my longtime partner on the *ESPN NFL Matchup* show, was with LeBeau for two seasons in Pittsburgh. "I never saw him belittle anyone," he said fondly. "He treated everyone with respect, even when mistakes were made, so guys would never want to let him down. That would be like letting down your own parents."

Dick's fatherly approach earned him the nickname "Coach Dad," but in 1992 he must have been a concerned parent when it came to Pittsburgh's defensive inconsistency. "We didn't have anybody on our line who could create real pressure on the quarterback," admitted Hoge. "It had to be done schematically. Dom, Marvin, and Dick all agreed something needed to be done, so Dick showed them how he could overload against one side of the offense by bringing more guys. In desperate moments, you often react and do stupid things. But sometimes you come up with something that changes the game, the way the Zone blitz did. It also comes down to whether you have the personnel who can intellectually handle the scheme. Our guys could do it."

"Dick taught his X's and O's in a way players could really understand," said Lake. "He took something that, from the outside looking in, might have appeared complicated. But he made it so simple for the players that they bought into it wholeheartedly. It just made sense, and there wasn't a lot of confusion when the plays were called. Everybody knew what they were supposed to do."

Lake is currently an assistant coach at UCLA, his alma mater, and he sounds like one when asked to explain why the '92 Steelers' new scheme caused opponents headaches: "The Zone blitz stretched the range where offensive linemen had to block. Instead of just focusing on the front four and linebackers where they could make adjustments fairly easily, now they had to look sideline to sideline when it came to potential blitzers. Before the Zone blitz, teams could bring out four wides and multiple routes, because they assumed the defense would have to spend extra manpower covering those receivers. They figured they could protect pretty well under those conditions. But with nickel and dime DBs as possible blitzers, that forced offenses to eliminate the four-receiver package. They had to put the tight end in the game and keep a back in to help block. Now they only had three receivers running routes, and the advantage flipped to the defense."

A system is only as good as the athletes who play in it, and in Pittsburgh LeBeau inherited a huge talent upgrade from what he'd had in Cincinnati. Solomon Wilcots came over to the Steelers that first season to help Dick break in the Zone blitz. "We had a lot of good people in the Bengals secondary," he said, "but our line and linebackers—except for nose tackle Tim Krumrie—were solid but not great players. The Steelers had, and would soon be getting, a lot of stars to plug into Dick's system. You start with [Greg] Lloyd, Woodson, and Lake. Once they added people like Chad Brown, Kevin Greene, and Levon Kirkland, things really took off with their Zone blitz."

When I came to the Philadelphia Eagles in 1977, my coach, Dick Vermeil, always cited our division rivals, the Dallas Cowboys, as the best-coached and most talented team in our conference. It was our goal, he insisted, to become their equals, then surpass them. If we could do that, Dick told us, we could beat anybody. And darned if he wasn't right, because within three years we became NFC champions by knocking off America's Team in the 1980 conference title game.

Similar conditions existed for the Steelers when Bill Cowher took over in '92. "The Buffalo Bills were the best team in our conference, and that's who we had to beat," he reflected. "We needed to figure out how to match up against a Bills team that ran three-wide-receiver formations. What could we do with the personnel we had to make things more disruptive?"

The Bills dominated the early nineties because they had Hall of Fame players in quarterback Jim Kelly, running back Thurman Thomas, and receiver James Lofton, along with wideout Andre Reed, whose numbers are good enough to put him in Canton. The Bills were also bigger than anyone else in that era. Five-foot-nine, 185-pound special-teams ace and receiver Steve Tasker was himself a midget among monsters. "In 1990 there were only seven guys in the NFL playing at over three hundred pounds," he said. "We had three of them— and they could all move."

Rapid motion became the foundation of Buffalo's attack after head coach Marv Levy copied Sam Wyche's Cincinnati No-Huddle offense and made it his own. "Jim Kelly ran our two-minute offense so well that we began running it other times in games," Levy remembered. "Eventually it became our offense for the next decade. The No-Huddle had repercussions we didn't even realize when we first started. We knew the opposition couldn't substitute easily. It shortened the period of time they could send in defensive formation signals from the sidelines. And it also diminished the turnovers we committed, because it was so basic. It had fewer plays. It simplified the decisions Kelly had to make on the field, and he loved that. Jim was tailor-made for that style of offense."

Kelly agreed. "My mom was always telling me to slow down, going all the way back to seventh or eighth grade. But that's how I've always been—just a guy who loves a fast pace, doing things quickly, and being on the go all the time." The offense even had a distinctive name: the "K-Gun." "Everyone thinks the offense is named after Kelly," said Levy. "But actually we had a great receiving tight end in Keith McKeller. When Keith came in, we were pretty much pass oriented, and that was why we called it the K-Gun—K for Keith. Plus his nickname was 'Killer,' so there's another K for you."

With their streamlined offense, the Bills operated at warp speed. "We had a menu of five plays that were included in our game plan every week," recalled Tasker. "We ran those against any team and any defense. Then we had another menu of five or ten plays that were specific to that game. Those would be just about all the plays we'd run. Back then, the No-Huddle was still relatively new, and nobody had yet figured out how to defend it. It was so compact that we got very comfortable with it, and because there was no free agency then, it was the same guys every year doing the same thing. And since we ran a new play an average of every sixteen seconds, it forced defenses to line up with virtually the same personnel on every snap. We had too much talent against predictable defenses, and we just killed people with it."

Fortunately for the Steelers, they could experiment with solutions to the K-Gun twice a year, when they played a division rival whose approach wasn't much different from Buffalo's. "We had the advantage of going against the 'Run and Shoot' with Warren Moon and all those great weapons on the Houston Oilers," said LeBeau. The Run and Shoot enjoyed its NFL heyday during the 1990s. It usually consisted of a single back, with no tight end and as many as four wide receivers that were given the freedom to adjust their routes on the fly. Those receivers included Haywood Jeffires, Curtis Duncan, and Drew Hill. They teamed with future Hall of Fame quarterback Moon, the perfect triggerman for this dizzying attack, given his rubber arm, ability to read defenses and the presence of mind to make quick decisions. "One of the only differences between them," noted LeBeau, "was that the Bills always kept a tight end on the field, while the Oilers didn't even have one on their roster! But they were both based on spreading opponents out, making you defend the entire field. The evolution of our defense was a reaction to defending the West Coast offense and Run-and-Shoot spread attack. With the defenders we had and later added, that gave us a leg up in defending against Houston. Before we got to Pittsburgh, the Oilers had been boss of the AFC Central. We changed that right away. Those were valuable games as preparation to play against the Bills' K-Gun."

Cowher's first game as Steelers head coach was in the Houston Astrodome against the Oilers, and the team quickly fell behind 14–0.

"But then we took control, intercepted five passes, and eventually won, 29–24," recalled Capers. "When we played them two months later, we did even better. Our players were more comfortable in our system, and we did a lot more blitzing. In that game, Woodson came off the edge and broke Moon's ribs. If you're a coach, you don't want to expose your quarterback to that kind of punishment."

Lake believed that, in one respect, playing the Bills would be less demanding than taking on the Oilers. "Against the Run-and-Shoot their patterns were executed a lot faster because they used so many receivers. When we played the Bills, where there's a back and a tight end, the game actually *slowed down* for defensive backs—and that allowed *us* to play faster. Our goal was to disrupt the timing of the Bills' offense. If we could force them out of their comfort zone and rush what they were doing, then mistakes were bound to happen."

In Cowher's first season, the Steelers went 11-5 and won the Central Division, earning them a home playoff game in the divisional round. The week before, in the wild-card game, the Bills staged the greatest comeback in NFL history, storming back from a 35–3 third-quarter deficit to beat the Oilers in overtime, 41–38. Capers still winces when he remembers that weekend. "By halftime, I'd already broken everything down and pretty much had our game plan all set. I thought I'd be able to relax the rest of the day, show up the next morning, and meet with the guys. When the Bills made that incredible comeback, I had to throw all my work in the wastebasket, go into the office, and stay up all night putting together a whole new game plan for Buffalo."

The Bills' historic rally had been led by backup quarterback Frank Reich, subbing for an injured Jim Kelly, and Jim was still not completely healed when the team arrived in Pittsburgh the following week. To the Bills, it didn't seem to matter. They were riding the momentum of an historic achievement. And besides, they'd already beaten the Steelers four straight times, including a win in early November. Based on what they knew, the Bills had to feel good about their chances.

This game is unique among those I've selected for this book: It's the only one where the featured team and coach *lost*. I know what you're thinking: How can this be an example of coaching genius if their team couldn't even win the game? In the case of the Steelers, the answer is simple. Pittsburgh's defense didn't cost it the victory. Had just one or two breaks gone their way, the Steelers would likely have won. But the greater reason for choosing this game is that it provided a widely viewed forum for a different approach to pressure defense. With the whole football world watching, the Steelers unleashed an innovative system that would frustrate and stifle the most prolific offense of that era.

1ST HALF

6 Bills Offensive Possessions

As expected, the Bills came out in their one-back, one-tight-end, three-wide set, a personnel package they would stay with virtually the entire game. Buffalo's top receiver, Andre Reed, aligned in the slot, where he would stay all afternoon. The Steelers countered with six defensive backs in a dime personnel package, assigning Carnell Lake as slot defender over Reed and Rod Woodson outside at left corner. Linebackers Greg Lloyd and Jerrol Williams set up as the defensive ends of a four-man front, although Williams would stand up during subsequent series in a conventional linebacker's position.

Pittsburgh went to Zone-blitz principles on the third play of the game, with Lake blitzing off the slot while defensive tackle Donald Evans dropped into coverage. Since the Steelers rushed only four men, this was technically a "zone exchange" rather than a Zone blitz, which calls for five or more rushers. The Bills completed a 5-yard pass to pick up a first down. Frank Reich then connected with wide receiver Don Beebe for 11 yards and another first down. It would be well into the second quarter before Buffalo successfully moved the chains again. The Steelers shut down three consecutive plays by Thurman Thomas, who rushed for 1,487 yards in 1992, the highest single-season total of his Hall of Fame career. On fourth-and-1, Buffalo gambled with a dive by Carwell Gardner. Linebacker David Little stopped the fullback cold, and Pittsburgh took over on downs. The Steelers responded with their first and only scoring drive of the day, a nine-play series ending with Gary Anderson's field goal to put Pittsburgh ahead, 3–0.

Buffalo's second possession was over in three plays. Pittsburgh deployed its base 3-4 personnel but continued to rely on Zone-blitz tactics. First Lloyd tackled Thomas for a 3-yard loss. On second-and-long, both Lloyd and Jerrol Williams rushed from their outside linebacker spots while nose tackle Joel Steed dropped underneath. Reich avoided pressure and connected with Thomas for 10 yards before Lake brought him down. Facing third-and-3, the Steelers called a rare all-out blitz; this was likely a Capers decision because Cover-Zero is something that LeBeau has historically avoided. Dom picked a winner this time, as the fierce pressure forced a tipped incomplete pass that ended the drive.

Buffalo made a defensive play of its own to regain possession when Nate Odomes intercepted Neil O'Donnell's pass about four minutes later. The Bills took over at their own 34 but didn't travel very far, as they were held to a second straight three-and-out series. Pittsburgh's defense returned to its dime package, allowing a short gain to halfback Kenneth Davis on first down. A throw by Reich was flicked aside by corner Richard Shelton, and then the Steelers really made the Bills look bad on third-and-long. The zone exchange was called, with Lake and Shelton rushing, while tackles Evans and Gerald Williams dropped off. Nobody picked up Lake, who breezed through untouched to sack Reich for a 4-yard loss. This was the zone pressure concept at its best: three confused Bills offensive linemen blocking Lloyd, while Lake came in cleanly off the edge. "What the Steelers were running was like Chinese to me," Bills center Kent Hull confessed sheepishly. "I directed our offensive line, and I looked at it like 'A-B-C.' The only problem was it turned out to be the *Chinese* alphabet. We simply didn't know who to block."

Pittsburgh's offense began the second quarter with a promising drive that got all the way down to the Buffalo 25 before O'Donnell was sacked for a huge loss, putting the Steelers out of field goal range. A Pittsburgh punt pinned the Bills back at their own 5, but a Reich-to-Beebe pass gained a dozen yards and gave Buffalo some breathing room. Staying in dime personnel, the Steelers swatted away two more pass attempts to Beebe and dropped Thomas for a loss on a running play, forcing Buffalo to punt once again. Four consecutive series had ended badly for the Bills, with the last three going no farther than their own 35-yard line. Pittsburgh's defense was dominating every facet of the game.

Current Bengals head coach Marvin Lewis coached Pittsburgh's linebackers in '92 and could easily understand the confused expressions on the Bills' faces that afternoon. "We had to have enough different defenses in our game plan so we could defend the No-Huddle. Since substitution was difficult, we'd try to mix things up with the personnel we already had on the field. We wanted the Bills to have identification problems, trying to figure out the different pressures we'd apply. One play someone could be considered a linebacker, then be a down lineman on the next snap."

Tasker voiced the Bills' obvious displeasure. "We'd always gone into games thinking we could do whatever we wanted. We had our set offense in the K-Gun, and we ran it as we liked. The Steelers were the first team we went up against where we were going to have to counter what *they* did to *us*. This was the first defense we played against that could control a game. We needed plans in place that deviated from what we normally liked to do. The Pittsburgh defense changed how we prepared."

Unfortunately for the Steelers, their offense was struggling as much as Buffalo's. Pittsburgh's next possession ended when defensive end Bruce Smith, a perennial All-Pro, forced a fumble by sacking O'Donnell. The Bills took over on their own 41, where their slumbering offense came to life. It took nine plays, but they finally scored when Reich hit Mitch Frerotte on a tackle-eligible touchdown pass from the 1-yard line. Oddly, Pittsburgh did not run a single Zone blitz scheme during the drive—and maybe it should have. Buffalo now had a 7–3 lead and held it into halftime after Bills corner James Williams intercepted O'Donnell at the one-minute mark.

Clearly the Steelers were frustrated, having played so well defensively through most of the half but having so little to show for their effort. Successful Zone blitz schemes had limited the Bills to just 121 net yards and 7 points—and this was the same Bills offense that had scored 41 the week before in their historic comeback win over Houston. Pittsburgh's problems did not end there. Late in the first half, Woodson left the game because of dizziness suffered from an earlier hit he'd taken on a punt return. Rod knew he was in trouble when he had to ask teammates for his coverage assignment. "I was in la-la land," he recalled. "It was just like being in a cartoon—trying to get your memory back." His replacement was backup Sammy Walker, who was legally blind in one eye. Even with perfect vision, Walker would not have been capable of playing at Woodson's All-Pro level. After the game, Steelers linebacker Hardy Nickerson told reporters, "As soon as he went out, you could sense Buffalo felt a little relief and started working to the spot where Woodson was."

2ND HALF

3 Bills Offensive Possessions

Pittsburgh opened the second half in its dime package, so the Bills temporarily shelved the pass and ran the ball against the Steelers' less fortified front. Their first two runs netted 18 yards. Then Reich finally threw, connecting with James Lofton for a dozen yards and a first down. At this point Pittsburgh returned to the Zone blitz, but Woodson's absence was painfully evident. Reich went to Lofton again, and the veteran receiver drew a pass interference flag against the clearly overmatched Walker. Two plays later, Walker was victimized again when Beebe hauled in a 9-yarder for another first down.

Dom Capers could see what was happening. Without Woodson, he had to compensate with his coverage schemes, and that cut down his more aggressive play-calling choices. Walker obviously needed help, so Capers gave him safety support, but it ended up costing the Steelers. With the Bills facing a third-and-10 at the Pittsburgh 25, Capers played safety Larry Griffin over the top of Walker. Reich read the coverage and dropped off a screen pass on that side to Thomas. With fewer defenders in position up front, there was ample room for the play to develop. Thomas gained 11 yards and another first down.

On the next play, Capers switched back to his 3-4 base personnel, placing Shelton instead of Walker at left corner. Two plays later, Shelton was handed the opportunity to make that substitution look like a stroke of genius. Reich made his worst throw of the game: a ball headed straight for Shelton. "I just made a bad read," Reich confessed after the game. "I thought Shelton was dropping off to cover [tight end] Pete Metzelaars. I don't know if I telegraphed it, but if Shelton had caught it, there was no way I was going to catch him." Unfortunately for Pittsburgh, the ball caromed right off Shelton's hands and hit the turf. Not a soul stood between him and the Bills' end zone. Afterward Shelton made no excuses. "I tried to run with it before I had it and dropped it. Maybe things go different there for us if I make the play."

Given this reprieve, Reich redeemed himself after the next snap. First Capers put Walker back in as part of the dime package. He then ran a Zone blitz, with Lake coming off the slot in a five-man rush, while tackle Donald Evans dropped off. But Lake couldn't get to Reich in time. The veteran quarterback feathered a pass to Lofton, who beat the bewildered Walker to the outside for a 17-yard touchdown. During the drive, the Bills made all three of their third down conversions, torching Walker on every one of them. Woodson's absence had changed everything. Buffalo led 14–3 with only a few minutes left in the third quarter.

Conditions only got worse for Pittsburgh on its next series. A promising drive quickly fizzled, and the Steelers had to kick away. Punter Mark Royals fumbled the snap and lost 15 yards, handing the ball back to Buffalo. Woodson returned to the game, looking to bolster his team's shaky pass coverage. "If it had been a regular-season game, I wouldn't have gone back in," he admitted. "I'd gotten my senses back and felt much better, but I didn't last very long because I broke my hand a few plays later and had to come out again." The Steelers were in real trouble. "I don't want to diminish what the Bills did that day, but we were pretty beat up at that point," said Capers. "We weren't the same defense we were from earlier in the season. A scheme can only take you so far."

With Woodson finished for the afternoon, the Bills moved swiftly into Pittsburgh territory and seemed on the verge of punching it in, but a textbook example of Zone-blitz pressure prevented another touchdown. From their 3-4 alignment, the Steelers rushed both outside linebackers, while nose tackle Steed dropped into coverage. A re-

verse from Andre Reed was quickly diagnosed by the charging Jerrol Williams, who dropped the Buffalo receiver for an 8-yard loss. The Bills settled for a field goal. Later they tacked on one last touchdown to wrap up the 24–3 win.

It was the Steelers' fifth straight loss to the Bills, but it had clearly marked a turning point in the series. For the first time, Pittsburgh had significantly incorporated zone-pressure concepts into its defensive game plan. The foundation of what is now recognized as the NFL's quintessential Zone blitz was firmly in place: blitzes out of dime personnel, pressures off the corner, the exchange of rush and coverage responsibilities, three-deep coverage—all the tools necessary to pressure a passer with far less risk at the back end. And it had been achieved against the best team in the AFC. The '92 Bills went back to the Super Bowl a few weeks later and made an unprecedented fourth straight Super Bowl appearance the following year. But their championship run would end there, and a significant reason for their fall was that the Steelers finally hit on the formula to contain Buffalo's prolific attack. The '92 playoff loss was the springboard to a string of dominant Steelers wins over Buffalo, wins that eventually propelled Pittsburgh to its own Super Bowl appearance in 1995.

"The Bills were still a notch above us then, but our performance in that game gave us a glimpse that showed us we could now play with anybody," LeBeau observed later. "It was a major stepping stone for our team in terms of gaining confidence and seeing what it took to go into big games against a top opponent—and eventually beat them."

Dick LeBeau is among the most culturally knowledgeable people I know in the coaching profession. He can quote from diverse sources, ranging from Bob Dylan to ancient European kings. "One of my favorite sayings comes from Frederick the Great, back in the seventeen hundreds. He said, 'He who defends everything defends nothing.' He knew his army wasn't big enough to protect all of Germany. But if he picked strategic parts to defend, then they'd be okay."

Steelers defenses applied this principle to all their opponents, but it was particularly effective against Buffalo. Whenever the Bills tried to spread the field, Pittsburgh countered with surgical strikes, coming from ever-changing starting points. And as the nineties progressed, Pittsburgh began to dominate. Even though the Bills got back to the Super Bowl in '93 and remained a playoff contender for most of the decade, they could not beat any Steelers defense coached by LeBeau. After finishing my study of the '92 playoff game, I watched tape of the next three games the teams played against each other: Monday night matchups in '93 and '94 and a divisional playoff game in '95. Each time, the Steelers added more defensive wrinkles, and the Bills seemingly couldn't handle *any* of them.

You'd think these lopsided losses on national TV might have motivated the Bills to address what was going wrong and to tinker with their offense. But their hearts were never in it, according to Tasker. "After Pittsburgh kicked our butts a few times, we tried some different things, but they didn't work that well. We started doing shifts and going back to huddles, but our offense sputtered. At the first sign of trouble, our guys would say, 'Fuck it, it's not working. Let's go back to the No-Huddle.' We didn't want to lose to beatable teams trying to run new stuff. We were unwilling to take a few steps backward to take a step forward."

The Bills came into their '93 game at 7-1, with a healthy Jim Kelly at quarterback. By the second quarter, Jim was in the care of team doctors. "We hit Kelly so many times—we were dropping people out of the sky on him," said Merril Hoge. "We'd start by bringing Woodson, then other people from all areas of the field. Then Rod came in from the other side. Then our safeties dropped down, and because Buffalo was worried about the perimeter, we could send guys up the middle. We really beat Kelly up bad. They had to take him to the locker room before halftime. I felt sorry for him."

The Steelers offensive players had basically been no-shows in the '92 playoff loss, but what a difference a year made! From his fullback position, Hoge was part of a ball-control juggernaut that maintained possession for nearly forty-five minutes. When the Bills got it back, they couldn't do anything against Pittsburgh's dime secondary packages and corner blitzes. "Normally, when an offense is playing against a 3-4, the best thing to do is spread them out," noted Woodson. "But it's harder to spread that defense out when you have a lot of good athletes who can play well in space and win those one-on-one battles. Plus, we were a good tackling team. We eliminated most of the big plays by running to the ball and making the hit right then and there." Altogether, Buffalo had ten offensive possessions. The team was forced to punt on eight of them, fumbled away another, and ended the half on the tenth. The final score was 23–0, and it easily could have been worse.

I was impressed by how much the Steelers had expanded Carnell Lake's role from '92 to '93. In this game, he displayed more versatility than ever as a blitzer, cover guy, and run stuffer. "I started from scratch with Carnell, and he ended up being one of the finest defensive backs ever to play in the NFL," said LeBeau. "He and I went through a real growing experience that helped make him a great football player."

Steelers Corner Blitz

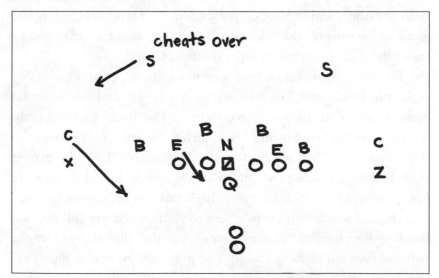

This play helped Woodson get into the Pro Football Hall of Fame. Rod takes off from the quarterback's blind side so it's not quickly recognized. It's essential for the free safety to cheat over and cover the X receiver, because otherwise that target would be wide open for a big play, should the passer elude Woodson's rush. This Zone blitz also demands that the right defensive end attack the inside shoulder of the offensive left tackle. This way, the left tackle will have to pick him up. If he's engaged with that block, then Woodson has a clean shot at the quarterback.

With the passage of time, Tasker has a better understanding of just how special Lake was. "Carnell was a precursor to players like Troy Polamalu, Ed Reed, Rodney Harrison and Bob Sanders—safeties who were different and could do nontraditional things," he pointed out. "Today a lot of defenses have a player like Lake, but what was asked of him then, he did before anyone else."

I also took note of LeBeau's increased use of "three under–three deep" coverage. That's a zone concept featuring not only a deep safety as a "center fielder" but also two additional people playing "left field" and "right field." Three under–three deep eventually became the predominant coverage of the Zone blitz. It facilitated pattern reading, based on the understanding of route combinations and route progressions. In the '93 game, defenders like Woodson and Lloyd knew where Bills receivers were going to be and could jump their routes to bat away or even intercept passes.

Although Pittsburgh deployed this coverage throughout the game, Steelers coaches called virtually none of their trademark Zone-blitz schemes. They weren't necessary, given how the Steelers dominated, both physically and in time of possession. "We were controlling the game and getting off the field quickly, so there wasn't a real reason to take a lot of chances that night," explained Capers.

The schedule makers set up a rematch in '94, another Monday nighter in Pittsburgh. The Bills lost again, 23–10, and this time elements of the Zone blitz were everywhere. The Steelers started early, with a defensive score in the first quarter. "Whatever alignment the Bills went to, we had a plan for it," said Cowher. "Two-by-two or three-by-one sets were pretty much all the Bills were ever in. And we knew their routes, which were usually dictated by formation."

The call was for an outside pass to Buffalo receiver Bill Brooks, but Woodson jumped the throw, moving in that direction before the ball was even out of Kelly's hand. The play remains one of the signature moments of Woodson's career. "It was a blitz off the right side," he recalled. "From what we saw on film, we knew that blitz would come wide open. I told our safety Darren Perry that if they came out in this certain formation, I was going to jump any underneath route I saw. It was exactly the play I thought it would be, I jumped it for an interception, and ran it in for a touchdown."

Kelly's agony had only begun. On the next series he was sacked twice, once by Kevin Greene and once by Chad Brown. Brown was especially active as a "joker"—the flexible player coaches move around to rush, blitz, or play coverage from multiple locations. In this game, the Steelers showed a lot more pre-snap movement, creating identification and recognition issues for the Bills. "When we played any other team, they never knew how to defend us," said Buffalo's Kent Hull. "Then we'd go into Pittsburgh, and they're dropping back tackles and blitzing linebackers. Some guy goes by you who wasn't your guy, and you just froze. The Zone blitz was absolutely the nemesis of the K-Gun offense. That defense just stopped what we were able to do."

A few minutes later, Kelly suffered through another series with back-to-back sacks, the first coming off corner pressure from Greg Lloyd. LeBeau calls Lloyd "probably the best football player I've ever seen or had the privilege of coaching. When you took him on, you buttoned every strap and put on every pad you had. He wasn't the biggest backer who ever played, but in terms of quickness and closing speed, he had it, with a great attacking personality to go with it." Lloyd loved LeBeau's system, because it always put him in position to make plays. "When I put on the Steelers uniform, it's like I was transformed into this superhero," he said. "It was like 'nobody can stop me, nobody can block me.'"

Lloyd was all over the field that night, but he lost out in his friendly rivalry with Greene for most sacks. Greene, the 1994 NFL sack leader, piled up three of them, and assisted on others. On one play, Greene recognized a screen pass was coming, so he abandoned his pass rush to cover the intended target. Kelly had nowhere to go with his throw and was a sitting duck for another Steeler to make the sack. "Greene and Lloyd were always on me about what I had the other guy doing," laughed LeBeau. "Neither one of them wanted the other fella to do anything any better, and they'd have such great competition in games, keeping track of what the other was doing. Kevin would say, 'Hey man, you're dropping me too much, come on!' But we could only blitz so many times."

"These breakdowns had nothing to do with physical execution," Kent Hull admitted. "They were all mental. If the other team was playing defense with six in the box, we could put five hundred yards up on 'em. But when they're moving people around, dropping, buzzing, then the odds really tilt in their favor. The Bills had better athletes than anybody—except Pittsburgh. Every one of those guys on that defense matched up well against us. We studied film for hours, trying to figure out their patterns, but it was tough. The Steelers gave no pre-snap indicators to tell us what was coming. All our protection rules we lived by went out the window against Pittsburgh."

That night, the Steelers picked up seven sacks, the most devastating coming from Woodson. Late in the third quarter, the Bills began an offensive series buried deep in their own territory. Woodson came off the slot, and Lake rushed from the same side—with no tight end in that area to help block. Greene fooled 305-pound Bills tackle Glenn Parker by taking a few steps forward to give the appearance he was rushing. Then Greene dropped off, but Parker was so focused on blocking a defender who was no longer there that he had no chance to react to Woodson's blitz. Rod blew past him, coming straight for Kelly. This was no blindside shot; it was a full-frontal assault. Kelly saw it all the way but could do nothing to avoid it. Rod hit Jim so hard that the ball went flying out of his hands. Steelers end Gerald Williams fell on it in the end zone, and Pittsburgh had its second defensive touchdown of the night.

Afterward Williams joked, "If I'm smart, I'll keep following Rod around, because he's making things happen." Woodson's stats for that game were staggering: nine tackles, two passes broken up, and a sack and an interception that each resulted in a touchdown. "Woodson may have been the greatest player I ever coached," Cowher claimed years later. "He was terrific athletically, very focused, and intellectually brilliant. I don't know of anyone who had a better feel for the game than Rod." The '94 Steelers went on to lead the league in sacks. "You can mark this down as the point where we really earned our nickname 'Blitzburgh,'" said Capers. "By now, the players were really well versed in our system, and nobody besides the Steelers was doing this back then, so we had opponents on their heels. We got opponents playing to us instead of the other way around. They were forced to play us differently than anyone else."

Tasker has a unique historical perspective on Pittsburgh's blitz schemes: "You know the saying 'There's nothing new under the sun.' My old coach Jerry Glanville was running some of the same stuff back in the seventies with the [Atlanta] Falcons and their 'Gritz Blitz.' The difference with the Steelers was that they had guys who could really play. Those Falcons teams were solid, but they didn't have people like Lloyd, Woodson, Lake, or Greene."

At year's end, the Steelers lost to the Chargers in the '94 AFC title game, but they redeemed themselves the following season. Dom Capers left the club to become head coach of the expansion Carolina Panthers, and LeBeau was named Pittsburgh's new coordinator. The Zone blitz became even more predominant with him in charge. The Steelers were once again AFC Central champions, and their reward was a divisional-round home game against none other than the Buffalo Bills.

Rod Woodson missed the entire '95 season with a leg injury. But Carnell Lake switched over to Rod's spot at corner and filled in brilliantly, earning a Pro Bowl berth at a new position. Lake celebrated with the first playoff interception of his career, but what saved the Steelers that day were two other interceptions made by linebackers Jerry Olsavsky and Levon Kirkland in the fourth quarter, with the game still close. Both picks were also textbook examples of Zone blitz principles working to perfection.

Olsavsky's came off a five-man overload blitz, originating from a 3-4 front. Lloyd rushed from Kelly's blind side, as did Kirkland. Nose tackle Joel Steed stunted around right end Brentson Buckner to create more movement and confusion. Buffalo's tight end moved inside to block Kirkland, but Lloyd got in cleanly and belted Kelly as he threw, never seeing Olsavsky underneath. This was the classic example of an offensive line being out*schemed* rather than out*manned*. Buffalo had six men to block, and the Steelers sent only five. Two Bills linemen needlessly went after Buckner, leaving no one to pick up Lloyd.

Kirkland's interception also came off of Pittsburgh's 3-4 defensive alignment. Kelly had planned to hit Brooks on a hitch to the outside, but Lloyd beat Buffalo's blockers and headed straight for the Bills quarterback. The pressure forced Kelly to come back inside toward Tasker, who was working his way over from the slot. Kelly threw late into the middle—a cardinal sin for a quarterback—and Kirkland appeared out of nowhere to intercept. Four plays later, the Steeler's offense punched in a final score to ice the 40–21 victory. "What set us apart in Pittsburgh was our ability to cover underneath receivers," said Marvin Lewis. "We took what people felt was unsound and made it very sound. We locked receivers down in coverage so that even if the quarterback did get the ball away, there weren't guys running free underneath."

A week later, the Steelers beat the Colts to earn a trip to Super Bowl XXX. Although LeBeau's defense played extremely well on Super Sunday, it couldn't overcome a late Neil O'Donnell interception that allowed Dallas to escape with a 27–17 win.

After another solid season in '96, Dick was hired back by Cincinnati and eventually became their head coach in 2000. Unfortunately, by then that struggling team richly deserved the dubious nickname sportswriters had hung on them: the Bungles. "I don't think Dick had good enough players as a head coach," stated Cris Collinsworth, who saw the team every day while covering them as a local radio personality. "He's been so ultrasuccessful in everything he's ever done, so I don't think the team's record had anything to do with his coaching style. In Cincinnati, you are not in charge of personnel if you're the head coach. That's someone else's job. Dick was only there for a brief time, coaching someone *else's* players."

At the end of the 2002 season, the Bengals hired LeBeau's ex-Steelers colleague Marvin Lewis to be their new head coach, and Dick found a job in Buffalo. He was there for just one season but transformed the Bills into the AFC's third-ranked defense. Pittsburgh took note, brought Dick back as defensive coordinator, and he's been there ever since—likely a Steeler for life. He coached the defense in its 21–10 win over Seattle in Super Bowl XL, and was again calling signals when the Steelers beat the Cardinals in the epic battle of Super Bowl XLIII.

"After we beat Arizona, we came back to Pittsburgh for the victory parade, and all of us were in our cafeteria getting a bite to eat," recalled Steelers linebacker James Farrior. Dick was already explaining to me a new scheme he wanted to try. I was like, 'Hey, Coach, it's time to celebrate, man. The season is over. We won the Super Bowl, and you're already thinking about defenses!' It was pretty funny, but this guy has so many schemes. He's probably got stuff that we've never even seen before in the back of his mind, and he's just waiting for the right opportunity to bring it out.

"We are a reflection of all the things that he's instilled in us," Farrior continued. "We believe in whatever he tells us; his word is gold. Whenever he talks, we keep our mouths shut, just waiting to hear him give us his knowledge. We all love him to death, and I think he feels the same way about us. There's a special bond here that a lot of other players and coaches don't have."

In today's NFL, every team features elements of the Zone blitz. The ultimate irony is that, off the top of my head, I can think of at least three games during the 2009 season when the Steelers lost to teams who beat them using Zone-blitz principles against Pittsburgh's offense. They say imitation is the sincerest form of flattery, but I can't imagine Dick was pleased when he saw his own team being victimized by ideas he'd created twenty years earlier.

But that is to be expected. When something works in our league, other coaches take notice. "Bill Belichick went full-go with 3-4 Zone-blitz concepts after he got to New England," insisted Solomon Wilcots. "He clearly copycatted this defense and won three Super Bowls with it." To me, that is a coach's ultimate sign of respect. "Look, we've played against it through the years, and it's still hard to beat," Belichick admitted. "When you play basically the same defense—and I'm telling you it's the *same* defense from 1992 through 2009—that, to me, is off the charts."

While LeBeau has kept his own basics in place, others have used his system as a jumping-off point for even more exotic blitzes. My *Monday Night Football* broadcast booth partner Jon Gruden has made note of these new wrinkles: "When college coaches ask how to beat the Zone blitz, I say, 'Which one are you talking about?' Because now there are so many. You'll see perimeter-Zone blitzes, Zone blitzes from a 3-4, 4-3, nickel, or dime. Seventy percent of your practice preparation had better be on picking up blitzes and recognition. Sometimes even that isn't enough. Your backs have to block the guy coming in clean, but there are some backs in this league who can't pick up a blitz to save their ass. That's when the Zone blitz can go wild."

Rod Woodson is now an analyst with NFL Network, and he's seen teams attempt to copy LeBeau's strategies, with mixed results. "When I look at different defenses around the league today, I always start from the secondary," he said, adding, "I learned that from Dick. When I see teams like the Eagles or Ravens—although both are great in their own right—they are sometimes fundamentally unsound on the back end. They'll blitz four or even five from a side, and one of their guys has to rotate over from the other part of the field. You don't usually see that in a Zone blitz; you see people in position to make plays." Carnell Lake agreed. "Other teams use the Zone blitz but don't involve the secondary as well as Dick does," he contended. "He is the master. They don't know how to tie the coverages in with the blitzes as efficiently. That's why it works so well in Pittsburgh."

You can see the Midwestern version of the defense in Green Bay, where current defensive coordinator Dom Capers has dusted off many of his "Blitzburgh" schemes and used them with the Packers. "You could look at one of my old Steelers games, compare it with what I'm doing now, and see a lot of similarities," he acknowledged. "I'm basically using [cornerback] Charles Woodson exactly the way I used Rod Woodson in the nineties. Both of them are nearly alike in size, speed, football instincts, and blitzing capabilities." Charles Woodson (no relation to Rod) came to Green Bay in 2006 after eight seasons as an Oakland Raider, and made the Pro Bowl in 2008 and 2009.

On-field talent is the X factor—the difference between the system's success and failure—according to Merril Hoge. "The Zone blitz doesn't work against everyone. Some teams run three wides, spread you out, and make you come from further distances. But if you have a safety like Troy Polamalu, it can still work. He does stuff you've never seen from any safety in the history of the game. He can drop back, then reverse field and run a blitz where the opponent loses track of where he was. Troy has allowed LeBeau to go to another level with the Zone-blitz concept."

Dick knows he has a one-of-a-kind player in Polamalu, and Troy feels the same way about his coach. "What makes LeBeau a great co-ordinator is that even after all his years in the NFL, he still listens to his players," he praised. "You can say to him, 'Coach, let's try this, let's do that.' He'll respond in one of two ways: either, 'I don't think that will work and this is why it won't work.' Or he'll say, 'That's a good idea, that could work, let's give it a try.' How could you not want to play for a coach like that?"

That may be Dick LeBeau's greatest virtue. He is seventy-three years old and has been in the NFL for more than a half century as he enters the 2010 season. And yet he's still eager to try new ideas, to come up with yet another fresh concept to confuse his competitors. "I guess in some ways it's kind of like music," LeBeau mused. "There's probably a finite number of ways which you can arrange notes, right? But here we are, thousands of years into human history, and we haven't reached the end yet. Every year, there are thousands of songs written, and thousands of new combinations of notes. So I guess there's *some* limit to what we can do on defense. But we haven't reached it yet."

Bill Belichick's "Bull's-Eye" Game Plan

SUPER BOWL XXXVI
ST. LOUIS RAMS vs. NEW ENGLAND PATRIOTS
Louisiana Superdome, New Orleans, Louisiana — February 3, 2002

Four weeks into the 1976 season, the Detroit Lions were floundering. After falling to 1-3, head coach Rick Forzano abruptly resigned, leaving football permanently to go into private business. Interim coach Tommy Hudspeth didn't have much time to ease into his new job, because Detroit's next opponent was the New England Patriots. The Pats were the hottest team in the NFL at the time, having beaten the defending world champion Steelers and the eventual '76 world champion Raiders in successive weeks. Now they were headed to the Motor City, and the Lions looked as if they'd be New England's next victim. Oddsmakers quickly installed the Patriots as three-touchdown favorites.

Six months earlier, the Lions had hired a young man barely a year out of college to help coach their special teams, receivers, and tight ends. His name was Bill Belichick. "New England had just beaten the Raiders by thirty-one points playing a lot of Cover-Three in their 3-4 defense," Bill recalled. "We had two really good tight ends with the Lions: David Hill and Charlie Sanders, who's now in the Pro Football Hall of Fame. Back then in the conventional pro set, it was very hard to get three receivers out to the weak side, because to do that, you'd have to release both backs. Against a 3-4, you just couldn't get them out quick enough. But if you switched to a balanced two-tight-end, two-receiver set, then you already have a guy at the line of scrimmage that can get to the weak side of coverage very quickly. So we decided to run this against the Patriots that week."

New England was completely baffled by Detroit's unexpected new formation. The Lions pounded the Patriots for nearly 200 rushing yards, and their tight ends accounted for three of Detroit's four touchdowns. New England suffered its worst loss of the season, 30–10. "Ultimately, Bill Parcells was at New England, along with other coaches like Ray Perkins and Fritz Shurmur," said Belichick. "And from that game on, every New England system since then has referred to that formation as 'Detroit.' Other coaches in the Parcells lineage—Ron Erhardt, Charlie Weis, myself—we still call that grouping Detroit. I'm not saying that formation was never run before, but as the years went on after '76, it became more popular. And today it's probably the lead personnel grouping in the league."

Belichick was only twenty-four years old when he put together this winning strategy. Thirty-five years later, he's still doing pretty much the same thing as the longest-tenured, and, arguably, most successful head coach in the National Football League.

Bill Belichick is the NFL's lightning rod. For much of this past decade, he has been the focus of football conversation. Just mentioning his name brings out every emotional response imaginable. Some people love the guy, others can't stand him, nobody's neutral. You can applaud him for his sustained on-field success, while also disapproving of the infamous "Spygate" incident, when the Patriots filmed opponents under circumstances that violated league rules. Belichick was admired for leading his team to a league record 16-0 during the 2007 regular season, but he was widely second-guessed for an unorthodox fourth-down gamble in a November 2009 game against the Colts. You'll remember New England attempted to protect their slim lead and keep the ball out of Peyton Manning's hands by throwing on fourth and short while still deep in Patriots territory. When that conversion failed, Manning and the Colts navigated the short field to score the winning touchdown. On one point, however, nearly everyone agrees: Within the coaching fraternity, he's the smartest guy in the room, and has been for some time.

Bill has showcased his creativity countless times during four decades of NFL coaching, but to my mind, his masterpiece is Super Bowl XXXVI in 2002. That night he took a Patriots team consisting largely of castoffs and kids and beat the highly favored St. Louis Rams. It was the biggest championship upset since Joe Namath and the Jets shocked Baltimore in Super Bowl III.

So far, every chapter title in this book has referenced both the coach and the signature strategy he introduced. The problem in this case is that Belichick's contribution is a game plan—and other than my creative former coach Sid Gillman, I haven't heard of too many coaches tagging their game plans with memorable nicknames. But *this* one should have one, and since no historian or coach has thought of a catchy title for Bill's blueprint, I made one up myself. I think it's warranted.

Against the record-setting Rams offense, Belichick mapped out tactics so radical that, even as I watched the game, I couldn't fully appreciate what I saw. It wasn't until after comprehensive film study that

I truly understood what he'd done. He drew up schemes that had never been tried in an NFL game and had his players ignore long-accepted defensive concepts. Somehow Belichick made it all work. In all my years in the NFL, this was the best-conceived game plan I had ever seen. And its unexpected success in the NFL's biggest game gave other coaches the green light to break the barriers of long-held football conventions.

My name for Bill's creation is the Bull's-Eye game plan. Why? Well, let's begin with the definition of the word, as cited in *Webster's* dictionary. *Bull's-Eye:* "the center of a target" or "something central or crucial." In thirty-five years as a player and analyst, I had never seen a defense focus so much energy on disrupting the actions of a single player. You might think, *Heck, that's not so rare.* Isn't the quarterback a defense's main target in most games anyway? To some degree, yes, but the Rams' Kurt Warner was *not* the guy being zeroed in on by New England.

It was star running back Marshall Faulk, who in 2001 had surpassed 1,000 yards for the seventh time in his first eight seasons. In the Super Bowl, he took a physical beating that must have left him sore for a month. Not just in running situations or third-down plays but just about *every* play, no matter where he was on the field. I never saw anything like it. There'd be a defensive end who couldn't care less about rushing the quarterback—he'd totally ignore Warner, sprint right to Faulk, and knock him on his ass. Marshall took hits from everybody: corners, linebackers, even defensive tackles. He was like a piñata at a kid's birthday party, because to Belichick, Faulk was where the candy was.

The Rams' head coach in Super Bowl XXXVI was Mike Martz, and he had good reason to make Faulk the centerpiece of his offense. According to Martz, "Marshall was the glue for everything we did. He basically redefined his position, widening what you could expect a running back to do. Not just where he ran the ball, but also in blocking and pass routes. He was more than willing to participate in all these areas; he had such a passion for football. Marshall also had better understanding of the game than any back I ever coached. He was intuitive, just knew where everybody was, and the split-second decisions he made were brilliant." Former Rams assistant coach Al Saunders agreed. "How many tailbacks in this league are smart guys? Not that many. Marshall Faulk was so sharp—he wanted to learn everything there was to know. You could ask him to do anything, move him anywhere, and he loved it."

My former Eagles teammate Wilbert Montgomery was Marshall's position coach in St. Louis and watched the guy every day in practice as well as on Sundays. Wilbert told me that Faulk could run the ball with equal ability out of any formation the Rams set up, including three- and four-wide sets. Naturally, this was a big help in slowing down an opponent's pass rush, because no runner of his era was more effective on draw plays. Tee off too hard chasing the quarterback, and Marshall would run it up the gut for a bundle. Wilbert also marveled at Faulk's pass-catching skills. He could line up consistently as a wideout; not just because he had good hands, but also because he ran routes as well as most NFL receivers. Traps, screens, quick outs, Go patterns—you name it. Faulk could do everything. He was the focus of the Rams offense, and that made him the "bull's-eye" for the Patriots' defense. Belichick was determined to stop him, even if it meant that some of his defenders would be forced to ignore their traditional responsibilities.

Let me say right off the bat that I'm a huge Mike Martz fan. First and foremost, he believes in an aggressive passing game, which is what I love. Some of his critics think he relies on it too much; that to compete you also need the straightforward "man-on-a-man-on-a man" physicality of the running game. I agree up to a point, but when it comes to offensive design and approach for today's NFL, Mike is on the money. If you have the right skill players in his system, it's unstoppable. With Faulk, wide receivers Isaac Bruce and Torry Holt, and other stars, he certainly had those athletes with his Rams teams from 1999 through the mid-2000s.

Mike grew up in San Diego, and as a kid rarely missed watching Sid Gillman's Chargers at Balboa Stadium or on TV. Eventually he played and then coached at local Mesa Junior College during the same time that Don Coryell was running his program at San Diego State. Martz soaked up Coryell's concepts like a sponge. *This* was the way offensive football was supposed to be, Mike believed. He cribbed ideas from both Gillman and Coryell as he moved up the college coaching ladder at stops such as Fresno State, the University of Minnesota and Arizona State.

Mike's fundamental passing beliefs became pretty much the same as Coryell's: aggressive calls, moving quickly downfield, relying on precise timing and rhythm between passer and receiver. Mike's mantra has always been "The ball is coming out fast, so run clean routes to beat your man. Be where you're supposed to be, when you're supposed to be there. Don't fool the quarterback."

After four years as an assistant with the Rams, Mike was hired in 1997 as Redskins quarterbacks coach under Norv Turner. Like Martz, Turner was also a true believer in the Air Coryell system, having won a pair of Super Bowls with it as the Cowboys' offensive coordinator in the early nineties. During his three years in Washington, Mike had an epiphany. He was crazy about his third-down play package, but game situations limited how often it could be used. Mike didn't like those restrictions and went to Norv with a suggestion. "Since we both love these plays so much," Martz asked, "why can't we run them whenever we want? Why wait till third down?" As a fellow disciple of Coryell, Turner agreed.

"So what happened," said Martz, "was that we decided to run these third-and-long plays regardless of down and distance or field position. To us it simply didn't matter anymore. This kept defenses guessing—they couldn't zero in on our tendencies, personnel packages, or formations, because they'd always have to be ready for the big pass."

Martz brought this mind-set with him to St. Louis when he became the Rams' offensive coordinator in 1999. That same year, under Dick Vermeil, Mike orchestrated "the Greatest Show on Turf," borrowing liberally from the Coryell playbook to create an attack that led the league in points and yardage. "There are two critical elements to Don's system that I made the foundation of the Rams' offense," said

Martz. "First, you build an offensive line that can pass protect without needing consistent help from the tight end or backs. Then you must have a runner who's a viable threat in normal down-and-distance situations.

"There's a significant difference between having to throw on early downs and *wanting* to throw on early downs. There's also a distinction between running a lot and running well. With this system, you can establish the run without running a lot." This kind of thinking played perfectly to the strengths of a Marshall Faulk. Put him in with a Kurt Warner, who could stand in the pocket under pressure and deliver to Bruce and Holt, and you've got yourself a championship offense. And, of course, that's just what happened. The Rams made it to the big game, then knocked off the Titans, giving my former team its first world championship since 1951.

Vermeil retired after winning Super Bowl XXXIV, and Mike was handpicked to take over. St. Louis made the playoffs in 2000, then did even better the next year. The '01 Rams won a league-high fourteen games behind one of the most dominating offenses in the game's history. Their quarterback, Kurt Warner, had to wait until he was twenty-seven to finally break into the league in 1998. All he did in his third full season was to lead the NFL in completions (375) and pass-completion percentage (68.7 percent), TD passes (36), average passing yardage per game (301.9), and passer rating (101.4). And his 4,830 total yards in the air—700 more yards than runner-up Peyton Manning of Indianapolis—was second only to Dan Marino's epic 1984 season in the annals of the game. (In 2008, New Orleans Saints QB Drew Brees bumped Warner to third place on the all-time single-season list.)

It was easy to see why St. Louis rolled into Super Bowl XXXVI as 14-point favorites. Only a year earlier Bill Belichick's maiden New England season had ended in a 5-11 disaster. Just past the midpoint of 2001, the Patriots' record sat at .500, the offense was led by a rookie quarterback named Tom Brady, and a third of the roster consisted of first-year players and waiver-wire pickups. The Pats got to the playoffs by winning their last six games but rarely overwhelmed their opponents during that stretch. Winter weather and a controversial referee's decision as to whether quarterback Tom Brady had fumbled the ball late in the fourth quarter had given them a playoff win many people felt they did not deserve over Oakland in the infamous "Tuck Rule Game." Even New England's championsip game victory over Pittsburgh was closely contested, with the Patriots staving off a Steelers second half comeback to win by a touchdown.

On paper, I didn't see the Patriots matching up very well with St. Louis. You go man-for-man across the board, and it should have been lights out in the Rams' favor. I truly thought the game would be a blowout. But as we've all since learned, you can never count out any team coached by Bill Belichick. He caused me problems when I played against him, and he has never ceased to impress me with his creativity since I became a football broadcaster.

By now, Belichick's career path is well known, even to casual fans. He's been around the game all his life, as the son of Steve Belichick, a former NFL player and college assistant at the U.S. Naval Academy. Bill played football at Wesleyan University, and after graduating in 1975, he turned to an old family friend for his first NFL job. "Don Shula and my dad went back a long way," Belichick recalled. "They both played college football in Ohio and had a relationship going back to the 1940s. When I talked to Coach Shula, I knew the Dolphins didn't have anybody doing film breakdowns on the staff, and I offered my services to him. I asked, 'Could I break down game film for you? I'd just like to learn your system and understand your organization.' He told me, 'I'm sure you'd do a great job, but I prefer my assistants do it so they'll learn those little details themselves, and not try to pass it off on somebody else.' I respected that. I think when you don't handle the details yourself, then sometimes things slip through the cracks and you miss something. Since then, I've always tried to keep that in the back of my mind. Even though we do have people handle those breakdowns for us now, I still try to be detail conscious myself, so that the 'little things' don't end up becoming 'big things' you miss."

Belichick ultimately landed that same job assisting head coach Ted Marchibroda with the Baltimore Colts, starting out at $25 a week. From there, he quickly moved up the coaching ladder, with stops in Detroit and Denver before joining the Giants in 1979. In New York,

Belichick spent a dozen years coaching the defense for Ray Perkins and Bill Parcells. Two of those seasons, 1986 and '90, ended with Super Bowl championships. That second ring got him his first head coaching job. From 1991 through 1995 he directed the Cleveland Browns but then resigned to go back with Parcells for stints with the Patriots and Jets before being named New England's head coach in 2000. After a rough first year, Belichick put together a run that has made the Patriots arguably the decade's most dominant team: nine straight winning seasons, seven division titles, four Super Bowl appearances, and three league championships. His success has made him the subject of many books, ranging from a biography by Pulitzer Prize–winning author David Halberstam to studies of Bill's management principles that have become business book list best sellers.

Bill's blueprint for success is built on core philosophies, beginning with his approach toward acquiring personnel. I've heard him say again and again, "It's not about collecting talent, it's about building a team. Some players fit better into one system or style of play than they do in another." Belichick assigns specific tasks for each of his players. He wants those tasks completed the way they're taught in practice. If each player does his job as instructed, Bill's team usually wins. "I want players that fit specific roles, and do the specific jobs they're asked to do," Belichick stated. "I'm more inclined to draft a consistent player, a guy who produces singles and doubles, instead of trying to draft a home run hitter or the next Hall of Famer, someone who makes big plays once in a while but may or may not have the total package to be successful in the NFL.

"In any season, we'll get critical plays from guys that maybe haven't had that many other plays during the year. But at a specific moment, it becomes 'their time,' and they come through. That's really what we're all about: everybody on the team performing and being prepared when called upon. Who knows exactly what those situations will be or when they'll come? My thing on preparation is that everybody needs to know what to do. You can't just count on one player—the quarterback or the middle linebacker, to know what to do in different situations, because everything happens so fast. I don't really feel like we're prepared until everybody knows how they should react in certain situations. It's our job as coaches to make sure they understand that, so we can react quickly and decisively in those critical situations. If we have a tough, smart football team that's ready and plays well under pressure, then we'll win our share."

This approach makes a lot of sense, but plenty of today's teams prefer stockpiling as many Pro Bowlers as possible. Good strategy is important, they'll concede, but ultimately they believe that better talent usually wins out in the NFL. Big guys crush little guys, fast people run away from slow people, and so on. For these teams, that principle isn't going to change. And there are also a number of NFL coaches who are steadfast in going with the same strategies all the time. They arrive at the stadium each Sunday and basically declare, "Here's what we do. We do it pretty damn well. We're going to run things like we always do—and it's the other team's job to try to stop it."

Belichick's view is much different. "Every week is its own challenge," he emphasized. "Every game brings its own set of circumstances, adjustments, play style, and matchups. We focus on what we want to do for that week, not what we did two weeks before or ten weeks before." Super Bowl XXXVI put that philosophy into action and showcased it as no game had done previously.

A little more than two months earlier, the Rams beat New England, 24–17, during the tenth week of the regular season. The Patriots played pretty well but ultimately failed to achieve their main goal: disrupting the precise timing of Mike Martz's offense. "They only scored twenty-four points," said Belichick, "but I never really felt like we had control of the game. It seemed like every time they needed a pass, they could hit one.

"We thought going in that night we couldn't just let St. Louis settle in and throw. We wanted to get them out of their rhythm, put pressure on Warner, force incomplete passes. So we blitzed—a lot. Unfortunately for us, their offensive line was great. By my count, we blitzed them forty-three times and never really got much heat on Warner. His line did a tremendous job, not only blocking us but also in making adjustments to pick up our blitzers. In the end, Warner always seemed to have enough time to make his throws."

Even though the Patriots were frustrated about losing, they

weren't totally discouraged. In the locker room afterward, the mood was surprisingly upbeat. Veteran safety Lawyer Milloy observed, "You would have thought we won the game, because everybody was saying, 'Hey, if they're supposed to be the next Super Bowl champs, what can we be?' That was the most positive we'd been after any game the whole year. And you know what? We didn't lose another game the rest of the season." Mike Martz also had high regard for the team he had just beaten. "That was the most physical game we played that year," he praised, "and I mentioned to the media at the time that this was a Super Bowl team. The Patriots were the best opponent we had played to that point."

One reason why New England was so tough was the versatility and flexibility of its defenders, the perfect example being Mike Vrabel, a free agent addition who hadn't found a home in Pittsburgh but was a perfect fit for Belichick's schemes in New England. He was equally adept coming out of a three-point stance or standing upright, and could attack from any angle. Another waiver-wire pickup, the highly intelligent thirty-three-year-old Roman Phifer, filled a specific role as New England's pass coverage linebacker. In Lawyer Milloy and Ty Law, the Patriots had defensive backs that were physical and tough, with the versatility to defend the run at the line of scrimmage and execute their responsibilities in pass coverage. They were also extremely effective blitzers.

More experience came from linebacker Bryan Cox and defensive backs Otis Smith and Terrell Buckley, smart veterans who quickly learned Belichick's new schemes—schemes with just enough wrinkles and variations that opponents couldn't have previously studied on tape. The Rams certainly weren't fully prepared to deal with them, and the results were evident on the scoreboard. Powerful St. Louis would be held to a single field goal through the first three quarters.

My first NFL head coach was Chuck Knox, a guy who won more games in his career than a lot of coaches who are in the Pro Football Hall of Fame. Chuck was legendary for dozens of sayings his players referred to as "Knoxisms." The one I remember best is, "What you *do* speaks so well. There's no need to hear what you *say*." Bill Belichick is very much of the same mind. "We don't have many signs in our locker room," he noted. "We have a quote from the great Chinese general Sun Tzu dating back to 540 B.C. It says, 'Every battle is won before it is ever fought.' We have another sign that says, 'Penalties lose games.' But that's it. What we *do* have are pictures of our players from games we've won, scenes of them making plays or celebrating a teammate's success. We're not big on signs. We're bigger on pictures."

I'm not sure if one particular photo is mounted on the walls of the Patriots facility, but if it's not, it should be: the image of *any* New England defender from Super Bowl XXXVI knocking Marshall Faulk on his ass.

1ST HALF

Rams Series No. 1
1st Quarter, 14:48 remaining: St. Louis 0, New England 0

The Patriots began the game in a 4-3 defensive set. This wasn't what New England had run during the early part of the season. But after six-year-veteran Tedy Bruschi proved he was more than capable of handling assignments from the traditional middle linebacker position, Belichick switched his base defense from a 3-4 to a 4-3. This gave Bill a blank canvas on which to draw up new alignments for his defenders to master—and his opponents to figure out.

During the Rams' opening drive, New England's secondary disguised its looks and schemes, shifting personnel after the snap and dropping some defenders into coverage as others moved into the box. The goal was to create hesitation and uncertainty; to disrupt Warner's usual rapid-fire processing of information and sharp dissection of coverage. The Patriots had made similar rotations the first time the two teams played but had then switched to constant blitzing. "We certainly aren't going to do *that* again after they picked us apart in the regular season," Belichick told his players. Indeed, the Rams rarely saw Bill dial up a blitz call in Super Bowl XXXVI. The switch in strategy wasn't a total surprise to Warner, but it did affect him. He was not the same quarterback this time around, which became evident early on.

Belichick's Bull's-Eye game plan was simply this: Whenever Marshall lined up in the offset position—either alongside or slightly angled from Warner—he was going to be hit. The Patriots were willing to sacrifice putting heat on Warner to neutralize Faulk. "Rather than disrupt the passing game by trying to pressure them," Belichick revealed later, "we were going to disrupt the passing game by trying to jam the receivers, and *most* importantly, take care of Faulk. We wanted to keep him out of the passing game. Everything was geared toward where Faulk lined up, with an emphasis on pass coverage."

An early example occurred in this first series when a penalty put St. Louis in a third-and-18 hole. Vrabel lined up as an end, yet was assigned to physically go after Faulk if he immediately released to the outside on a pass route. After the snap, Faulk pretended to block, then took off. Vrabel intended to blast Faulk but landed only a glancing blow. Marshall slipped free for a screen pass, but it didn't gain enough yardage for a first down, so the Rams punted. It would be one of the few times that Marshall avoided severe head-on contact all day.

Rams Series No. 2
1st Quarter, 8:15 remaining: St. Louis 0, New England 0

St. Louis picked up the game's first score but had to grind for every yard as New England's defense tightened the screws. St. Louis ran nine plays on the drive. The Patriots played man-to-man, with their corners in press coverage on seven of those plays. They had safety help over the top, which is why they were able to do this, but, conceptually, they were in physical man-to-man coverage. Although Warner completed six passes, none gained more than 14 yards. The third play of the series, a 3-yard pass to Bruce, spoke volumes about New England's get-tough approach. Tight end Ernie Conwell crossed into the middle, covered by Phifer. Out of the corner of his eye, Conwell detected a blur. It was Bruschi, who was free to roam because *his* man, fullback James Hodgins, had stayed in to block. Tedy promptly knocked Conwell off his feet. At the same time, cornerback Ty Law ran all the way from the other side and stopped Bruce cold with a textbook open-field tackle.

Four plays later, Faulk absorbed his first truly brutal collision. Seeing that Marshall was lined up offset, Willie McGinest moved from his crouched defensive end position, switching to outside linebacker. Following the snap, Faulk released outside. As if shot from a cannon, McGinest ran straight into Faulk and pushed him backward, even though he wasn't primarily involved in the call. At the same time, Phifer busted up a botched tight-end screen to Conwell, who lost yardage on the play.

Despite these setbacks, completions to Bruce, Faulk, and the seldom-used Hodgins moved the ball to New England's 32-yard line. On third-and-3, the Rams came out in one-back, four-wide-receiver personnel, with Faulk aligned in a wide receiver's position in the left slot. It's known as an "empty set," with no one in the backfield behind Warner. But the play's design was to the right, *away* from Faulk. The three wideouts to that side attacked the press coverage. Bruce broke open to the sideline against Law, who was clearly playing to the inside. But a confused Warner threw to the wrong man, trying to force it to tightly guarded veteran wide receiver Ricky Proehl. The pass was incomplete, and St. Louis settled for a Jeff Wilkins field goal to take a 3–0 lead.

It was only two drives, but patterns were emerging. Clearly, Be-

Bull's-Eye Blitz

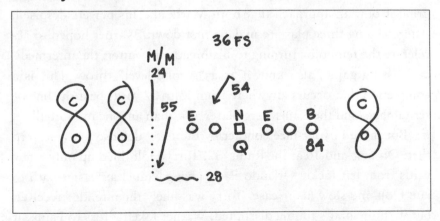

New England's specialty pressure package designed to make life miserable for Rams running back Faulk. When Faulk was offset in the backfield, the Patriots blasted him every chance they had. On this play, defensive end McGinest drills Faulk, then continues his rush to the quarterback. It forces a hurried screen pass to the tight end for just a few yards. Belichick was willing to sacrifice a lot on defense to keep Faulk out of the flow, rightfully convinced that a Faulk-less Ram offense could be better contained.

lichick's heightened aggression was bothering the Rams. "The game plan was to hit those guys, knock 'em down, beat them up," admitted Bryan Cox, "Every play, run or pass, getting the ball, *not* getting the ball. You had to hit the Big Three—and that was Holt, Bruce, and Faulk." Vrabel could also see the difference from their regular-season game. "Bill was obviously not going to give the Rams the same looks after they'd beaten us the first time," he recalled. "So we changed things up. I also think we were a better team in the Super Bowl than we were in November. We had a better understanding of what we wanted to do. We just tried to jam their receivers with our corners and line-backers—and, obviously, hit Marshall as much as possible."

Rams Series No. 3
1st Quarter, 1:59 remaining: St. Louis 3, New England 0

The Rams' offense thrived on quick-striking play selections, a pace that hurried opponents first into uncertainty, then into making mistakes and breakdowns. By being physical and disrupting the timing of routes, New England allowed the Rams to pick up yardage only in small bites, as opposed to their usual big gulps. The Patriots were forcing St. Louis out of its comfort zone, and it happened again on this drive. Except for one big pass completion, the Rams were forced to grind it out, an approach that both Martz and his players despised. After needing three plays to make a first down, Warner hoped to accelerate the tempo by turning to his bread and butter: the intermediate passing game, also known as a "second-level" throw. This is a completion that occurs anywhere from 15 to 22 yards past the line of scrimmage, and the Rams were better at it than anyone in football.

But more in-your-face contact by the Pats' defense put a stop to that. On first-and-10 at the Rams' 37, Torry Holt lined up only a few yards from left tackle Orlando Pace, giving Vrabel an easier path to jam Holt and slow his release. Torry was likely the intended receiver, but with the play's timing disrupted, Warner faked a toss to Faulk. It didn't fool New England defensive end Bobby Hamilton, who, unblocked, breezed in and sacked Warner for a 5-yard loss.

The next play was more of the same. This time Vrabel belted

Faulk when he tried to release outside, while McGinest popped wide-out Az-Zahir Hakim coming out of his stance. With his two main targets out of position, Kurt's internal clock told him he'd better bail out, but all he did was step up into *more* pressure. Warner's throw to Hakim was high, not one of his customary accurate darts, and Az paid dearly by absorbing his second nasty hit of the play—a vicious shot in the rib cage from Phifer. Not surprisingly, Hakim dropped the pass. The Rams' skill players, from Faulk on down, were taking their lumps, and they weren't liking it.

Hakim got some revenge on the following play, when the Pats rushed only three players on third-and-15. The offensive line gave Warner plenty of time to set up, and Kurt connected for a 29-yard completion, the longest Rams play of the first half. It was vintage Warner—a terrific throw against two-man coverage. Hakim also did his job, beating Buckley by running a Rams' staple: the intermediate in-breaking route.

From there, the drive sputtered. On first-and-10, New England was in its base 4-3, with the corners playing press man coverage on the outside, and the linebackers and safeties playing zone concepts on the inside. The call was supposed to be a pass to Faulk down the seam, but the inside-zone scheme took it away. Instead Warner went to Conwell, who was running an underneath pattern. It ended badly, as Lawyer Milloy drilled the St. Louis tight end, and the pass was dropped. On second down, Warner picked up 5 yards on a designed quarterback draw, but he was not so fortunate on third-and-5.

New England went into its dime package of six defensive backs, with its corners in press coverage. It was then that Belichick called his first blitz of the game. The blitzer wasn't a linebacker but safety Tebucky Jones, and the blitz was both well disguised and unexpected, given that the Rams had seen nothing like it in the twenty-two previous plays they'd run. Warner's hurried pass was tipped by six-foot-six rookie Richard Seymour at the line, forcing the Rams to try another field goal. This time, Wilkins's kick went wide. Another frustrating slow-as-molasses series for St. Louis that produced no points.

Of the nine plays in this drive, the Patriots played man coverage in seven of them. Six of those plays found New England corners pressing their assigned receivers. This was a very aggressive posture for Belichick, considering the extraordinary talent of St. Louis's skill players. Something you rarely see in the NFL was unfolding: matchups that would remain virtually unchanged throughout an entire game. Ty Law on Bruce, Otis Smith on Holt, and Terrell Buckley on Hakim. And Bill was showing surprising confidence in his other nickel and dime backs, Terrance Shaw and Antwan Harris, neither of whom was considered to be at the same talent level as the Rams they were covering. But within the Pats' aggressive scheme, they were more than holding their own.

Rams Series No. 4
2nd Quarter, 10:08 remaining: St. Louis 3, New England 0

St. Louis started out well, with two Faulk runs picking up 20 yards. It looked as if the Rams were finally settling into their customary rhythm. But then Belichick made his best defensive call of the game, resulting in one of the most shocking plays in Super Bowl history.

With first-and-10 at the Rams' 39, the Patriots deployed their 4-3 base personnel but didn't show that alignment. For the first time all day, New England went into a 5-2 set—Vrabel aligned across from Conwell in a three-point lineman's stance. Following the snap, all five players on the front, including Vrabel, rushed Warner. Right offensive tackle Rod Jones turned his attention inside to the hard-charging Bobby Hamilton and did not react to Vrabel. With Conwell free-releasing into his route and Faulk working to the other side, there was no one in position to account for Vrabel.

The defensive play call was named "Turkey Zero," and there was more creativity to its design than simply the surprise element of sending Vrabel. Once the play began, Hamilton took one step forward toward Jones, and then worked his way inside to Seymour in a line stunt. Seymour initially aligned head-up on center Andy McCollum, came to the outside, and drove hard into Jones, which made it impossible for the right tackle to look back outside as Vrabel barreled in. The result was a hurried throw by Warner under intense pressure. "They kind of forgot about me," noted Vrabel. "I think Kurt was pretty surprised that I was there and free, and just kind of let it go. Ty Law made a great read on it, playing the ball and not the man." Law cut in front of Isaac Bruce, stole the pass and ran untouched 47 yards for the first touchdown of the game.

But why did Belichick make such a call at this particular moment? The Rams had already run twenty-five plays and New England had shown *nothing* like it until now. What happened was that Bill took advantage of a perceived weakness in St. Louis's line. The starting right tackle for most of the year had been Ryan Tucker, but he wasn't in the game at the time; in fact, Jones started in his place. This was Rod's first season in St. Louis after five years in Cincinnati. He'd played in only six games all year, so he may have not have been totally certain of his responsibilities. Recognizing this possibility, Belichick went right after Jones, showing him an alignment and pressure scheme he wasn't used to, then neutralizing him with Seymour's brutal hit coming off a line stunt. The turnover gave New England the lead, even though its own offense was struggling. The Superdome crowd was absolutely

Turkey Zero Blitz

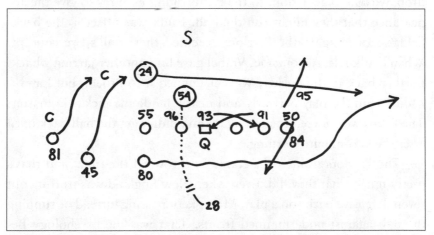

Pressure from outside linebacker Vrabel, who was aligned with his hand on the ground as a 5th down lineman, sparked the single most pivotal play of the game. St. Louis right tackle Jones did not account for Vrabel as a rusher, moving inside instead. That gave Vrabel a clear path to the quarterback. Warner's hurried throw was easily intercepted by cornerback Law who returned it for a touchdown, the moment that jump-started one of the greatest upsets in Super Bowl history.

stunned. There would be no blowout, and any remaining aura of Rams invincibility vanished. "The whole mood of the fans changed," said Milloy. "You heard some of those people who weren't sure who they wanted to root for start rooting for the Patriots. That play was huge. It put us on the map."

Rams Series No. 5
2nd Quarter, 8:49 remaining: New England 7, St. Louis 3

The touchdown completely energized the Patriots' defense. Vrabel continued where he left off, shedding a block by receiver Ricky Proehl to nail Faulk for minimal gain on the first play. The Rams picked up 11 and 9 yards on their next two tries, bringing up second-and-1 at midfield. St. Louis ran a toss to Faulk, but Bruschi had him in his crosshairs and blew him up with a great open-field tackle. Facing third-and-inches, Martz went with a curious play selection.

Most teams would probably have tried to power their way for the first down, but Mike Martz is a different breed of cat. Given his druthers, Mike usually goes with the pass, and that's what he called here. He lined up with four wide receivers. Warner went to a five-step drop, with no play-action, so the Rams didn't even *try* to give the appearance that they might run the ball. Faulk was offset in the backfield, so once again the Patriots executed their Bull's-Eye concept. When Faulk released outside, Vrabel gave him another jarring whack. Further back in the pocket, Warner gunned it to Proehl, but Lawyer Milloy read the play perfectly and nearly made the pick. No matter: The Rams were forced to punt again and didn't get the ball back until after the two-minute warning.

The Patriots *wanted* the Rams to throw all the time, and that's pretty much what they did. Even when New England was trotting out seven defensive backs on a play, Martz kept passing instead of running the ball against undermanned fronts. That was the psychology Belichick understood. He believed that, no matter what, Mike had no intention of relying on his running game. Mike's offensive philosophy was pass, pass, pass. He probably should have run the ball more often, which would have forced the Pats to switch over and play a more conventional defense.

Belichick researches his opponents as comprehensively as any coach in the NFL. I'm absolutely certain that he broke down the coaching tape of the 1999 NFC title game between Tampa Bay and the Rams team that went on to win the Super Bowl. Tony Dungy's Tampa-Two defense gave St. Louis all it could handle that day. They were really the only team that stopped the Rams that year, and nearly pulled off the upset before falling, 11–6. "They weren't a patient group," recalled Dungy. "They went after big plays and made a ton of them. They always felt like they were going to score forty points. We felt that mind-set would play into our hands. We knew if we could pressure Kurt Warner, we'd make some plays and get some takeaways, and that's what happened. They moved the ball a lot. They did hit some big plays on us, but we tackled well. We kept them out of the end zone until the end, and we got our share of turnovers. Up till then, people thought the Rams were unstoppable."

In Super Bowl XXXVI, I think Mike's ego got in the way, and I'll use a story I heard from Proehl as an example. Ricky went to Martz during the game and pointed out that New England was putting six and seven DBs on the field, so why not run more often? Mike basically told Ricky to shut up; that he was going to win the game "his way." Now, I think Mike's players basically liked this mind-set because, to a man, they were aggressive and loved to pass. But in my opinion, variation isn't a sign of weakness, and an unexpected play call can open up all kinds of possibilities. At any rate, Belichick knew in his heart that Mike wasn't going to change, so Bill never really varied his defense all day. Martz has since admitted that he should have run the ball more out of passing formations, especially on third down. But, he also added, "It's difficult in a Super Bowl to call runs on third-and-four, or third-and-six—even with Faulk as your running back."

Rams Series No. 6
2nd Quarter, 1:52 remaining: New England 7, St. Louis 3

Starting from their own 15, the Rams began cautiously but were helped by a penalty that put them at the 25 with plenty of time left. New England went with seven defensive backs, leaving only four rushers to pressure Warner. That number dropped by one because, with

Faulk aligned in the offset position, Vrabel went right for him again—and jammed Marshall as he went outside. This time, though, the play went away from Faulk, and at first it looked as if the Rams would hit the jackpot. Proehl caught the ball after running an angle route and busted loose for what appeared to be a huge gain. Instead the play ended in disaster for St. Louis.

"We were trying to get down close enough for three points and hopefully pick up some momentum," Martz remembered. "We hit Ricky on what we call a Z-post. We cleared out, he ran underneath, caught it, and now we've got a nice little convoy of players in front of him. Ricky took off, but he didn't see the tackler [Antwan Harris] come in and put his helmet right on the football. He just made a terrific play, knocking it out—and New England recovers. I don't know if there was anything you could do about it. Just one of those things that happens, and what can you say?"

Looking at this play, I'm almost at a loss for words myself. During the two-minute drill, with a mere 4-point lead, Belichick stayed committed to his Bull's-Eye game plan: It was more important to minimize Faulk as a viable option in the passing game than to pressure Warner in the pocket. It was all part of Bill's overall approach featuring press technique by his cornerbacks, in both zone and man coverage, to disrupt the timing of the Rams' second-level passing game. Messing with that rhythm would force Warner to look to Faulk as his outlet, but with Marshall *also* getting smacked around, any ability to get the ball to him in open space was severely compromised. The strategy enabled the double-digit underdogs from Massachusetts to take a 14–3 lead into the locker room. That's because Tom Brady needed only five plays after Proehl's fumble to complete a touchdown pass to wide receiver David Patten in the final seconds.

By any measure, Belichick's decision was proving to be the correct one. He was sacrificing pass-rush pressure to disrupt Faulk whenever he lined up in space. It was more important for the Patriots to minimize the running back as a viable option in the passing game than to harass Warner in the pocket. This was all part of a comprehensive approach that featured press technique on the outside, utilizing both zone and man coverage. The idea was to slow down the Rams' intermediate passing game. It was a brilliant overall strategy from Belichick that worked throughout the first half—and would continue in the second. As a receiver, Marshall Faulk would never be a factor in Super Bowl XXXVI.

2ND HALF

Rams Series No. 1
3rd Quarter, 11:58 remaining: New England 14, St. Louis 3

The Superdome crowd was uplifted by an inspiring halftime show from the rock band U2, honoring the victims of the 9/11 attack that had occurred just a few months earlier. A new surge of energy seemed to be emanating from the Rams as well. It was obvious that Martz had made some adjustments in the locker room, because St. Louis came out throwing more effectively in their first drive of the second half. Torry Holt caught an 18-yard pass to start things off, but a holding penalty on Conwell wiped it out. St. Louis quickly erased the mistake, though, with a 20-yard completion to Az Hakim. The play worked because its design called for Warner to roll right, out of his customary dropping point and safely away from New England pressure. I liked that tactic by Martz—changing Kurt's launch point, which allowed Warner to get comfortable right out of the chute. Hakim, with more time to work his route, beat the press man-coverage by nickel back Buckley, enabling him to make the catch.

Warner followed this with a deep-drop progression that ended with a 22-yard completion to Bruce, who beat single coverage from Ty Law. On its surface, you'd look at this play as simply another successful intermediate St. Louis throw. But to me, it also underscored the Patriots' commitment to their overall defensive goals. Here it was, first-and-10, the second play of the half. The Rams were aligned in base personnel, yet the Patriots were in a nickel package. The inference here is plain as day: For Belichick, it was critical to defend the pass, first and foremost. You could argue that he was daring Martz to run, but I believe Bill had already made the tactical judgment that the Rams' passing attack was far more dangerous, and therefore more critical to stop. This jibes with one of Belichick's most sacred coaching concepts: You take away what the opposing offense does best.

One wrinkle I noticed on this play was that defensive tackle Richard Seymour ignored pass-rushing chores and dropped into the flat to pick up Faulk. Bruschi was also converging on Marshall, so I'm not sure whether Seymour made a mistake in his coverage responsibilities. But his unconventional move was certainly consistent with previous New England defensive calls. It wasn't a factor on this play, and the Rams now seemed to be looking more like the team that had scored over 500 points in the regular season. After a Patriots pass interference call, St. Louis was at New England's 41 and clearly on the move.

Belichick deserves a ton of credit for his defensive game plan, but it's also important to remember that key plays from great players can be just as big a factor in winning. That's just what happened on the next call. Up to this point, New England's defenders had been playing primarily in two-man and man-free coverage, but on this play they switched to a two-deep zone scheme, one of the few times it would be deployed all game. In two-deep coverage, all the defenders are responsible for *areas* on the field—not individual receivers.

Following the snap, safety Tebucky Jones mistakenly stayed too far inside, not getting enough width in his two-deep coverage responsibility. This allowed Holt to get wide open down the left sideline, in the outside void between Jones and the underneath zone corner. Warner saw him and set up to make the throw. Martz had made the perfect call. The Pats were caught flat-footed in busted coverage. But seconds later, with the play concluded, Kurt was on his back, and St. Louis had been handed a 7-yard loss.

What the heck happened? I'll tell you what happened. Rookie Richard Seymour made an incredible individual play. He overpowered veteran guard Adam Timmerman, a very reliable 310-pound pass-blocking lineman, and sacked Warner before he could pass.

In my view, *this* was as big a game changer as the Vrabel blitz that brought about Law's touchdown interception. The Rams were rolling. If Warner had been in a clean pocket, this would have been a touchdown. Kurt didn't miss these kinds of throws. But he didn't get to make this one, thanks to Seymour. What he did had nothing to do with any Belichick scheme but had everything to do with a young athlete beating a more experienced blocker to make a terrific play. Stuff like this sometimes gets lost in the shuffle, but I assure you that this was as critical a moment as any in the game.

On the next play, Warner saw that New England was once again in two-deep zone coverage, so what the heck, he figured: let's go back to Holt in the same area. Patriots linebacker Roman Phifer was in Cover-Two, running down the middle seam, so it was essential for Tebucky Jones to play his assignment correctly. He didn't, failing to get enough depth or width, so Holt beat him badly down the left sideline. But Warner threw the ball too far outside, and Holt could not stay in bounds for the completion. Another missed opportunity for the Rams.

The next call killed the drive for good. New England went into dime coverage, with all four corners in press position. Belichick called for a safety blitz from Lawyer Milloy toward Faulk's side. Once again, Faulk was in offset alignment. Any chance that Marshall could possibly be a pass target quickly went up in smoke. He *had* to stay in and pick up Milloy, or Warner would be on the turf again. Meanwhile, Phifer, who originally had Faulk man-to-man in the coverage scheme, now was free to go after the quarterback. Roman not only knocked the ball down but also laid some wood on Warner. The result was an incomplete pass and another Rams punt. End of promising drive, no points, Patriots' ball.

Looking at this play again, I am still astounded at Belichick's defensive choice. It's third-and-17, a situation where many coaches play the percentages and go with safe coverages: Play zone, force a short throw, make the tackle well short of the first down, and get the ball back. Instead Bill had his guys attacking with pressure, calling a safety blitz with the rest of the secondary staying stride for stride with receivers who were better skilled than the people covering them. This all went back to Bill's basic belief that Faulk was the key to the offense and had to be neutralized, one way or another, on every down. A great way to accomplish that was to force him to stay in the backfield as a blitz protector.

Rams Series No. 2
3rd Quarter, 6:40 remaining: New England 14, St. Louis 3

In this game, there was only one offensive series during which Mike Martz departed somewhat from his basic principles—and this was that drive. He ran Faulk four straight times to start things, picking up 30 yards on the first three carries and none on the fourth. After a pass play to Holt picked up 5 yards, St. Louis faced a third-and-5 at the Patriots' 45-yard line. Martz could have chosen to run Faulk again. Belichick gambled that he wouldn't, calling for a dime package in the secondary, but this time with three corners and three safeties, not four corners and two safeties. He also had defensive end Willie McGinest line up wider than normal. After the snap, Milloy came crashing through on another safety blitz.

The Rams immediately faced a truckload of problems. Because Faulk once again aligned in the offset position, McGinest was able to line up at this wide angle and was free to blitz. This meant tackle Ryan Tucker had to rotate outside to block Willie, so he couldn't help with Milloy. Martz's called formation had no tight end on that side to block Milloy, either. Guess who got stuck with *that* chore? Yep, Faulk had to stay in and block, so he was eliminated from yet another play. Then St. Louis got more bad news. "Holt slipped coming out of his break on a slant route, and Kurt threw a pick over there on the sideline to Otis Smith," Martz recalled. "Otherwise we'd have had a nice pickup and kept driving." The turnover was especially damaging to St. Louis, because Smith ran it back 30 yards, which put the Patriots in range to convert a field goal.

Rams Series No. 3
3rd Quarter, 1:18 remaining: New England 17, St. Louis 3

Up to now, the Patriots defenders had performed far beyond anyone's expectations, but they were starting to wear down. These guys had played their hearts out but knew how dangerous the Rams still were. It would have been virtually impossible to hold down St. Louis for a whole game.

Martz also liked his chances, even trailing by two touchdowns. "Look, we'd moved the ball up and down the field, but all we'd done is pick up what I call 'empty yards,'" he acknowledged. "We gained over four hundred yards in the game, and until late in the fourth quarter, I don't think New England had more than one hundred twenty to one hundred forty yards in total offense. So statistically it was lopsided in our favor. What killed us were the turnovers. Sure, they stopped us on some plays, but we also stopped ourselves.

"The thing that's remarkable about my players was that they were so resilient. We get into the fourth quarter, and Kurt says to them, 'Okay, let's go, let's get it back, let's do it.' Sure, there was a sense of frustration, but not panic. They felt they had enough time to get the points we needed and that now was the time to get it done."

As expected, St. Louis went into its hurry-up offense, but I didn't know until Martz told me later that he seriously considered utilizing it much earlier. "We thought about *starting* the Super Bowl in the two-minute drill to kind of put them on their heels and take them out of their complex defensive schemes," he disclosed. "Once we finally did get into the No-Huddle offense, we went down the field pretty quick and really got into a rhythm."

This drive was the Rams' best of the game, covering 12 plays and 77 yards, and eating up about five and a half minutes. Martz continued to tinker with his adjustments, and those changes paid off. At the same time, the Patriots' defense was getting tired. Their offense hadn't given them many breathers, and the talent differential between St. Louis's skill players and New England's patchwork quilt of free agents and long-in-the-tooth veterans was finally starting to show.

The Rams began the drive by orchestrating a favorable matchup: Isaac Bruce against Mike Vrabel. This was vintage Martz. He shifted to an empty set with Faulk split wide left, outside the numbers. Then he had Bruce motion across the formation to the slot, inside of Faulk. The formation and the motion dictated the matchup. If Bruce gets off the line unobstructed, Vrabel loses that one every time, and after getting a clean release, Ike picked up fifteen yards. The Rams tried a similar call on the next play, with Holt going to the opposite side. This time Vrabel was ready, blasting Holt right after the snap. But Warner still made the play work, hitting Faulk on an outlet throw to pick up 7 more yards. The reason Faulk was available as a safety valve for Warner was because of the Rams' formation. Marshall lined up as an I-back, so the Patriots did not hit him after he released.

An adjustment of Martz's became evident two plays later. The Rams' offense depended on its wide receivers having clean releases off the line of scrimmage, or "free access," as it's sometimes called, to get into their routes. It enabled them to generate the necessary velocity for executing their speed cuts. One way to get that free access was to put a receiver in motion, which they did with Hakim on this play. This made it extremely difficult for any Patriot to jam or reroute him. Coming out of his offset position, Faulk, as usual, got clobbered on his outside release, this time by Vrabel. But the play was to Hakim, whose earlier motion allowed him to avoid press coverage and pick up 14 yards for the first down. On the next play, both Holt and Bruce ran Go routes down either sideline. Warner, under heavy pressure, bought time, and hit Ernie Conwell on a check-down for 9 yards.

I want to digress for a moment to point out something you might not know. There were no audibles in Martz's system back then, and he *still* doesn't think much of them today as offensive coordinator with the Chicago Bears. Given the fluctuating defenses of the modern game, this is amazing, but that's what he believes in. Mike's quarterbacks make their adjustments on the move, which is totally different from a Sid Gillman offense. Sid liked having the built-in big play rather than having to react in the form of a sight adjust after the ball was snapped. With Martz, you had the chance for a big play, but more on a look-in pass or slant as a blitz beater, not in the original design of the call. In 2001 Warner was in only his third full NFL season, still comparatively short on game experience. But when it came to understanding and seeing the field, he was very sound. I think his Arena League experience really helped him here. In the confined space of the AFL playing surface, there was always pressure, and the ball had to be out fast, so decisions were made on the move. In the Martz system, you have to react to the defense after the snap with sight adjustments, much like Kurt did as an Arena quarterback. Warner really showcased those skills during the fourth quarter of Super Bowl XXXVI.

It had taken almost fifty minutes, but the Rams were finally look-ing like their old selves. After a short run picked up another first down, Martz put in both tight ends, along with the fullback Hodgins. For the first time all game, St. Louis had a tight end on the same side as Faulk when he was lined up in an offset position. This extra beef kept him from being smacked around, as tight end Jeff Robinson successfully tied up Vrabel. With no defender in his face, Marshall was able to get a free release out of the backfield, breaking open on an angle route. Warner drilled it to him, and the Rams gained 22 yards before Tebucky Jones finally dragged Marshall down. This was a really good adjustment by Martz. I'm not sure why he didn't call it sooner.

Three minutes into the fourth quarter, the Rams were, at last, in-side New England's 10-yard line. On a check-down, Warner hit Robin-son inside for a 6-yard pickup, bringing up second-and-goal from the 3. But two great individual plays from Patriot defenders kept St. Louis out of the end zone—at least for the moment. The first came from McGinest, who steamrolled Tucker, forcing Warner into a hurried throw that was nearly intercepted by Milloy. The second great play came after Bruce ran a stutter fade route into the right corner of the end zone. Warner's pass got there, but Law had Bruce blanketed, and the pass was incomplete.

It was now fourth-and-3 with ten and a half minutes remaining. A field goal was out of the question. The Rams had finally put together a decent drive, and settling for 3 would have deflated their morale and only made the score 17–6. Warner dropped back to pass and got flushed out of the pocket, running to his right. Phifer blasted Kurt, and the ball popped free in the direction of Tebucky Jones.

Lawyer Milloy had a front-row seat for what happened next: "The ball's now in the hands of our fastest guy on defense, and he's running untouched the other way, ninety-seven yards! At that point I'm think-ing, *We've won this game. This thing's over. No way they come back from 24–3.* As Tebucky's running down, I looked around for any flags. Unfortunately, there was one, but it was behind us, near the goal line, where the infraction happened, so I didn't see it. I'm celebrating with Tebucky, but the next thing you know, the refs are waving it off. That was a huge momentum swing in the Rams' favor."

For one of the few times in the game, Belichick's Bull's-Eye strategy did more harm than good. McGinest was supposed to be Faulk's designated hitter on the play. And at first, it appeared as if Willie was going to be a real hero, wrecking Bruce's pattern with a hard jam, then taking off to find Faulk. McGinest found him, all right, but he didn't hit him—he *held* him—and it was a flagrant hold the official easily spotted. Jones's touchdown return was wiped off the books, and the Rams got a fresh set of downs just short of the goal line. Two plays later, Warner scored on a quarterback keeper, and after an uninspiring three-and-out series by the Patriots' offense, the Rams were back in business, down by only a touchdown with plenty of time on the clock.

Rams Series No. 4
4th Quarter, 7:44 remaining: New England 17, St. Louis 10

The Rams had the ball but were also stuck with lousy field position, beginning the drive on their own 7. Some teams would have tried a running play or two to get some breathing room. Martz doesn't think that way, and called for a four-wide-receiver set on the first play. Across the line, the Patriots were equally as aggressive. New England's corners crouched tightly to the line in press position, with only one safety to help out deep. This is a very risky defense to play when you've got 93 yards of open field to defend, but Belichick wasn't going to stray from his original game plan.

As expected, the Rams passed, and passed some more. St. Louis threw on its first six plays of this drive, picking up enough yardage to get into Patriots territory. New England rotated its secondary schemes on almost every down, with mixed results. On one play, the Patriots came out in the nickel, but it wasn't a standard set. The inside defensive backs played man-to-man while the outside defenders went with zone coverage. Bothered by fierce front pressure, Warner had to throw the ball away, and he took a vicious hit in the process.

On the next play, the Pats went for broke with the very risky Cover-Zero, a well-disguised double-safety blitz, which meant there was *no* help behind the corners if they got beat. It was the first time all day that New England called this, and it came at a critical point in the game. It was a decision made by a coaching staff confident in its belief that it had the St. Louis offense out of rhythm. But on this play, the Rams were in perfect synch. With Jones and Milloy rushing the passer, Faulk was forced to stay in and block. Marshall kept Warner out of harm's way, and after a seven-step drop, Kurt gunned it to Proehl, who'd badly beaten Law on a corner route. Proehl picked up 30 yards, the Rams' longest play of the night. After a 12-yard completion to Robinson, St. Louis found itself on the New England 39 with more than five minutes remaining.

Martz then called the drive's first running play: a trap to Faulk that Phifer and Vrabel shut down easily. Smarts, rather than strength, was the difference on the next play. When primary receiver Ernie Conwell went in motion prior to the snap, Milloy ran parallel to him, convincing Warner he'd be facing man-to-man coverage. Once the play began, however, New England dropped into a three-deep zone with a safety sitting in the middle of the field, taking away Conwell's availability on a seam route. Kurt's check-down target was Robinson, but Vrabel matched up in his zone and cut it off. By then, the Rams' protection had collapsed, and McGinest buried Warner for a drive-killing 16-yard sack. After a feeble third-and-long pass hit the ground, the Rams were forced to punt.

A little over three and a half minutes remained. All the Patriots had to do was pick up a couple of first downs and drain the clock. They did neither. The Rams defense played one of its best series of the game, forcing a three-and-out. Then New England punter Ken Walter got off his worst kick of the game. His 30-yarder rolled out of bounds at the Rams' 45, and St. Louis was given one last chance.

Rams Series No. 5
4th Quarter, 1:51 remaining: New England 17, St. Louis 10

All night long, the Patriots had been successful with press coverage on the outside and a solid commitment to aggressive man-to-man schemes. So when this Rams drive began, I was surprised to see New England switch over to prevent coverage. Maybe the team made the change because the Rams had already burned all their time-outs. Belichick's reasoning may have been that he hoped to force short throws underneath, keep everything in front, and make tackles on the field of play to keep the clock moving.

It was good strategy on paper, but it had to be executed properly for it to work, and this time New England wasn't able to do it. From the shotgun, Warner faced virtually no pressure on his first call. Faulk got jammed, of course, but he wasn't getting the ball anyway. Hakim ran a drag route underneath, caught the pass, and took off. Mike Vrabel played one of his finest games ever in Super Bowl XXXVI, but on this play he failed to make the tackle. Az picked up eighteen yards and was able to run out of bounds to stop the clock.

The ball now rested on the Patriots' 37, and here we see another on-the-fly Martz adjustment. Mike put in his fifth receiver, named Llewellyn "Yo" Murphy, who'd played most of his career in Canada and had made the Rams squad primarily as a kick returner. In this formation, Murphy was the I-back, with Faulk in the fullback's position! That's classic Mike Martz: tinkering with tactics no matter how critical the juncture of the game. New England responded with seven defensive backs, including Antwan Harris, who took off for Warner right after the snap. I'm not certain, but I believe Harris's responsibility on the play was Murphy, who had not caught a single pass all year in a Rams uniform. Anyway, the hard-charging Harris ran headlong into the right tackle Tucker and got splattered. Murphy ran past Harris and found himself wide open in the flat. Warner flicked it to the ex-CFL star, who picked up 11 yards before stepping to the sidelines at the New England 26.

The clock read 1:37 to play, giving the Rams plenty of time—and perhaps an opportunity for a surprise Faulk running play out of passing formation against a soft front. But that's not what Mike Martz does, especially in a two-minute situation. Instead Mike came up with a brilliant play selection that clearly outmaneuvered the Patriots' coverage.

With all four corners in press position as part of their two-man coverage, Bruce and Proehl aligned right next to each other on the outside, with Bruce on the line of scrimmage and Proehl slightly off the line. This concept is referred to as a "stack." Frankly, I was a little surprised that the Rams didn't go with this alignment more often. The Patriots relied heavily on press coverage, and a stacked release is a great way to neutralize and defeat that scheme. There are three problems a stacked release poses for defenders:

- If the DBs try to press, they run the risk of colliding into each other, leaving their receivers uncovered.
- Even if they don't press, there's still that moment of indecision. Does the defensive back switch to the receiver coming toward him, or stay with the guy he's supposed to cover? In the NFL, just one moment of hesitation can be deadly.
- The stacked release puts receivers in great position to make legal picks or rubs, blocking out defenders, while putting at least one of the pass targets in open space.

After the snap, the two Rams receivers crossed each other on their releases. Bruce basically ran a pick play on slot corner Terrance Shaw, which kept Shaw from getting outside to cover Proehl. Ricky appeared to be running a wheel route, which is a quick out, followed by a move upfield in a curved pattern. This worked beautifully against New England's press coverage, giving Proehl free access to the outside, away from the deep safety Jones. A wide-open Proehl caught Warner's throw, then juked Jones, and ran into the end zone, tying the game at 17 with a minute and a half remaining in regulation.

We all know what happened next. Despite initial intentions to protect the football and play for overtime, Tom Brady reversed course, led the Patriots downfield and got his team into field goal range. With just seconds remaining, Adam Vinatieri drilled a 48-yard kick through the uprights, and the underdog Patriots were world champions.

If New England hadn't made that kick, and if the Rams had won the game in overtime, much of what the Patriots did that day might have been forgotten—at least by the general public. But either way, members of the coaching profession would have noticed and appreciated Bill Belichick's Bull's-Eye game plan and play-calling mastery. The fact that New England was even able to limit this incredible Rams attack for as long as it did was enough for defensive coordinators around the league to scream "Get me that coaching tape right now! I've gotta see how he did that!"

Since Belichick came to New England in 2000, I've seen him devise defensive alignments that I never saw him use when he coached with the Giants or the Browns. I don't remember stuff like defensive linemen standing upright, or a defense with no pass rushers. His creative juices have clearly flowed during his time with the Patriots. And as his schemes got better, so did his players. He beat the Rams with solid but unspectacular defensive personnel, but with each year, that personnel improved. Belichick won two more world championships in 2003 and '04. In 2007 New England came within 39 seconds of claiming yet another Lombardi Trophy and the first 19-0 perfect season in NFL history. When he lost Brady in the first quarter of the first game in '08, cynics predicted a quick demise for the Patriots. "We'll see how good a coach Belichick is without the best quarterback in the league," many observers sneered. Well, Bill turned in one of his best coaching performances, winning eleven games with backup Matt Cassel, a quarterback who previously hadn't started a game since high school! Then in 2009, Bill led a young and injury-riddled Patriots team to its seventh division title of the decade.

I personally believe that Bill achieved his greatest coaching accomplishment with his 2001 team, but good luck pinning him down on that. "I have three children," Bill said. "It would be the same question as 'Who is your favorite child?' They're each unique, and I love all of them. So I wouldn't rank one child ahead of another, and I don't know that I could rank one championship team ahead of another. To me, they're all special."

Patriots teams that followed after 2001 clearly had better athletes, but they've rarely possessed the league's best pure talent. They've managed to remain among the NFL elite because New England is one of the smartest and best-coached clubs in football. When you have a coach who modifies schemes and play design on a weekly basis, you'd better have bright people who can learn these changes quickly. I don't have stats on this, but I wouldn't be surprised if New England has more guys on its roster with college degrees than any other team. These players hit the books, study opponent's tendencies, and just seem to have a better grasp of what's supposed to happen in any circumstance. That's why, with their personnel department, it's critical they find people with both athletic skill and intelligence.

When Bill talks to his scouts about a prospect, he never asks what that player *can't* do but what he *is* capable of doing. Then he can take that athlete's strength and plug it into spots where he'll help the team. When the Patriots run an unorthodox scheme, they don't put people in a position to fail. Bill slots them in situations where they can be successful, playing to their strengths. This philosophy seems so obvious, but you'd be surprised how many NFL coaches do not buy into it. They fall in love with what they've created in their playbook and believe that simply through repetitive drills and their own teaching talents, they can hammer a square peg into a round hole. I prefer Belichick's approach. The other way I find limiting and self-defeating.

In 2007 our ESPN crew was in Baltimore to cover the Patriots-Ravens game. The day before, Mike Tirico, Tony Kornheiser, and I met with Belichick to get background information for our *Monday Night* broadcast. Usually these meetings are routine; boilerplate chatter that doesn't reveal much. Most fans think Belichick must be like that all the time anyway, because they only see him speaking in his monotonous drone during press conferences, a forum he obviously loathes.

But at our meeting, Bill really got animated, because being in Baltimore was his homecoming. He wasn't far from Annapolis, Maryland, where his dad coached at Navy when Bill was growing up. He could look out of his hotel window and see the building where he held his first pro job evaluating film for Ted Marchibroda back in 1975. Belichick really began to glow when reminiscing about coming to old Memorial Stadium, working in what was little more than a broom closet, next to the office of Orioles manager Earl Weaver. Inside that confined space was nothing but a projector and a chair, and Bill would sit in that sweatbox all day, painstakingly poring over game film. It was a memory he spoke about with great fondness. This was the place where his career path had begun.

As a head coach, Bill has to deal regularly with public relations and marketing aspects of the game, stuff he doesn't really care about. They're necessary, but a distraction from what he enjoys best. Belichick loves coaching football players and has as much respect for the game's history as anyone I know. But Bill is happiest when he once again becomes that twenty-three-year-old kid down in the basement of Memorial Stadium. When he's alone in the dark, projection clicker in hand, studying game tape, watching tiny flickering football images on a blank wall, in search of the next innovation that will someday help his team win.

Y ou may remember my stating in the introduction that football doesn't change only from year to year but from week to week. These changes are often triggered by teams reacting to innovative strategies they've encountered on the playing field. But another catalyst can be the heightened demand for success from owners and fans. In this day and age, pro football is a results-oriented sport. Management can grow impatient and give up on a particular coach or his philosophy if improvement doesn't happen quickly.

In my view, this mind-set was ushered in by the unexpected success of the '99 Rams. St. Louis went from worst to first and won a Super Bowl, but before that it had been the worst team of the nineties. Other owners saw this and said, "If they can do it, so can we." Since then, coaching turnover has increased. Free agency has changed how organizations are built and players are developed, as more specialized role players are emerging than ever before. Technological advances have altered how game trends are evaluated. The sheer size of coaching staffs has grown, so the man-hours for study have also increased. Off-season programs and drills are more complicated and time consuming. Today, football truly is a year-round job, and players and coaches run on a treadmill that is accelerating to even faster speeds.

When the seven games selected for this book were played, the NFL was a different league from what it is today. Even my most recent game choice, the Patriots' upset in Super Bowl XXXVI, happened a decade ago—and a lot has changed since then. At that time, it would've been almost impossible to predict the current state of football. Evaluating these games and coaches who've influenced the NFL took nearly three years of study, but at least I was analyzing events that had already taken place. I had game tapes sitting on my desk, and I could run them back and forth whenever I wanted. It's a far more difficult task to foresee tomorrow's NFL trends or identify which young coaching wizards might be the next Don Coryell or Dick LeBeau.

Whenever you make predictions, you risk looking like one of those scientists I read about as a kid, the ones who envisioned flying automobiles and moving sidewalks. We're all still waiting for those modern marvels to appear, and my own forecasting skills might turn out to be just as inaccurate. But I'm willing to take the risk discussing trends that could be in pro football's future.

In my senior year at college, two of my teammates on the Youngstown State football team joined me on a weekend trip to Buffalo. The Bills were opening their 1972 schedule against the New York Jets, and the three of us wanted to see Joe Namath play in person. Though I'd been a Bills fan since I was a kid, Joe had been my idol since high school, and I'd patterned much of my quarterback technique on him. After my two buddies, Dave Ferguson and Bob Ferranti, cut a deal with a ticket scalper, we made our way into War Memorial Stadium. This would be the Bills' final season in the Rockpile before moving to their new home in the suburb of Orchard Park, and it still featured many of the same familiar trappings I remembered noticing as a kid, including that dilapidated snow fence surrounding the field. As we entered, the Jets had just begun their warm-ups, and not more than a hundred feet from where we stood was Joe Willie himself, having a catch with future Hall of Fame receiver Don Maynard.

I'd seen Namath other times from the vantage point of my old Bills season ticket seats, but never from this close. Leaning against the snow fence, I was able to study his footwork, grip, and throwing motion better than any time before. As I watched him, it suddenly hit me: I could do exactly what he was doing. These were skills I also had. For the first time in my life, I truly felt that I could succeed as an NFL quarterback. You can call it an epiphany, a bolt from the blue, whatever you want. But from that moment on, I intuitively felt I understood what a pro quarterback was supposed to do. There would be another year of college play—and seasons learning from the finest NFL coaches before I became a polished pro—but on that day, my pro football journey officially began. It's a journey I'm still experiencing and enjoying almost forty years later.

Because I've both played and studied the quarterback position for so long, I believe I understand its requirements and demands better than any other position. But you don't need anything remotely resembling my background to realize that today's NFL is predominantly a passing league. That's what drives the game. During the 2009 season, a dozen teams threw for at least 4,000 yards—the highest total in the last decade. Despite those attention-grabbing numbers, I believe quarterback talent at the pro level has become diluted over the past few years. I don't think there are more than ten top-flight quarterbacks in the NFL right now; not even a third of the current starters. When I played, I felt that at least half the league had quarterbacks with consistent pro skills, and you pretty much knew what you were going to get every week. The number is clearly less today, and it has a great deal to do with how the position is presently being coached at the high school and college levels.

Colleges have determined that it's much easier to achieve success with mobile quarterbacks in spread offenses. Movement passing systems are much simpler to teach than the pro style, because quarter-backs don't have to learn to read as many coverages. What you end up with are more run-oriented, sprint-option guys, not the drop-back passers that the pro game requires. In baseball, a team's top athlete becomes the shortstop; in football, the best college athletes are being switched to quarterback. "If everybody is playing spread in college, where are you going to find the quarterbacks that can pass from a pro set?" asked Tony Dungy. "They're going to be fewer and farther between, and you still have to win. We're going to have to adapt in the NFL. If this is the product that's coming to us, we're either going to create some type of developmental system to get these guys ready—or we're going to have to adapt to the skills that the guys have who are coming into the league."

Let me assure you that even as more of these spread quarterbacks enter the pros, there is no way the NFL is going to morph into a higher-grade version of college football. It can't happen, because the two are not even the same game, and here's the difference: College game action generally flows from the "outside in," whereas action in the pros mostly originates from the "inside out." Why? Two simple reasons, really. One is the vast disparity between the talent levels of athletes; the other is that colleges play on a differently configured field than the pros. A lot of the wild gadget calls you see each Saturday in the Southeastern Conference or Pac Ten simply won't work in the NFL. "When you put the ball on the hash marks in college, you have a wider side of the field to work with, and defenses are based on that," explained Bill Cowher. "But the pro game is played in the middle of the field, which means you can attack or be attacked from both sides. So it's much more complex for college kids making the next step to the pros, because overall play is not as clearly defined in the pros as it is in colleges."

Bill Belichick believes that the college hash mark placement produces many of its big plays. "Fast guys in college can make a lot of yardage just by outrunning people on defense. But in the NFL, because the ball is in the middle of the field, and because NFL defenders are close to being as fast as offensive guys, you just don't see many plays in the pros where one man outruns the whole team. And when you put the ball in the middle of the field, you don't have that extra ten yards of space to outrun them."

"In college you can get away with an athletic quarterback who isn't that accurate with his passes," noted former head coach of the Arizona Cardinals Dave McGinnis, currently the Tennessee Titans linebackers coach. "Because the NFL's hash marks are different, everything is squeezed into the middle of the field, so the passing lanes close much quicker. The speed of the linebackers and defensive backs is faster. Quarterbacks can run in college, but not so much in the pros, because more defenders close more quickly."

This doesn't mean that NFL coaches aren't looking to steal good ideas from their college counterparts. Quite the contrary. And they'll often find formations or schemes that can be readily applied to the pro game—one recent example being the "Wildcat" formation. The Wildcat, of course, was introduced by the Miami Dolphins in 2008—a modern version of the old Single Wing formation from the 1930s and '40s. It removes the quarterback and replaces him with a running back, who takes the snap and has the freedom to run or pass from unconventional locations in the backfield. Numerous teams around the league have since added Wildcat formation plays to their offensive repertoire. Most of the time, however, the differences between the two games are simply too stark for any system to be adapted smoothly. Bill Belichick exhausted a ton of man-hours one off-season poring over college film, hoping to find solutions that would improve New England's ground attack. "I went through all of Navy's games," he recalled, "because they'd led the nation in rushing, even though they obviously don't have the best players. I thought there might be something that we could apply to help our running game. But after watching every game and every play they ran, I saw that all of them involved a running quarterback. Either he ran the ball, or the defense had to play him as if he was going to run. None of our opponents is ever going to defend Tom Brady running the ball. Unless you have the absolute right guy, you'd be giving up a lot in the passing game. Navy's running game is as good as any in college—or pro football. It's a great system. But we couldn't use it in the pros."

Although a majority of schools depend on spread formations and mobile quarterbacks, a number of them still teach the pro passing system. They include USC, Georgia, Arkansas, Ole Miss, Rutgers, and Miami. After evaluating the quarterbacks from these schools, it's evident that even their underclassmen already have the look of NFL quarterbacks. By that, I mean that their drops, mechanics, and delivery truly resemble what you see at the pro level. They simply play the game a lot differently from the movement quarterbacks you see in spread systems. "The top two quarterbacks selected in the first round of the 2009 draft weren't running the spread," noted Jon Gruden. "They ran a more conventional offense. Matthew Stafford [drafted by the Lions] and Mark Sanchez [the Jets] were easier for scouts to evaluate because they were more familiar with pro sets."

Just a few years ago, these types of passing prospects were virtually the only ones who were drafted. "In years past, for college teams to recruit top players, they tried to run pro-style offenses," pointed out Sam Wyche. "This way, they could say they were training them to play in the NFL. Now the pros are looking at all of these great quarterbacks coming out in the spread, and they're modifying their offenses. They're trying to accommodate the new talent experienced in it. There are clearly spread quarterbacks in college who are quite capable of throwing the ball from the pocket.

"But because of their spread capabilities and their ability to run, they could become the 'other quarterback'—as a changeup to the pure passer on the team," Sam believed. "My theory is: God did not create thirty-two quality starting NFL quarterbacks to play at one time. A lot of the guys in the NFL are starting quarterbacks because there's nobody better to take their place. So you'll have teams searching for additional help. And the teams that do have a Manning or a Brady might say, 'Why don't we have a little wrinkle in here; pose a threat aside from our normal stuff?'"

Sam thinks that if pro teams carried such a double-barreled weapon, keeping both conventional- and spread-formation quarterbacks on NFL rosters, they would pose real problems for defenses; "I see guys like Armanti Edwards from Appalachian State becoming the 'other quarterback' in the lineup—where the opponent is going to have to prepare for two offenses. As long as that quarterback is a threat to throw the ball, defenders have to worry about him. Quarterbacks that can throw but also move like running backs could be big in the future. Teams that draft these guys are going to have a giant edge, because they'll force opponents to split their practice time in half, defending two styles of offense."

If NFL teams try this, they'd better make sure that division of labor is clearly defined. As Brian Billick observed, "What's the biggest problem in the league now? If your number one quarterback goes down, you are screwed. If teams go to the spread more regularly, do you really want to expose your quarterback with less protection? It's pretty risky. You can't let your quarterback take those kinds of hits in the NFL."

With some teams, the difference between their first-string and backup quarterback isn't that much, but if your number one guy is a superstar, it's an entirely different story. One time, Jon Gruden and I were attending a Colts practice before one of our ESPN games, and we were standing next to their offensive coordinator, Tom Moore. Tom is "old school" in every sense of the word. He's been in the NFL for over thirty years and has signaled in every play call of Peyton Manning's career. As we watched, we were surprised to see Manning taking virtually all the reps in the session. Jon asked Tom why he wasn't giving some snaps to Peyton's backups. Moore is a man of few words, but when he talks, those words have weight. He looked us both in the eye, paused for a moment, then said in that gravelly voice of his, "Fellas, if '18' goes down, we're fucked. And we don't practice *fucked*."

Bill Cowher is optimistic that today's best collegiate spread quarterbacks will be capable of making the adjustment to the NFL. "It may take some of the college spread quarterbacks a little longer to develop," he stated, "but I don't think there's been a better time, with so many good quarterbacks. I attribute that to the fact that there's so much more passing going on in college now. They have a better feel for the passing game."

I hope Bill's right, but I wonder whether these young guns possess the skill set needed to be a solid NFL quarterback. As I see it, there are four basic abilities a pro passer must have:

- the ability to read coverages during dropback
- the ability to plant the back foot while knowing where to throw
- the ability to deliver the ball with timing and anticipation
- the ability to pass accurately

In the NFL, the elite quarterbacks are the ones who sit in the pocket and deliver the ball on time. The best of them right now include Peyton Manning, Drew Brees, Aaron Rodgers, Tom Brady, and Philip Rivers. But these types of guys are a diminishing breed in the college game, and that trend is filtering down to the high school level. If a teen isn't learning drop-back skills in high school or college, it may be too difficult for him to pick this up by the time he reaches the NFL. Eventually, I'm not sure there will be enough qualified drop-back passers to go around. So I expect that you'll eventually see more movement-oriented quarterbacks at the professional level.

One interesting change that might result from an increase in the number of mobile NFL quarterbacks could be an increase in the number of running backs who offer versatility and can pass proficiently. And there could be quarterbacks who excel at traditional running plays. It's entirely possible that we'll see plays out of the I formation with run/pass options built in, depending on the defense they're facing. You certainly couldn't build your entire offense around this because your quarterback would get killed, but it would be very exciting as a change of pace.

Jon Gruden sees it as more than an either/or choice, saying, "Teams today are almost *required* to have components of the spread as part of their system. The quarterback has to be able to run and make at least one guy miss. He needs durability, elusiveness, and the ability to dominate in one-on-one situations. [Denver's] Tim Tebow runs like a fullback. It almost seems as if he *likes* the punishment. As a pro, he could end up running the ball ten times a game. If you have Tebow on your roster, you have to do that. Just understand that you can't bring in a guy like that and think you can quickly train him to throw like Joe Montana. He can learn the pro passing system, but he'll be better adding elements that weren't there before."

Jon's right when he says it would be too much to expect rookie spread quarterbacks to be successful right away, because the NFL spread formation is considerably different. In college, quarterback reads are simple. I had a conversation with 49ers quarterback Alex Smith, and he told me he never even *read* coverages when he was at the University of Utah—he had to make only half-field reads, where he threw to spots. Even though college personnel can be spread just like pro personnel can, the design of their offenses doesn't call for them to attack the full field. This makes it harder for scouts to project how well spread quarterbacks will react to what they see across the line in the NFL.

In addition, the intelligence requirements are much tougher in the pros than in college. Today's NFL quarterbacks need a high football IQ to play against pressure defenses. It certainly helps if kids in high school and college are taught how to read coverages, become more familiar with pre-snap looks, and understand what the defenses are trying to do, but even that doesn't guarantee full understanding. I retired in 1989, which wasn't that long ago. But I never even *thought* about doing some of the things asked of quarterbacks today. Calling out protection schemes, shouting dummy snaps two or three times during the cadence, changing the play, changing the snap count—I never had to worry about *any* of that when I played. I really tip my hat to the guys who now play the position.

Because of the current rules, emphasis on the ground game is greatly reduced from my era. The old adage of running the football and then playing great defense still works up to a point, but I don't think it gives you your best chance to win a Super Bowl. Today's game is all about explosive plays. The running game must fit the passing game. Too many teams look at them as separate entities. The more proficient teams are better able to mesh the two, both through formations and play calls. Teams that can run the ball well out of passing formations will be the teams with the most explosive offenses. "The hardest thing in the pro game today is to run the football," claimed Gruden. "The multiplicity of defenses makes it tough. It's hard to know what defense you're blocking. It's hard to make that first down late in the game when you run. And it's hard to run it in on the goal line. There are no real fullbacks. And the tight ends now are *receiving* tight ends—they can't make the blocks you need on third-and-short."

That's why I categorically state that having a quarterback who is able to make throws from the pocket is the most important asset an NFL team can have. Everything else stems from this. Although the Vince Youngs and Michael Vicks of the world pull off amazing plays with their feet, it's harder for them to win consistently, because they don't make enough accurate throws from the pocket. They've proven they can win NFL games here and there, but over the course of a full schedule, it's hard for them to execute enough big plays in the passing game to reach a championship level. You see the problem of relying on these types of quarterbacks when you've got to throw on third down or if you're behind. When you're in a situation where you *have* to throw, those bootlegs aren't going to be worth much.

Bill Belichick's great teams of the past decade are a testament to this belief. "The running game is very important," he said. "But the score can take you out of it. And we've seen that numerous times where a team falls behind and a great back isn't getting those carries anymore. When you're stuck in that situation, you'd better be able to throw it—or you're going to lose. There are exceptions. If you can control the game with your defense and not turn the ball over, like the Ravens did back in 2000, then you might be okay. But overall, if you can't throw from the pocket in this league, you can't win."

Pocket passers can't make throws of any kind if they're on their backs, so they must have the ability to neutralize the sophisticated blitz packages prevalent in today's NFL. One way to slow down those nasty guys is through play-action, and I believe you're going to see even more of it in the future. "In the past few years, I've seen a huge increase in the amount of play-fakes," said Dick Vermeil. "You never saw that much play-action in the seventies and early eighties. Are teams using it more because they run it more effectively, or do they use it for pass protection? I think it's for protection."

Play-action demands great field vision and understanding from the quarterback. Before the ball is snapped, it's essential that he gets a good look at the defense's formation. After the snap, he must briefly turn his back on the rush to make the play-fake. For a moment, there's a blind spot: a second where he's not seeing the defense. He must possess the ability to turn his head around, readjust, then find receivers quickly. That's why there's a premium on play-action quarterbacks, because they're asked to make instant reads, refocus, reset, and then throw accurately. I think you see more play-action now for two reasons: First, it affords you great protection, because you usually have more blockers available for protection. Second, it disorients defenders, confuses them, and messes up their assignments. In tape study, I see so many defensive mistakes out of play-action, and I think coaches are recognizing the success that teams are having with it. Ultimately, it's a deception play. You are asking defenders to react to something that isn't really happening. Executed properly, it can be extremely effective.

Confusing defenses is just one tactic available to offenses. Another is tiring them out. There's no better way to achieve both of those aims than with the No-Huddle offense, and I believe you'll be seeing an increase in No-Huddle attacks. According to Brian Billick, "If you can manipulate the other team at the line of scrimmage and take the coaching out of it, the No-Huddle can work. It also simplifies the offense for the quarterback. It will stretch the defenses, while also limiting their packages and substitutions."

In this era of specialization and rotating personnel packages, defenses are in trouble if they can't get the right people onto the field to combat what the offense is doing. "Late in my career, it became more of a hassle matching up your personnel with the opponent's," recalled Joe Collier. "It got to be so that you had a coach up in the booth whose sole job was to spot their substitutions, then relay them back to us on the bench, so we could put people in to get a more advantageous matchup. The changes were so wholesale that it became a rat race on the sidelines. Today you need a lot more good defensive backs to compete with all the wide receivers on the field, and finding good secondary help is tough. They're a rare breed. With spread formations, it's a different game."

Because of the increase in three- and four-wide packages, slot receivers are taking on even greater importance. The single most important asset for a player in the slot is intelligence. He has to be able to read and understand coverages, almost like a quarterback. He is working in a high-traffic area, with defensive linemen dropping, safeties coming in. The slot man has got to be able to navigate and read on the run. Speed isn't as vital as quickness—being able to move adroitly in small areas, and then being able to get open, even with defenders all around him. New England's Wes Welker led the NFL in receptions in 2009 and right now is the league's best slot receiver. Other good ones include the Ravens' Anquan Boldin and the Vikings' Percy Harvin, who should really improve with experience. The Saints' Marques Colston isn't that fast, but he's very strong and has a big body that's ideal for slot play. Finally, there's Pittsburgh's Hines Ward, who may be the best slot receiver we've ever had in the NFL.

Slot men aren't always big and muscular, but size does help in those high-traffic areas. As players grow bigger, there are some who worry there might not be a place for little guys in pro football's future, but I'm not among them. Speed and quickness in open space are skills that you must have in today's offensive-oriented NFL. Smaller backs and receivers with separation skills will continue to play a major role in offensive game plans. With the emphasis on spread formations, you're seeing coaches calling plays to get the better athletes in space. There they can use their athleticism better than in confined areas, and that's more entertaining for fans. Having someone like San Diego's Darren Sproles with the ball in the open field is a lot more exciting than watching a big fullback diving into the line. People want to see big plays.

But at the other end of the weight scale, I also think we could soon be seeing four-hundred-pound linemen, a practical possibility because of training and nutritional advances. You could also have three-hundred-pound linebackers for special personnel packages. Used correctly, guys this size would pose real matchup problems for offenses attempting to block massive blitzers with just a running back. Ultimately, the size of a team's line depends on its coach. He'll make that choice based on the style of play he prefers. There are offensive lines like those of the Cowboys or Eagles: big, mauling, heavy guys who come off the ball in force and are hard for pass rushers to get around, and then there is the running game of the Houston Texans. Their linemen are smaller and lighter, utilizing blocking schemes similar to those we saw with Mike Shanahan's offensive lines back when he coached the Denver Broncos. Undoubtedly, Mike will bring this style with him to Washington now that he's coaching the Redskins.

Teams are pressuring more with faster second- and third-level players, so it's possible that some offensive linemen of the future might be lighter than road graders like the Cowboys' 375-pound Leonard Davis. Presently, you have defenders lining up in the A-gap who are faster. Are big, fat guys going to be able to handle these speed blitzers? It's a real debate. On tape, I've seen some of these 350-pound tackles get just an arm on a blitzing corner and knock him right to the turf. But more and more, you're seeing agile guys like Denver's Ryan Clady, Cleveland's Joe Thomas, and Jake Long on the Dolphins. They aren't 360-pound guys, like Flozell Adams was in Dallas. These kids are playing at weights in the low 300s, and even at that size, they're amazingly quick and athletic.

League executives like high scores and big pass plays. So do the fans. The result: NFL defenses today are at a real disadvantage. The rules overwhelmingly favor the offense. Increased penalties for hits that used to be legal are taking away some of the defense's aggressiveness. But bless their hearts, they keep trying to come up with ways to at least slow down, if not completely stop, the wide-open attacks of the modern NFL. "Defenses today want you to have to block more people so they can have more defenders covering fewer receivers," noted Al Saunders. "Most zones now are matchup zones: man coverage in a zone scheme. If you've got more guys protecting, then defenders have the guys who are out in the pattern almost always double covered. That's where you get the quarterback holding the ball. He's looking around with nowhere to throw it, because the few receivers he has aren't really open. Defensive coaches can scrutinize protections based on formations, personnel, and down and distance. Technology has really helped in this area."

What defensive coaches see in game tape will determine how they respond to each offensive challenge. "Defenses of the future will go where offenses take them," predicted Bill Parcells. "The more offenses spread out, the more defenses will try to exploit the opportunities to knock the quarterback down or pressure him into bad throws. The chess match today is the offense trying to appear that it's going to be spread out but then motioning guys back to get max protection so they can throw downfield. It's between pressure and stretch. Passing is too efficient now, and defenses have to find ways to disrupt it. Overloading one side is one way they're trying to do it."

That's exactly what we're now seeing in New York with Rex Ryan's defense. The Jets are savaging offenses with overload schemes, bringing four pass rushers from one side, yet always getting at least one of them in clean. The beauty of these overloads is that they're still safe blitzes, because Rex keeps seven defenders in coverage. This might be the first time I've ever seen four on one side—a lineman, two linebackers, and a safety or corner—all crashing in from one area.

Jon Gruden told me that blitzes like that can't really be picked up. Nothing is tipped off from the pre-snap read. And if you're the left tackle, and your guy drops off, you have no one to block. There's no offensive tackle on the planet fast enough to get to the other side in time to help fight off the overload. Assistants can't even coach the proper technique to deal with this blitz. The team with the ball just has to hope that blocker is an athlete who can react quickly enough to help in some way.

Rex has a high volume of these kinds of pressure plays, much more than other teams. He will take some risks, however, and is sometimes willing to be fundamentally unsound in his coverages. Most coaches would do anything to avoid that. You've got to be a little bit crazy to do this, and Rex is just like his dad that way. But Ryan's approach seems to be working. In 2009 he became the first rookie head coach in NFL history to have his defense lead the league in both fewest yards and points allowed in a season, rankings that got his team all the way to the AFC championship game. I watch what the Jets are running, and I wonder how some of it's even possible. They're doing things I've never even seen in coverage before. Rex is simply responding to the multiple looks he's getting from offenses, but being aggressive in doing so.

Ryan isn't alone when it comes to blitz package innovation. The Packers' Dom Capers is a bit more cautious, but he remains among the most creative NFL defensive minds. Philadelphia's Sean McDermott learned well from the late Jim Johnson and is a young guy to watch. In New Orleans, Gregg Williams has stayed very aggressive, using zero-coverage and other varied looks. You saw how his blitz schemes and rotating fronts battered both Kurt Warner and Brett Favre in the 2009 playoffs, then shackled the Colts' offense at key moments in Super Bowl XLIV. Just days before that historic upset over Indy, Williams told reporters, "My job is about effecting change. If you don't effect change, you're out of the league as a coach, as a player."

Most pressure packages, no matter what their design, are initially triggered by the big guys up front. The current drafting trend is for bigger and heavier interior linemen. Nose tackles are pluggers and space eaters—your least athletic linemen. But more and more, you'll see defensive ends like Justin Tuck and Trent Cole, who are lightning fast. These aren't linemen, they're linebackers playing defensive end. They might weigh as little as 230 or 240. Defensive ends in 4-3 formations are becoming leaner, faster, and quicker as the defensive tackles grow heftier and stronger.

"You're going to see more Dwight Freeney types on the defensive line, because you won't need bulk on the line against the spread," observed Dave McGinnis. "Big ends aren't as important; the NFL power-run game isn't there any longer." Because of new pressure schemes, we're witnessing a paradigm shift to size and skills at virtually every defensive position. "With the advent of spreads in the pros, that means your linebackers will have to be smaller and quicker," McGinnis maintained. "Safeties are going to have to become cover guys. The era of in-the-box safeties is gone. Your slot defenders become more valuable, so you'll need hybrids with the skills of both safeties and linebackers."

Finding smaller, quicker pass-rushing ends on draft day is a constant goal for personnel directors. Another specialized position that's vital today, but wasn't even considered a priority in my era, is the nickel cornerback. The nickel corner now plays, on average, around 60 percent of the snaps because of the passing game's predominance. This guy can no longer simply be a spare part—as, until recently, many thought him to be. Traditional corners have the benefit of playing near the sideline, which acts like an extra defender, but when you're a nickel back or a slot defender, you have to defend both sides of the field. He doesn't have to be as good in coverage as the regular corners, because he'll usually get help from the linebacker and the safety. But the nickel corner has to be a good run defender, because even teams that line up in three-wide as their base offense will often run out of those formations. This transforms the nickel corner into a strong-side linebacker playing over the slot. So he's got to be big and tough enough to play the run—he can't be five foot seven and 170 pounds. The nickel corner also has to be able to blitz. Twenty years ago, these skills simply weren't required of a nickel back.

Some of the best nickel corners at work today include Tampa Bay's Ronde Barber, Antoine Winfield with the Vikings, and Green Bay's Charles Woodson. I never thought I'd see the day a nickel corner would be named NFL Defensive Player of the Year, but Charles earned that honor in 2009. He's able to make more plays as a nickel than he ever could as a conventional corner, because he can blitz more easily and cause more fumbles. There's nobody in the history of the NFL who strips the ball better than Charles Woodson.

All these twenty-first century defenders are doing what they can to limit explosive plays, but the truth is that it's harder than ever to do so, given the way the game is currently played. The funny thing is that you would think the wide formations used by the spread generate coast-to-coast plays, but I've found that isn't necessarily the case. True, such formations create more seams, but when that happens, the ball becomes almost like a magnet, and defenders flow to it. The runner or receiver might pick up 10 to 12 yards this way, but he's probably not going any farther.

By contrast, if you gash the defense in tighter formations, you've got safeties closer to the line of scrimmage and fewer additional defenders out in space. If someone breaks past the line, there aren't enough people at the third level to stop him. I think most big plays—the 40- and 50-yarders you see on highlight shows—come from the tight formations. Ron Rivera told me that the vast majority of big plays result from gap breakdowns by the defense: mental errors that balloon into physical errors. One guy goes the wrong way, a gap opens, and that's it. This might sound mean spirited, but it's true: Big plays come from guys screwing up their assignments and going where they're not supposed to go. "Players must understand they are but one of eleven parts, and their role fits into those eleven pieces," said Dick LeBeau. "You're only as strong as your weakest link. You can't go flying off all over the damn field. If I tell them to go left, and they go right, they darn well better get to the ball."

If defenses can avoid mental breakdowns as they apply more varied and unfamiliar pressure schemes, they might be able to close the gap between themselves and today's offenses. "I think you're going to see a lot more of the mixed bag packages," predicted Tony Dungy. "Some teams are using those highly skilled two-hundred-fifty-pound guys, mixing them up and bringing different blitz packages to put pressure on quarterbacks. If you're playing against a great quarterback and can't pressure him some way, you're probably going to lose the game."

And *more* of those games are coming. I believe the NFL will eventually go to an eighteen-game schedule, and coaches are going to have to respond with both strategic and personnel modifications. Players want to play; that's how they're trained. It's also how they're paid: There are incentive bonuses in their contracts. Beyond that, it affects the mind-set of a guy when he's asked to sit out a game or two that's deemed unimportant. And an extended season only increases the potential for more games at the end of the year that don't mean much. Coaches will be trying to protect their players, but to me that's the antithesis of how you should play the game. You take away some of the competitive edge, and that part bothers me. There's also the obvious wear and tear on the athlete. This is a violent, physical, demanding sport, and adding more games is going to be tough on the health of the players. The body can take only so much abuse, and players need time to rest and heal.

One solution is that roster sizes will have to be adjusted, even expanded. Right now teams pay fifty-three guys but dress only forty-six on game day. Why not have all of them eligible, and then add even more players to a developmental squad? The players will go for that because it means more jobs. And with a fresh influx of revenue from the additional games, team owners should be able to afford those new salaries. It would improve the quality of play because then you'd preserve the health of starters. They'd no longer have to play on special teams, where they're more vulnerable to injury.

A longer season will also affect how the game is coached on the field. But that's where my crystal football begins to fog up. I can't begin to guess what changes will occur, but you can be certain that an extended schedule would have a bearing on what you'd see each Sunday. When the NFL jumped from fourteen to sixteen games in 1978, things worked out fairly well. Players and coaches are, if nothing else, adaptable creatures. And fans will be happier watching more games that affect the standings and fewer preseason snoozers that have never been more than glorified scrimmages. If recent TV ratings are any indicator, this move should be successful. Fans can't seem to get enough of the NFL—and I feel exactly the same way.

No matter how much the game changes, fundamentals will remain at its core. "It still comes down to basics," stated Joe Theismann. "If you have good health and good players on both your offensive and defensive lines, then you are going to be near the top in a lot of categories, and you are going to have a chance to win a championship. We're so caught up in headliners in our society: the wide receivers, the quarterbacks, and ball-hawking corners. But the basis of success in the NFL is tutoring and training the offensive and defensive lines. That's the area where personnel guys place their focus. I look at it the way I look at a plate of food. Blocking and tackling are, and always will be, the meat and potatoes of our game."

I'll carry Theismann's observation even further. If blocking and tackling are the meat and potatoes, then the desserts are schemes like formation variations, men in motion, blitz packages, and situational specialists. The most creative recipes on this dessert menu have the power to make the meal or to ruin it. But to take this food analogy one more step, it's important to understand that these exotic items have a relatively brief shelf life. Eventually defenses catch up to the offenses. Offenses counter with their own moves to neutralize clever defensive strategy. Every year, there will be something that takes the league by storm, and you can't easily predict what it will be until it happens.

Coaches work fourteen to sixteen hours each day, seeking new ideas that will give them an edge. Someone will find something—and then it will spread like flame through a woodpile.

"Everyone's a copycat in this league," noted Dick Vermeil. "Some coaches think, *I'd better give this a try. That's the way to win. I've only got so many years left in my contract. We're not successful the way we're doing it right now. We've got to find a way to do it better.* And then, all of a sudden, those teams go down and another trend comes up. It still comes down to who's got the best players. If you don't have enough of them, then your packages are limited. And if you don't have players that can make big plays, then you'd better design something to manufacture those plays."

Fortunately, the influx of player talent is as impressive as it's ever been. Athletes entering the pro ranks now are as big as veterans, and kids coming out of high school look like grown men! Their skill sets are more complete than even just a few years ago, and they have the advantages of healthier nutrition, comprehensive exercise regimens, and better coaching. The pros clearly have better raw talent to work with today. Now it's up to their staffs to create winning strategies.

Shortly before he passed away, Bill Walsh observed, "Like everything else in society, coaching has become more sophisticated. There's much more science to coaching, more research. The game is more refined, strategies and tactics have changed. It's certainly a faster game, more wide-open. People are better teachers, more exacting in what they want. The staffs are so much larger and have a broader base of expertise." Bill made this statement a few years ago, but it's as true now as it was the day he said it. There's never been a more exciting time for coaches to experiment with new ideas.

Through all my film study, the one constant I see is that there's no single way to win a football game. There are many paths to a championship. I wince when I hear people say, "This team needs a better running game or breakout receiver to win it all." Other than a top-flight quarterback, there isn't any one component a squad *must* have to contend for the Super Bowl. If it has coaches who are innovative and adaptable, and who can successfully teach their system to a core group of solid players, that team can win in this league—and maybe make a little history of its own along the way.

Acknowledgments

Any quarterback will tell you that he's only as good as the guys who block for him and the receivers who catch his passes. Putting this book together was no different. There were many people who helped us throughout the researching and writing process, and we'd like to extend our thanks to all of them.

The bedrock of this book was the coaching and archival film that allowed us to revisit and analyze each of our chosen games. Thanks go to Bob McCartney with the Steelers, Berj Najarian of the Patriots, and Rusty Sullivan at the New England Sports Museum for sharing their football footage. We'd also like to thank our colleagues at NFL Films who tracked down game footage and vintage broadcasts, including Jeremy Swarbrick, Michael Villanova, and Chris Willis. A big shout-out goes to Nick Kehoe, Lou Russo, and Sean Coffey on the *NFL Matchup* production team. Additional thanks to Maryann Wenger, James McCormick, and Diane Kimball for their assistance with interviews. NFL Films was also a valuable source for hundreds of transcripts, publications, and produced programs that greatly enriched our narrative. We'd like to thank Howard Katz and Steve Sabol for making all those resources available. Thank you, Steve, for also writing the foreword to this book. We appreciate your kind words and support.

Another vital source for any football research project is the Pro Football Hall of Fame. We are indebted to their archivists Pete Fierle,

Saleem Choudhry, and Jon Kendle. Thanks also to various team representatives for their assistance: Dan Yuska from the Bears, Philadelphia's Derek Boyko, the 49ers' Bob Lange, Stacey James with the Patriots, Dave Lockett with the Steelers, and Jim Steeg in San Diego. Additional thanks go to Pittsburgh's Mike Fabus, the Chargers' Todd Tobias, Anthony Bonagura of the Eagles, the Bears' Bill Smith, Michael Zagaris with the 49ers, and Brent Hensel and Christy Berkery in New England for their help in providing photographs.

More than sixty players and coaches were kind enough to sit for often lengthy interviews, and we are grateful to them for being so generous with their time and insights: Bill Arnsparger, Pete Banaszak, Tom Bass, Hank Bauer, Bill Belichick, Brian Billick, Glenn Blackwood, Dom Capers, Harry Carson, Joe Collier, Cris Collinsworth, Bill Cowher, Randy Cross, Len Dawson, A. J. Duhe, Tony Dungy, Larry Eisenhauer, Gary Fencik, Tom Flores, Dan Fouts, Leslie Frazier, Joe Gibbs, Peter Giunta, Jon Gruden, John Hadl, Jack Ham, Merril Hoge, Kent Hull, John Jefferson, Carnell Lake, Dick LeBeau, Marvin Lewis, Mike Martz, Dave McGinnis, Matt Millen, Ron Mix, Jim Otto, Bill Parcells, Doug Plank, Ron Rivera, Andy Russell, Rod Rust, Sam Rutigliano, Rex Ryan, George Saimes, Al Saunders, Marty Schottenheimer, Don Shula, Phil Simms, Mike Singletary, Mike Stratton, Steve Tasker, Joe Theismann, Dick Vermeil, Mike Wagner, Danny White, Woody Widenhofer, Solomon Wilcots, Kellen Winslow, Rod Woodson, and Sam Wyche.

We were blessed to have one of the finest editors in the business working with us in Mark Tavani at Ballantine Books. Mark's a Philadelphia native, so we knew we were in good hands. That's also true in the case of Philip Bashe our wonderful copy editor. We're deeply appreciative of Mary A. Wirth who applied her considerable graphic arts talent to each chapter's coaching diagrams. Many thanks to our literary agent, David Black, and his staffers Gary Morris and Antonella Iannarino for helping us navigate through the intricate world of publishing. We're also grateful for the labors of Steve Mandell, Gary Lozoff, and James Gregorio, who were critical in the early phases of the project.

This book would not have been possible without the tireless support of our wives and families. Thank you, Liz, Joleen, Jessica, and B. J. Jaworski; Debora, Emily, and Jess Cosell; and Joan, Jonathan, and Rebecca Plaut. We appreciate your putting up with our craziness over the past three years. We all promise to now be more available for household chores—at least until the start of next football season.

Ron Jaworski
Greg Cosell
David Plaut
Mount Laurel, New Jersey
MARCH 2010

APPENDIX

BOX SCORES

BOSTON PATRIOTS vs. SAN DIEGO CHARGERS
JANUARY 5, 1964

Boston	7	3	0	0	-	10
San Diego	21	10	7	13	-	51

SD	-	Rote, 2 run (Blair kick)	0–7
SD	-	Lincoln, 67 run (Blair kick)	0–14
BOS	-	Garron, 7 run (Cappelletti kick)	7–14
SD	-	Lowe, 58 run (Blair kick)	7–21
SD	-	Blair, FG 11	7–24
BOS	-	Cappelletti, FG 15	10–24
SD	-	Norton, 15 pass from Rote (Blair kick)	10–31
SD	-	Alworth, 48 pass from Rote (Blair kick)	10–38
SD	-	Lincoln, 25 pass from Hadl (pass failed)	10–44
SD	-	Hadl, 1 run (Blair kick)	10–51

	BOS	SD
First Downs	14	21
Rush-Yd-TD	16-75-1	32-318-4
Comp-Att-Yd-TD-Int	17-37-228-0-2	17-26-305-3-0
Sacked-Yd	6-42	2-13
Net Pass Yd	186	292
Total Yd	261	610
Fumbles-lost	1-0	1-1
Turnovers	2	1
Penalties-Yd	1-18	6-30

Patriots rushing: Crump 7-18, Burton 7-3, Garron 3-15, Lott 3-15, Yewcic 1-14, Parilli 1-10
Patriots passing: Parilli 14-29-189-0-1, Yewcic 3-8-39-0-1
Patriots receiving: Burton 4-12, Colclough 3-26, Cappelletti 2-72, Graham 2-68, Crump 2-28, Lott 2-16, Garron 2-6
Patriots interceptions: none

Chargers rushing: Lincoln 13-206, Lowe 12-94, Rote 4-15, McDougall 1-2, Hadl 1-1, Jackson 1-0
Chargers passing: Rote 10-15-173-2-0, Hadl 6-10-112-1-0, Lincoln 1-1-20-0-0
Chargers receiving: Lincoln 7-123, Alworth 4-77, MacKinnon 2-53, Norton 2-44, Kocourek 1-5, McDougall 1-4
Chargers interceptions: Maguire 1-10, Mitinger 1-5

PITTSBURGH STEELERS vs. OAKLAND RAIDERS
DECEMBER 29, 1974

PITTSBURGH	0	3	0	21	-	24
OAKLAND	3	0	7	3	-	13

OAK	-	Blanda, FG 40	0–3
PIT	-	Gerela, FG 23	3–3
OAK	-	Branch, 38 pass from Stabler (Blanda kick)	3–10
PIT	-	Harris, 8 run (Gerela kick)	10–10
PIT	-	Swann, 6 pass from Bradshaw (Gerela kick)	17–10
OAK	-	Blanda, FG 24	17–13
PIT	-	Harris, 21 run (Gerela kick)	24–13

	PIT	OAK
First Downs	20	15
Rush-Yd-TD	50-224-2	21-29-0
Comp-Att-Yd-TD-Int	8-17-95-1-1	19-36-271-1-3
Sacked-Yd	0-0	2-22
Net Pass Yd	95	249
Total Yd	319	278
Fumbles-lost	3-2	0-0
Turnovers	3	3
Penalties-Yd	4-30	5-60

Steelers rushing: Harris 29-111, Bleier 18-98, Bradshaw 4-1
Steelers passing: Bradshaw 8-17-95-1-1
Steelers receiving: Brown 2-37, Bleier 2-25, Swann 2-17, Stallworth 2-16
Steelers interceptions: Ham 2-19, Thomas 1-37

Raiders rushing: Davis 10-16, Hubbard 7-6, Banaszak 3-7, Stabler 1-0
Raiders passing: Stabler 19-36-271-1-3
Raiders receiving: Branch 9-186, Moore 4-32, Biletnikoff 3-45, Davis 2-8, Banaszak 1-0
Raiders interceptions: Wilson 1-37

OAKLAND RAIDERS vs. SAN DIEGO CHARGERS
SEPTEMBER 14, 1980

Oakland	3	7	7	7	0	-	24
San Diego	3	7	0	14	6	-	30

SD	-	Benirschke, FG 52	0–3
OAK	-	Bahr, FG 35	3–3
SD	-	Jefferson, 4 pass from Fouts (Benirschke kick)	10–3
OAK	-	Branch, 48 pass from Pastorini (Bahr kick)	10–10
OAK	-	Jones, 11 fumble return (Bahr kick)	10–17
SD	-	Winslow, 25 pass from Fouts (Benirschke kick)	17–17
SD	-	Williams, 4 run (Benirschke kick)	17–24
OAK	-	Chester, 18 pass from Plunkett (Bahr kick)	24–24
SD	-	Jefferson, 24 pass from Fouts (no kick)	24–30

	OAK	SD
First Downs	25	30
Rush-Yd-TD	41-186-0	32-76-1
Comp-Att-Yd-TD-Int	16-34-256-2-3	29-44-387-3-5
Sacked-Yd	1-7	2-15
Net Pass Yd	249	372
Total Yd	435	448
Fumbles-lost	2-1	3-2
Turnovers	4	7
Penalties-Yd	14-94	8-59

Raiders rushing: King, 13-70, van Eeeghen 14-60, Whittington 7-30, Pastorini 4-24, Jensen 2-2, Plunkett 1-0

Raiders passing: Pastorini 15-33-238-1-3, Plunkett 1-1-18-1-0

Raiders receiving: Branch 4-99, Chester 3-53, King 3-20, Casper 2-17, Bradshaw 1-32, Chandler 1-15, Jensen 1-12, van Eeghen 1-8

Raiders interceptions: Davis 1-49, Millen 1-9, Hendricks 1-5, Hayes 1-0, Owens 1-0

Chargers rushing: Williams 17-38, Cappelletti 13-29, Fouts 2-9

Chargers passing: Fouts 29-44-387-3-5

Chargers receiving: Winslow 9-132, Jefferson 9-110, Williams 7-79, Joiner 4-66

Chargers interceptions: Edwards 2-0, Buchanon 1-0

NEW YORK GIANTS vs. SAN FRANCISCO 49ers
JANUARY 3, 1982

New York	7	3	7	7	-	24
San Francisco	7	17	0	14	-	38

SF	-	Young, 8 pass from Montana (Wersching kick)	0–7
NYG	-	Gray, 72 pass from Brunner (Danelo kick)	7–7
SF	-	Wersching, FG 22	7–10
SF	-	Solomon, 58 pass from Montana (Wersching kick)	7–17
SF	-	Patton, 25 run (Wersching kick)	7–24
NYG	-	Danelo, FG 48	10–24
NYG	-	Perkins, 59 pass from Brunner (Danelo kick)	17–24
SF	-	Ring, 3 run (Wersching kick)	17–31
SF	-	Lott, 20 interception return (Wersching kick)	17–38
NYG	-	Perkins, 17 pass from Brunner (Danelo kick)	24–38

	NYG	SF
First Downs	13	24
Rush-Yd-TD	22-65-0	34-135-2
Comp-Att-Yd-TD-Int	16-37-290-3-2	20-31-304-2-1
Sacked-Yd	2-9	3-16
Net Pass Yd	281	288
Total Yd	346	423
Fumbles-lost	4-2	2-0
Turnovers	4	1
Penalties-Yd	9-61	14-145

Giants rushing: Carpenter 17-61, Perry 2-1, Brunner 2- –2, Bright 1-5
Giants passing: Brunner 16-37-290-3-2
Giants receiving: Perkins 7-121, Gray 3-118, Carpenter 3-18, Young 2-15, Mistler 1-18
Giants interceptions: Currier 1-2

49ers rushing: Ring 10-29, Cooper 7-52, Patton 7-32, Easley 4-9, Montana 3-9, Solomon 1-12, Clark 1-6, Davis 1-4
49ers passing: Montana 20-31-304-2-1
49ers receiving: Solomon 6-107, Clark 5-104, Patton 2-38, Young 2-22, Wilson 2-21, Ramson 1-11, Elliott 1-5, Ring 1- –4
49ers interceptions: Lott 2-32

CHICAGO BEARS vs. DALLAS COWBOYS
NOVEMBER 17, 1985

Chicago	7	17	3	17	-	44
Dallas	0	0	0	0	-	0

CHI	-	Dent, 1 interception return (Butler kick)	7–0
CHI	-	Butler, FG 44	10–0
CHI	-	Richardson, 36 interception return (Butler kick)	17–0
CHI	-	Fuller, 1 run (Butler kick)	24–0
CHI	-	Butler, FG 46	27–0
CHI	-	Butler, FG 22	30–0
CHI	-	Thomas, 17 run (Butler kick)	37–0
CHI	-	Gentry, 16 run (Butler kick)	44–0

	CHI	DAL
First Downs	18	12
Rush-Yd-TD	40-216-3	16-52-0
Comp-Att-Yd-TD-Int	10-25-197-0-1	15-39-167-0-4
Sacked-Yd	4-35	6-48
Net Pass Yd	162	119
Total Yd	378	171
Fumbles-lost	1-0	1-1
Turnovers	1	5
Penalties-Yd	8-105	6-65

Bears rushing: Payton 22-132, Fuller 4-21, Thomas 4-19, Suhey 4-11, Gentry 3-24, Sanders 2-8, Perry 1-1

Bears passing: Fuller 9-24-164-0-1, Payton 1-1-33-0-0

Bears receiving: Wrightman 2-61, Suhey 2-46, Gault 2-24, McKinnon 1-24, Gentry 1-22, Moorehead 1-16, Payton 1-4

Bears interceptions: Richardson 1-36, Frazier 1-33, Taylor 1-18, Dent 1-1

Cowboys rushing: Dorsett 12-44, Lavette 3-0, Hogeboom 1-8

Cowboys passing: White 9-17-107-0-1, Hogeboom 6-22-60-0-3

Cowboys receiving: Renfro 3-45, Newsome 3-25, Cosbie 2-25, Hill 2-15, Dorsett 2-12, Cornwell 1-32, Fowler 1-9, Gonzalez 1-4

Cowboys interceptions: Bates 1-2

BUFFALO BILLS vs. PITTSBURGH STEELERS
JANUARY 9, 1993

Buffalo	0	7	7	10	-	24
Pittsburgh	3	0	0	0	-	3

PIT	-	Anderson, FG 38	0–3
BUF	-	Frerotte, 1 pass from Reich (Christie kick)	7–3
BUF	-	Lofton, 17 pass from Reich (Christie kick)	14–3
BUF	-	Christie, FG 43	17–3
BUF	-	Gardner, 1 run (Christie kick)	24–3

	BUF	PIT
First Downs	19	18
Rush-Yd-TD	39-169-1	27-129-0
Comp-Att-Yd-TD-Int	16-23-160-2-0	15-29-163-0-2
Sacked-Yd	1-4	7-52
Net Pass Yd	156	111
Total Yd	325	240
Fumbles-lost	0-0	4-1
Turnovers	0	3
Penalties-Yd	4-33	2-23

Bills rushing: Davis 10-104, Thomas 19-54, Gardner 7-22, Reich 2- –3, Reed 1- –8
Bills passing: Reich 16-23-160-2-0
Bills receiving: Beebe 6-72, Thomas 3-25, Lofton 2-29, McKeller 2-22, Metzelaars 2-11, Frerotte 1-1
Bills interceptions: Odomes 1-1, Williams 1-0

Steelers rushing: Foster 20-104, O'Donnell 4-26, Thompson 1-3, Royals 1-0, Stone 1- –4,
Steelers passing: O'Donnell 15-29-163-0-2
Steelers receiving: Mills 8-93, Davenport 3-54, Foster 3-7, Stone 1-9
Steelers interceptions: none

ST. LOUIS RAMS vs. NEW ENGLAND PATRIOTS
FEBRUARY 3, 2002

St. Louis	3	0	0	14	-	17
New England	0	14	3	3	-	20

STL	-	Wilkins, FG 50	3–0
NE	-	Law, 47 interception return (Vinatieri kick)	3–7
NE	-	Patten, 8 pass from Brady (Vinatieri kick)	3–14
NE	-	Vinatieri, FG 37	3–17
STL	-	Warner, 2 run (Wilkins kick)	10–17
STL	-	Proehl, 26 pass from Warner (Wilkins kick)	17–17
NE	-	Vinatieri, FG 48	17–20

	STL	NE
First Downs	26	15
Rush-Yd-TD	22-90-1	25-133-0
Comp-Att-Yd-TD-Int	28-44-365-1-2	16-27-145-1-0
Sacked-Yd	3-28	2-11
Net Pass Yd	337	134
Total Yd	427	267
Fumbles-lost	2-1	0-0
Turnovers	3	0
Penalties-Yd	6-39	5-31

Rams rushing: M. Faulk 17-76, Warner 3-6, Hakim 1-5, Hodgins 1-3
Rams passing: Warner 28-44-365-1-2
Rams receiving: Hakim 5-90, Bruce 5-56, Holt 5-49, M. Faulk 4-54, Proehl 3-71, Robinson 2-18, Conwell 2-8, Murphy 1-11, Hodgins 1-8
Rams interceptions: none

Patriots rushing: Smith 18-92, K. Faulk 2-15, Edwards 2-5, Patten 1-22, Brady 1-3, Redmond 1- –4
Patriots passing: Brady 16-27-145-1-0
Patriots receiving: Brown 6-89, Redmond 3-24, Wiggins 2-14, Edwards 2-7, Patten 1-8, Smith 1-4, K. Faulk 1- –1
Patriots interceptions: Law 1-47, Smith 1-30

Index

ABOUT THE AUTHORS

RON JAWORSKI is one of the broadcasters of *Monday Night Football*, and one of the most popular analysts covering the NFL today. He appears regularly on a number of ESPN shows and specials. Jaworski attended Youngstown State University, then played seventeen NFL seasons. In 1980, he led the Philadelphia Eagles to Super Bowl XV and was named NFL MVP. Jaworski then became a sports commentator and TV show host. The president of Philadelphia's famed Maxwell Club, Jaworski is involved in charitable activities and a variety of business ventures.

GREG COSELL and DAVID PLAUT are senior producers with NFL Films. Cosell is the creator and supervising producer of the NFL Matchup program, as well as a frequent guest on national sports radio programs. He lives in Mount Laurel, New Jersey. Plaut is a multi-Emmy Award–winning producer with NFL Films, former book critic for *USA Today Sports Weekly,* and the author of four previous books. He lives in Moorestown, New Jersey.

ABOUT THE TYPE

This book was set in Sabon, a typeface designed by the well-known German typographer Jan Tschichold (1902–74). Sabon's design is based upon the original letter forms of Claude Garamond and was created specifically to be used for three sources: foundry type for hand composition, Linotype, and Monotype. Tschichold named his typeface for the famous Frankfurt typefounder Jacques Sabon, who died in 1580.